QUALITATIVE
INTERVIEWING

SECOND EDITION

QUALITATIVE
INTERVIEWING
THE ART OF HEARING DATA
SECOND EDITION

HERBERT J. RUBIN
NORTHERN ILLINOIS UNIVERSITY

IRENE S. RUBIN
NORTHERN ILLINOIS UNIVERSITY

SAGE Publications
Thousand Oaks ▪ London ▪ New Delhi

For information:

Sage Publications, Inc.
2455 Teller Road
Thousand Oaks, California 91320
E-mail: order@sagepub.com

Sage Publications Ltd.
1 Oliver's Yard
55 City Road
London, EC1Y 1SP
United Kingdom

Sage Publications India Pvt. Ltd.
B-42, Panchsheel Enclave
Post Box 4109
New Delhi 110 017 India

Library of Congress Cataloging-in-Publication Data

Rubin, Herbert J.
Qualitative interviewing: the art of hearing data / Herbert J. Rubin, Irene S. Rubin.— 2nd ed.
    p. cm.
Includes bibliographical references and indexes.
ISBN 0-7619-2074-9 (cloth) — ISBN 0-7619-2075-7 (pbk.)
    1. Interviewing. 2. Interviewing in sociology. I. Rubin, Irene. II. Title.
H62.R737 2005
001.4′33—dc22

                                                    2004005677

Printed in the United States of America on acid-free paper.

04   05   06   07   08   09   10   9   8   7   6   5   4   3   2   1

Acquiring Editor:	Al Bruckner
Editorial Assistant:	MaryAnn Vail
Production Editor:	Tracy Alpern
Copy Editor:	Patricia Oman, Publication Services, Inc.
Typesetter:	C&M Digitals (P) Ltd.
Indexer:	Gloria Tierney
Cover Designer:	Glenn Vogel

Contents

Preface

Learning about the world through qualitative interviews has extended our intellectual and emotional reach, and by turns, roused and satisfied our intellectual curiosity. Qualitative interviews have operated for us like night-vision goggles, permitting us to see that which is not ordinarily on view and examine that which is often looked at but seldom seen. Interviewing has enabled us to jump social barriers, of race, income, national origin, sex, and occupation. We have examined foreign-aid programs and probation offices, talked to community organizers rebuilding inner-city neighborhoods and to federal officials responding to threats of agency termination. We are continually absorbed by the sense of discovery and pleased by the depth, thoroughness, and credibility of the final reports. In *Qualitative Interviewing: The Art of Hearing Data* we hope to transmit not only a set of techniques but also some of the exhilaration we have experienced in doing our research.

You should use the model we present—choosing interviewees who are knowledgeable about the research problem, listening carefully to what they tell you, and asking additional questions about their answers until you really understand them—whenever you need to learn about something in depth from another person's point of view. We call this approach *responsive interviewing* because the researcher is responding to and then asking further questions about what he or she hears from the interviewees rather than relying on predetermined questions. We describe the philosophy that underlies the model, underscoring the importance of working with interviewees as partners rather than treating them as objects of research.

Depth interviewing contrasts sharply with quantitative research. Many of our colleagues believe that only statistical techniques are rigorous and dismiss all forms of qualitative research as mere storytelling, useful at best as prologue to a statistical study. These colleagues have little idea of the richness of the findings from depth interviews or of the careful standards, the built-in credibility checks, and the systematic analysis that guide depth interviewing. Rather than stripping away context, needlessly reducing people's experiences to numbers, responsive interviewing approaches a problem in its natural setting, explores related and contradictory themes and concepts, and points out the missing and the subtle, as well as the explicit and the obvious.

Qualitative Interviewing distills our experiences from careers spent in the field, supplementing our experiences with lessons drawn from a wide array of published research, as well as examples supplied by professional colleagues. In particular, Professor Jim Thomas shared with us his work on criminals and Professor Steven Maynard Moody sent us copies of his interviews with street-level bureaucrats.

Although we know our approach works, we are not suggesting a new orthodoxy that must be practiced exactly as presented. Instead, we are offering a way for novice researchers to begin, fully expecting that they will modify our model based on their own experiences.

Modifications to the Second Edition

In this second edition, we have updated the examples and clarified topics that our students found difficult, particularly, how to choose a topic, how to recognize concepts and themes that suggest follow-up questions and then guide the analysis, and how to create an overall structure for the interview. We discuss in detail how responsive interviews are built around *main questions*, which address the overall research problem; *probes*, which help manage the conversation and elicit detail; and *follow-up questions*, which explore and test out new ideas that emerge during the interviews. We emphasize how to figure out and word follow-up questions meant to explore new concepts and themes.

We have expanded the discussion of computer techniques, explaining what you should and should not expect from your software. We have added material and explained more clearly how to analyze interviews in ways that suggest new questions for subsequent interviews, how to resolve research puzzles, and how to theorize about the implications of the research findings. We have maintained the distinction between topical and cultural interviews, but instead of discussing each in separate chapters, we have contrasted them throughout the text.

In this revision we show more explicitly that the stages of research—design, data gathering, and analysis—are intimately linked. We try to drive home the idea that researchers perform analysis throughout their projects, not just at the end, so that as they learn more, they can modify both the research problem they are exploring and the questions they ask. In responsive interviewing, ongoing analysis necessitates continual design as researchers figure out how to explore new information they discover.

We emphasize the importance of developing and maintaining a partnership with the interviewees and stress the necessity of behaving in an ethical way. Since the first edition, universities and government agencies have strengthened their institutional review boards (IRBs), which are set up to ensure that research subjects are not harmed. We discuss how to work out proposals that will meet the requirements of IRBs while maintaining the flexibility needed for qualitative interviewing.

Though we have made numerous changes in this edition, our underlying approach to research remains the same: Find interviewees who know about your research problem from first-hand experience or direct knowledge, ask them questions about their experiences and knowledge, and listen intently to their answers. Then keep questioning until you have a good, rich, and credible answer to your research problem.

1

Listening, Hearing, and Sharing Social Experiences

I'll tell you one thing. It has been a very interesting conversation with you because I think in the course of conversation it's given me the time . . . to reflect . . . on what we are doing and how we are doing it. . . .

—An interviewee working to restructure her organization

People strive to comprehend the world in which they live and work to help them manage their relationships, their jobs, and their problems. They learn from conversations with friends, relatives, neighbors, technicians, clerks, and associates at work and in school, as well as from newspapers and television. This informal learning is important but restricted, because in daily encounters people rarely ask how things occur or why and are unlikely to think about groups other than their own. To get deeper understanding, you need to study the world more systematically. Sociologists, psychologists, political scientists, public administrators, educators, and professionals in the medical, social, and human services apply a more methodical approach to learning called *social research*.

Social research utilizes an array of techniques. *Survey researchers* ask people standardized questions, such as what they think about gun control or whether they have been the victims of crime in the past year. *Demographers* analyze official data, such the U.S. Census. Demographers can tell you whether neighborhoods are becoming more segregated or whether housing is becoming less affordable. Some social researchers *experiment*, that is, intentionally make a change and then look for the impacts of that change. For example, researchers may assign some garbage pickup routes to a private company and others to city employees to see who does a better job and at what cost.

We can answer many important questions by surveying, analyzing official data, and experimenting, but these techniques have limits. Statistical summaries may not communicate, because numbers do not tell a story people easily understand. Further, boiling down answers into numbers strips away the context, losing much of the richness and complexity that make research realistic. You could measure poverty by counting the dollar income people earn, before taxes. But you would learn little about how people survive on their income, whether they share apartments with boarders, whether they fix the plumber's car in exchange for plumbing services, or whether they eat at relatives' houses at the end of the month when they run out of money.

Fortunately, there are social research tools that allow researchers to explore more complex questions. *Naturalistic, qualitative social researchers* gather information by *observing* and by *talking with and listening* carefully to the people who are being researched. Naturalistic researchers study people in their ordinary settings, where they live or work or play, analyze what they have heard and seen, and then convey to others, in rich and realistic detail, the experiences and perspectives of those being studied (Lincoln and Guba 1985). Naturalistic researchers obtain data through *participant observation* and *qualitative interviewing,* which are done sometimes separately and sometimes together. When doing participant observation, naturalistic researchers watch their research setting from the sidelines or join the activities of those they are studying and take notes on what they see. Interviewing projects rely less on watching and more on asking questions. This book focuses primarily on how to prepare, conduct, interpret, and report in-depth qualitative interviews, leaving discussions of participant observation to other fine texts on the topic.

The Uses of Qualitative Interviewing

You do not need to conduct depth qualitative interviews to find out how frequently people wash their hair, watch a television program, or buy a particular product. These are matters that can appropriately be counted. But if you want to know what people think about personal hygiene, why they watch so much television, or whether they feel that they gain status by buying a particular product, then qualitative interviewing is the right approach. If what you need to find out cannot be answered simply or briefly, if you anticipate that you may need to ask people to explain their answers or give examples or describe their experiences, then you rely on in-depth interviews.

Through qualitative interviews you can understand experiences and reconstruct events in which you did not participate, from becoming a fundamentalist Muslim to organizing a mine workers' union, from participating in a beauty contest to fighting a war in central Africa. You can extend your intellectual and emotional reach across age, occupation, class, race, sex, and geographical boundaries. Sociologists study debutante balls and garage sales; political scientists study dirty campaign tactics and court administration; anthropologists study migrant workers and gay marriages. Women can study men's Saturday night poker games, and men can study women's health clubs. Through in-depth qualitative interviews people in health care, social-work agencies, the news media, law enforcement, and the courts are able to reconstruct stories of what happened to clients, witnesses, and victims whose lives are very different from their own.

Qualitative interviewing projects are especially good at describing social and political processes, that is, how and why things change. What happens to ordinary working-class people when the town's major employer leaves? How did a once-flourishing neighborhood become a burnt-out zone? How did a corrupt police department change into a model of public integrity?

Depth interviews can help fill in historical blanks and in doing so make older people more understandable to the younger, by showing how wars, revolutions, and cultural expectations shaped previous generations. Often the formal record ignores slaves, women, religious or political minorities, conquered peoples, or people with particular illnesses. The glories of military victories may need to be tempered by descriptions of the sufferings of the soldiers on the front lines. Sometimes the formal record focuses only on the winners, forgetting the role of the challengers. Interview projects can help remedy these omissions.

Using qualitative interviews, researchers delve into important personal issues. Studies have explored what marriage means to husbands and wives and how marriages sometimes fall apart; they have examined how people live with and adapt to the constant humiliation of racism or sexism. Why do unmarried teenagers get pregnant? How do gay couples divide household work?

Decision makers use the results of qualitative interviewing studies to shed new light on old problems. Suppose a city had devised a program to improve reading scores of children in inner-city schools through a peer tutoring program but reading scores showed no improvement. What then? Researchers may talk to the children and learn from their stories that there are other factors contributing to the lack of educational progress, such as the fact that they are hungry, or that they have no quiet place to study, or that their younger siblings tear up their books. Based on the interviews, policy makers could decide to take a new approach, such as providing quiet study rooms after school.

Research based on depth interviews also helps us understand our work lives. Depth interviewers have asked how people deal with stress on the job, why workers defy the rules of the workplace and how they justify those breaches, and how workers build enough trust among themselves to form a union and strike. Interview data help explain barriers to promotion for women and minorities, often called the *glass ceiling*.

Naturalistic researchers examine both sides of an issue, the supervisors and the supervised, the suits and the blue collars, production and sales, the top-floor and the street-level workers. Though ordinary life roots you in one position, when you are interviewing, you see life in the round, from all angles, including multiple sides of a dispute and different versions of the same incident. Observing life from separate yet overlapping angles makes the researcher more hesitant to leap to conclusions and encourages more nuanced analysis. Qualitative interviewers explore new areas and discover and unravel intriguing puzzles. This search for answers keeps the researcher's imagination fresh and his or her work exciting.

A FAMILY OF QUALITATIVE INTERVIEWS

Quote

Qualitative interviews are conversations in which a researcher gently guides a conversational partner in an extended discussion. The researcher elicits depth and detail about the research topic by following up on answers given by the interviewee during the discussion. Unlike survey research, in which exactly the same questions are asked to each individual, in qualitative interviews each conversation is unique, as researchers match their questions to what each interviewee knows and is willing to share.

There are many approaches to depth qualitative interviewing that differ in how *narrow* or *broad* the interviewer's questions are. For example, imagine a researcher just beginning a project on graduate education. He or she might start with a broad question or statement—for example, "Let's talk about how it feels to be a graduate student"—and let the conversational partner answer any way he or she wishes (Douglas 1985). Such *open-ended, unstructured interviews* are meant to obtain a general flavor of what it is like to be a graduate student. Later, as the researcher discovers patterns, he or she might want to prepare a series of more specific, *semistructured* (also called *focused*) questions (Merton et al. 1990) that are suggested by the answers to the initial questions. Semistructured questions about graduate study might focus on preparation for comprehensive exams, choosing a thesis topic, the extent of faculty mentoring, and the amount of peer support among the graduate students.

Other interviews are narrower in focus, for instance, when the researcher is interested in the meaning of one core idea, such as what nursing staff think about pain management or what campaign promises mean to elected officials. Or the interviewer could be looking for a specific piece of information to figure out how a specific event occurred, for example, who made the decision to buy new software, or who is responsible for the death of an orangutan in the National Zoo.

A second way that qualitative interviews differ is whether they are about eliciting *understandings* or *meanings* or whether their purpose is to describe and portray specific *events* or *processes*. Is the purpose to find out how people understand the word *empowered* (a study on meanings) or is the goal to describe street demonstrations (events) that the community group carried out to persuade City Hall to pay attention to neighborhood problems?

Using these two dimensions—breadth of focus (narrow or broad) and subject of focus (meaning or description)—we have grouped various types of qualitative interviews, as shown in Table 1.1.

Table 1.1   The Variety of Qualitative Interviews

	Narrowly Focused Scope	In-Between	Broadly Focused Scope
Focused Mainly on Meanings and Frameworks	Concept clarification	Theory elaboration	Ethnographic interpretation
In-Between	Exit interview	Oral histories Organizational culture	Life history
Focused Mainly on Events and Processes	Investigative interviewing	Action research Evaluation research	Elaborated case studies

We will describe the corner cases and then those that fall in-between. Keep in mind that researchers sometimes use more than one pattern in a single study. For example, they may be conducting an elaborated case study, and in the middle of an interview examine a narrow concept.

CONCEPT CLARIFICATION

People who live in the same family or neighborhood or who work in the same organization or otherwise meet and interact regularly share a common history and vocabulary. When they talk to each other, they may use special words to describe their work or to describe bosses, customers, or colleagues. They may even use phrases that refer to whole episodes that everyone in the group knows about. The purpose of a *concept clarification interview* is to explore the meaning of these special, shared terms.

As you listen to your interviewees, you may notice that particular words are not being used in their ordinary sense. In one study, Irene Rubin was trying to learn how a city's budget process changed and had asked a fire chief to describe how his department viewed the budget office. The chief replied, "We view them as suits and they view us as unable to see the whole picture." Irene had to figure out what "suits" meant in this context. She listened to find out how other interviewees used this word, looked for examples, and then clarified these examples in subsequent discussions. She learned that to the fire fighters, those in the budget office acted like executives, dressing up like bankers, telling everyone what to do, whereas the people in the fire department wore hard hats, blue-collared shirts, and got things done. The clothes symbolized these differences.

INVESTIGATIVE INTERVIEWING

Investigative interviewing is narrowly focused to learn what happened in a specific instance. For example, managers might want to investigate excessive use of the photocopy machine, journalists might look into a case in which a man on death row claimed to have been wrongly convicted, or lawyers might examine the background of clients to find mitigating circumstances to reduce punishments. Each one of these investigations requires the researcher to do qualitative interviews on a narrow topic.

ELABORATED CASE STUDIES

The purpose of interviews conducted as part of *elaborated case studies* is to find out what happened, why, and what it means more broadly. The goal is not just to figure out who is using the photocopy machine without permission, but also to understand when and why employees feel entitled to use office equipment for their personal needs, if people consider such use wrong, and what people believe belongs to the employer. The study might address what factors increase or decrease employees' sense that office equipment and supplies are there for the taking. The hope in an elaborated case study is to be able to generalize to broader processes, to discover causes, and to explain or understand a phenomenon.

ETHNOGRAPHIC INTERPRETATION

Ethnographies are studies that sketch an overall cultural setting, such as that shared by an ethnic group, a village, or a neighborhood. This type of research describes the key norms, rules, symbols, values, traditions, and rituals in that setting, and shows how they fit together. Research about college students that portrays the major aspects of their lives, including partying, studying, sports, dating, working, and music, examines the rules underlying how to meet and whom to date and whether to cheat and how much to study, and includes experience with and attitudes toward professors, administrators, counselors, and fellow students would be an ethnographic study of college life.

THEORY ELABORATION

Interviewers engaged in *theory-elaboration* research pick a specific problem that is examined and from that study pull out themes that have some broader significance. Starting with something as narrow as insurance fraud, an interviewer might ask what kinds of fraud are common, who perpetrates them, and what differentiates successful and unsuccessful scams. The goal of the theory-elaboration study is to use a particular case to learn more about fraud and its perpetrators in general. In research on students, a theory-elaboration study might look at cheating on tests or how those in study groups help one another and then try to elaborate what is learned to figure out where the border line is between mutual help and dishonesty.

ORAL HISTORY

Oral-history interviews explore past events ranging from broad topics such as describing the war in Iraq or the administration of President Ronald Reagan to narrow concerns such as the events surrounding the shutdown of a chicken processing plant in Maine. By piecing together the stories of conversational partners who experienced specific events, such as the Great Depression or the Cuban Missile Crisis, the researcher reconstructs past history.

Some oral-history interviews focus on elites, such as those who were in the cabinet of a particular president, while others pay attention to ordinary people and their experiences. Studs Terkel's books on the Great

Depression and World War II provide moving accounts of how ordinary people responded to traumatic times (Terkel 1974, 1984). Other oral histories describe the extermination of Jews and others by Germany in World War II, portray those who survived the mass killings in Cambodia, or narrate the revolution in Iran when the Shah was deposed and religious fundamentalists took over the state. Such research helps explain the traumas that shaped a specific generation, perhaps suggesting how destructive rulers survive or what makes governmental regimes collapse.

ORGANIZATIONAL CULTURE

Organizational-culture research includes a more focused ethnographic study, homing in on a particular organization or work group to figure out rules of organizational behavior that are taken for granted from stories, shared metaphors, and lessons taught to new members. Organizational-culture studies may be triggered by a seemingly cataclysmic event, such as the meltdown of an accounting and auditing firm such as Anderson, which although dependent on its reputation for integrity, permitted the destruction of evidence in a legal case. Among other matters, organizational-culture studies explore why employees violate rules, why they obey orders when their moral compass says they shouldn't, and why some organizations are much more creative and adaptive than others (Frost et al. 1985; Schein 1985).

LIFE HISTORIES

Life histories are similar to oral histories, but rather than reflect on external happenings—for example, the protests of the 1960s, the Vietnam war—individuals are asked to provide a narrative about the stages of their life, their childhood, education, jobs, marriages and divorces, children, illnesses, and other crises they have weathered, as well as the good times. Life histories of important people may reveal their formative experiences, for example, what shaped the values and ambitions of a president of the United States. Life histories of ordinary people enable researchers to learn about the way people live (Cole and Knowles 2001; Tierney 1999), often focusing on documenting a way of life that is disappearing (Frisch 1990; Grele 1985; Lummis 1988; McMahan 1989).

A collection of life histories of people of different ages can illustrate change over time. For example, were the women interviewees born in the early 1900s expected to go to college, get a job, or marry when they graduated from high school? What about women who grew up in the 1930s,

1940s, or later? Or researchers could compare the life experiences of African Americans who grew up before the Civil Rights era, during that tumultuous period, and after that major change.

EVALUATION RESEARCH AND ACTION RESEARCH

The purpose of *evaluation research* and *action research* is to discover if programs and policies are working, for whom they are working, and what could be improved. For example, in determining whether welfare reforms are succeeding, evaluation researchers would interview former welfare recipients to learn how they were faring. An *exit interview* is a focused evaluation interview in which companies or schools or hospitals try to learn about people's experiences when they were employed, being educated, or hospitalized. People may be interviewed when they leave and asked to recall their lives there and to identify problems that need to be repaired.

Action research aims to change the status quo by documenting the extent of some problem, or by examining proposed solutions to see which might work best. An action researcher would examine problems faced by those in a neighborhood to figure out what can be done to solve them. Or action researchers who want to help the homeless might interview them to find out what legal problems they have had or what medical problems they face, so as to be able to work with those in need to redesign programs to help solve the problems uncovered.

Cultural and Topical Interviews as Ideal Types

All qualitative interviews share much in common, but differ in how the overall research projects are carried out. To highlight these differences, we have loosely grouped interviews into two broad categories, *topical* and *cultural*, the former examining what happens in specific circumstances, the latter exploring the ordinary, the routine, the shared history, the taken-for-granted norms and values, the rituals, and the expected behavior of a given group of people.

CULTURAL INTERVIEWS

To learn about culture, researchers ask members of a group about what is socially approved, listen for and discuss terms that are specific to a group or setting, and examine what people have learned through experience and then passed on to the next generation. Cultural interviews are designed differently from topical interviews. Often the interviewer has no preset agenda of issues to cover, allowing flexibility in what is discussed in any conversation. Because cultural knowledge, by definition, is widely shared, finding interviewees who have specific knowledge is less of an issue in cultural interviews than in topical studies. In interviews of people with similar cultural backgrounds and shared cultural knowledge, similar questions, ideas, and themes that emerge in the early interviews can be pursued in greater detail in later ones. With no preset agenda, interviews can be more relaxed and interviewers can build trust before broaching emotional or difficult topics.

Cultural interviewing involves more active listening than aggressive questioning. The researcher asks the interviewee to describe a typical day or ordinary occurrences, allowing the conversational partners plenty of room to portray what is important to them. Or the interviewer asks for examples that illustrate widespread assumptions, norms, or common behaviors. Whether the example is factually true or not is less important than how well it illustrates the assumptions and norms. If followers of David Koresh, who later immolated themselves when surrounded by government agents, described Koresh as a messenger of God, what matters is not whether he was a messenger of God but that his followers apparently believed it.

Conversational partners, however, may have difficulty directly explaining their culture because they take it for granted and hence it is invisible to them. So, before initiating cultural interviews, researchers often do participant observation and then ask for explanations of what they have seen, especially behavior that is culture-laden, such as a public ceremony or an object—for example, an award or a picture—associated with an important occurrence. Interviewers may also try to get at culture by eliciting stories that people pass on from one generation to the next, that embody relevant past experience and tell people how to behave and what to avoid (Boje 1995; Hummel 1991; McCall 1990). Researchers learned in a cultural study of one university that new faculty are told in tones of wonder and approval a story about a job candidate who had 18 books on his job resume. The clear implication is that writing many books is a cultural ideal irrespective of the exact number.

In writing about culture, to the extent publishers permit, the author presents the report in the words of the conversational partners, allowing readers who have the raw material of the interviews close at hand to make their own interpretations. In preparing a cultural report, the researcher is like a photographer, making choices about what to frame within the picture, but reproducing exactly what was there.

TOPICAL INTERVIEWS

Topical studies explore what, when, how, why, or with what consequence something happened. How did the Soviet Union, to some the epitome of the evil empire, collapse and fall apart? Why did a judge move a multiton sculpture of the Ten Commandments into a public building in apparent defiance of the constitutional requirement for the separation of church and state? Topical studies seek explanations for puzzling situations in a specific time and place. Unlike cultural research, in which the interviewer has to figure out what is of interest in routine events, in topical research the problem is highly visible at the beginning of the study.

The goal of topical interviews is to work out a coherent explanation by piecing together what different people have said, while recognizing that each person might have his or her own construction of events. The researcher sorts, balances, and analyzes what he or she heard, creating his or her own narrative that can be as simple as the summary phrases "the program works" or "the program fails" in an evaluation study, or as complicated as the minute details of how environmentalists created effective coalitions that preserved open space in a growing county (H. J. Rubin 1988a). The topical researcher is more like a skilled painter than a photographer, selecting details and creating an image from them.

In creating this narrative, the researcher tries to figure out the facts of the matter. Because the interviewer often needs a particular piece of information and must ascertain whether or not something is true, questioning in topical interviews is often somewhat more directive and aggressive than in cultural interviews. While there is no justification for any form of bullying—if people do not want to tell you something, you need to back off—topical interviewing is considerably more focused and preplanned than cultural interviewing.

In topical-research interviewing, researchers play a more active role than in cultural research. Though they listen carefully to learn the perspectives of the interviewees, the researchers themselves choose the initial topic. Topical interviewers spend time and effort finding interviewees most likely to know the answers, and through the questioning they try to make sure the conversation stays on target. In the final write-up, there may be proportionally fewer extended quotes from the interviewees and more judgments and conclusions from the researcher than in cultural interviews.

In practice, interviewing projects typically involve some cultural and some topical approaches, though usually more of one than the other. If you can master each style, you will be prepared for virtually any contingency that arises during an interviewing project.

Shared Characteristics of
In-Depth Qualitative Interviews

Though varying in purpose, style, and design, all forms of qualitative interviews share key features. First, projects using qualitative interviews build on a naturalistic, interpretive philosophy, a topic that we explore in depth in the next chapter. Second, qualitative interviews are extensions of ordinary conversations. Third, the interviewees are partners in the research enterprise rather than subjects to be tested or examined.

QUALITATIVE INTERVIEWS AS
EXTENSIONS OF ORDINARY CONVERSATIONS

Qualitative interviews and ordinary conversations share much in common. As in normal conversations, questions and answers follow each other in a logical fashion as people take turns talking. Researchers listen to each answer and determine the next question based on what was said. Interviewers do not work out three or four questions in advance and ask them regardless of the answers given. The interview, like an ordinary conversation, is invented new each time it occurs.

Because interviews are invented new each time, they can be wonderfully unpredictable. The conversational partner may take control of the interview and change the subject, guide the tempo, or indicate that the interviewer was asking the wrong questions. Sometimes interviewees become hostile, overly friendly, threatening, or flirtatious. Occasionally, bizarre events occur, such as happened to us in our first study when we arrived at our appointment and found the interviewee sitting in the middle of the room with a shotgun in his lap. Part of the skill of the qualitative researcher is in being able to adapt quickly to a situation that is totally unexpected.

Qualitative interviewing builds on the conversational skills that you already have. In ordinary conversations, people routinely ask questions and listen to the answers. "These pills are two years old—are they still good?" "I am lost. Where is Alden Place?" Such conversations follow well-known rules. People understand whose turn it is to talk and that it is impolite to interrupt. People know it is okay to change the subject and how to do it with grace. Everyone accepts that, for the most part, it does not matter exactly what they say, because ordinary conversations are as much about being in a relationship as they are a means of sharing information.

However, to conduct a qualitative interview and hear the meaning of what people say requires skills beyond those of ordinary conversation. Developing those skills takes considerable practice. How do you think of questions for a topic that you have chosen? How do you get people to stay focused? Whom do you interview and why? How can you trust what people are telling you?

On a more technical level, how do you persuade a person to become an interviewee? How specific should a question be? Is the wording too biased? How do you get people to elaborate on what they say? How do you put together different tellings of the same event? When do you take on-scene notes and when should you rely on memory? Do you use an audio recorder or a video camera?

Even the rules of ordinary conversation are a little different during an interview. For the most part, ordinary conversations are held between acquaintances. At least at the beginning of research, most qualitative interviews are between strangers, so part of the interviewing process requires establishing a connection that allows for an openness of exchange. Further, whereas some ordinary conversations may be guided by planned agendas, some hidden and some open, most are primarily sociable, moving from sports, to family, to complaints about work, with little apparent order. In contrast, many of the topics in depth interviews are intentionally introduced by the researcher, who encourages the interviewee to elaborate on a limited number of concerns. The result is more structured than is common in ordinary discourse.

Interviewers often focus the discussion on a narrow range of topics and then try to learn about these in detail. The depth, detail, and richness sought in interviews, what Clifford Geertz (1973) called *thick description,* are rooted in the interviewees' first-hand experiences and form the material that researchers gather and synthesize. To get to this level of detail, depth, and focus, researchers work out *main questions, probes,* and *follow-ups.* Main questions get a conversation going on a specific matter and ensure that the overall subject is covered, whereas probes are standardized ways to ask for more depth and detail and encourage the conversational partner to continue. To achieve richness and depth of understanding, those engaged in qualitative interviews listen for and then explore key words, ideas, and themes using follow-up questions to encourage the interviewee to expand on what he or she has said that the researcher feels is important to the research.

Researchers not only ask about what they have just heard, but may also ask about gaps and omissions. For example, if in describing a marriage the interviewee skips from the courtship to having children to the stresses of a divorce, the researcher might want to ask about the events that led to the divorce. Through intense and often physically fatiguing concentration, qualitative interviewers listen for what has not been said, as well as what has been said. *Qualitative interviewers listen to hear the meaning of what interviewees are telling them.* When they cannot figure out that meaning, they ask follow-up questions to gain clarity and precision.

Overall, qualitative interviewing requires more intense listening than normal conversations, a respect for and curiosity about what people say, a willingness to acknowledge what is not understood, and the ability to ask about what is not yet known.

INTERVIEWEES AS CONVERSATIONAL PARTNERS

Unlike survey interviews, in which those giving information are relatively passive and are not allowed the opportunity to elaborate, in qualitative interviews, interviewees share in the work and the fun of discovery, often guiding the questioning in channels of their own choosing.

In this book we call those who respond to interview questions *interviewees, informants,* or *conversational partners. Interviewee* is a relatively neutral word, but the term also refers to the subjects in survey research. *Informant* usually means someone who tells us about the research setting, and not just about his or her own experiences. However, the word *informant* also is used by the police to describe an individual who talks about another person's crime, so this term has to be used with caution. Our term *conversational partner* has the advantage of emphasizing the active role of the interviewee in shaping the discussion and in guiding what paths the research should take. Moreover, the term suggests a congenial and cooperative experience, as both interviewer and interviewee work together to achieve a shared understanding. Keeping in mind that the person being interviewed is a conversational partner reminds the researcher that the direction of the interview is shaped by both the researcher's and the interviewee's concerns.

The term *conversational partner* also emphasizes the uniqueness of each person with whom you talk, his or her distinct knowledge, and the different ways in which he or she interacts with you. Some conversational partners are self-revelatory, others more restrained and formalistic. Some need prodding to elaborate; others won't stop talking. Some have keen memories and provide lots of evidence, whereas others speak tentatively or are given to speculative conclusions.

The researcher customizes questions for each interviewee, accommodating both to what the person knows and to the topics that make the conversational partner most comfortable. Asking everyone the same questions makes little sense in qualitative interviewing. An interview is a window on a time and a social world that is experienced one person at a time, one incident at a time.

Our image of a partnership with the interviewee does not always work but represents the goal of integrating the concerns of those with whom we speak into how we do our research. If the partners can direct the conversation to matters that they know about and that they think are important, the interviews are likely to be of a higher quality. If you impose on them questions about what you think is important, you may substitute your ill-informed view of the field for their experienced and knowledgeable one.

The Organization of the Book and the Responsive Interviewing Model

Qualitative interviewing is both art and science. As a science there are some general rules and normative standards that should be followed, but as with all arts, techniques are modified to reflect the individual style of the artist. Some interviewers are more comfortable with meandering discussions; others need more structure. For a few researchers, aggressive questioning is a way of discovering information, whereas for many, passive listening is the approach to take. A range of personal interviewing styles is required to mesh with the variety of situations that qualitative researchers face.

This book introduces a model that we call *responsive interviewing*, an approach that allows a variety of styles yet incorporates what is standard in the field. The term *responsive interviewing* is intended to communicate that qualitative interviewing is a dynamic and iterative process, not a set of tools to be applied mechanically. In this model, questioning styles reflect the personality of the researcher, adapt to the varying relationships between researcher and conversational partner, and change as the purpose of the interview evolves. Responsive interviewers begin a project with a topic in mind but recognize that they will modify their questions to match the knowledge and interests of the interviewees. You would not talk to major league baseball players about foreign policy or to officials in the State Department about the politics of major league baseball teams. Instead, in responsive interviewing, the specific focus of a study emerges from the interaction between researcher and conversational partner. *Qualitative research is not simply learning about a topic, but also learning what is important to those being studied.*

As in nearly all research, qualitative projects end with a careful analysis of what has been learned that is written up in reports, dissertations, articles, or books. However, unlike many other forms of research, in the responsive interviewing model, *analysis is not a one-time task, but an ongoing process.* Interviews are systematically examined—analyzed—immediately after they are conducted, to suggest further questions and topics to pursue. Interviews are later reexamined as a group. If gaps are seen even when writing a report, the researcher may go back to conduct more interviews. Analyzing and interviewing alternate throughout a study.

In this book we examine both the philosophy and techniques of depth interviewing. In Chapter 2 we discuss the intellectual frameworks that shape qualitative interviewing methods and show how the procedures emerge from an interpretive, constructionist philosophy of knowledge.

Qualitative interviewing is flexible, but it is not random or happenstance. Rather, it adapts as circumstances change. Chapters 3 and 4 describe this process of adaptive planning that we term *iterative research design.* Chapter 3 examines how researchers choose topics initially and then through iterative and flexible redesign refine their topic in response to what they learn from the conversational partners. The chapter also addresses how to design research to ensure that you end up with sufficient evidence to make a convincing argument. Chapter 4 continues the discussion on iterative design, examining how researchers achieve credibility through careful choice of interviewees and research sites, thoroughness in questioning, and accuracy and transparency in reporting.

Chapter 5 discusses how to encourage conversational partners to share their experiences. This chapter also examines research ethics that are central to conducting open-ended qualitative interviews, emphasizing the obligations of the interviewer to protect the conversational partner from harm as a result of the research.

The next four chapters focus on the phases of developing actual interviews. Chapter 6 explores the dynamics that occur between researcher and conversational partner during an interview. Chapter 7 looks more closely at the purposes of main questions, probes, and follow-up questions and how to integrate them in a single interview. Chapter 8 suggests ways of wording main questions and probes. Chapter 9 describes how to figure out what to follow up and how to phrase the follow-up questions.

The logic and techniques of qualitative data analysis are covered in Chapters 10 and 11, which describe how to identify concepts and themes and combine them to answer the research problem. Chapter 12 is about sharing the results of this analysis through writing up the findings in ways that are richly descriptive and delicately nuanced, clear, absorbing, and convincing, and that ultimately can be published.

THE AUTHORS

The responsive interviewing model recognizes that researchers as well as conversational partners are individuals with emotions, biases, and interests. To give a feeling for how personal characteristics and interests affect interviewing, we have used many examples from our own research. The two of us—Irene Rubin, a public administrator, and Herb Rubin, an urbanologist— have engaged in a variety of projects. Years ago, Herb and Irene studied the impact of Thai government economic development projects on poor farmers. Herb has examined the too-rapid growth of suburbia and, in another project, talked with those whose job it is to promote economic growth in the United States. He has conducted hundreds of interviews with community activists and national advocates who spend their lives trying to improve the job prospects, housing, and safety of poor people. Irene has looked at how governments cut back and balance their budgets, how budget processes change, and whether and how governments learn to solve problems. Where do bureaucracies store what they learn and how do they retrieve it when then need it? Irene is now trying to figure out the implications of governments contracting with the private sector to offer some services.

Our experiences include formal interviews with assistant secretaries of cabinet-level departments, casual conversations in rice paddies with Southeast Asian farmers, and informal interviews in retirement homes. At different times, we have conducted evaluation interviews, action research, elaborated case studies, and investigative interviews. We have had interviews with those who have put one over on us and we have had interviews whose depth and frankness have embarrassed us. On occasion, we have had to act aggressively, like an investigative reporter; more often, we have listened in a less directive way to what our conversational partners wanted to communicate. The text is laced with examples of problems we have run into and usually managed to get out of. We want to show that real research is not always a smooth operation; the unpredictability of qualitative interviewing requires a continual, thoughtful set of solutions to emerging problems. Qualitative interviewing is forgiving; you can make mistakes and recover from them if you are alert and a little bit lucky. Most importantly, by sharing our work, we hope you will feel some of the excitement we feel each time we learn something new.[1]

Since our work reflects only a tiny fraction of what can be accomplished through depth interviewing, we have supplemented personal examples from our colleague, Jim Thomas, a criminologist. As we were working on this book, we noticed that most of our conversational partners were in mainstream professions and usually on the right side of the law. Jim was nice enough to share with us his experiences with people in jail and others that the mainstream labels as deviant. We have also added many examples from published research projects on urban life, health, schools, police, and the economy. Choosing the examples has been difficult, since there are so many good studies to pick. We have selected only a small, and we hope representative, sample of what is out there, including Wilson's (1996) and Anderson's (1999) studies of urban poverty, Charmaz's (1991) reports describing those with chronic illnesses, Lather and Smithies' (1997) group interviews with women with AIDS, and Chase's (1995) discussion of women school superintendents. We also rely on Duneier's (1999) description of street venders in New York City and MacLeod's (1995) observations and interviews of teenage street gang members, as well as an oral life history of how the closing of a poultry plant affected one woman (Chatterley et al. 2000). We use these books (and others mentioned throughout this text) because they are fine studies and often display interviewing styles that differ from our own and because these studies opened up new worlds to us. We hope they will have the same effect on you.

Note

1. Most of our responsive interviewing research is on problems of the public sector or on advocacy organizations that seek to influence the public sector. See H. J. Rubin (1973, 1984, 1988a, 1988b, 1993, 1994, 1995, 1997, 2000) and I. S. Rubin (1977, 1982, 1985, 1992, 2002, 2003).

2

Why We Do What We Do

Philosophy of Qualitative Interviewing

D uring our 35-year-long research adventure studying the social and political world, we have relied on a wide variety of data-gathering techniques. Using participant observation we watched interactions between bureaucrats and peasants in a developing country. With in-depth interviews we explored how cities, universities, and the federal government respond to budget deficits, how institutional racism affects urban redevelopment work, and how government agencies learn. We've designed telephone surveys and mail surveys on a variety of topics. Early in our careers we used whatever data-gathering method seemed to fit the research problem. After a number of years, however, we found we were relying nearly exclusively on observations and depth interviews because we got fuller and more creative results. Over time, many other researchers in sociology, political science, public administration, education, and health have also found that qualitative methods are what to use when studying a complex and nuanced world.

In this chapter, we contrast two different philosophies of research, a *positivist* and an *interpretive constructionist* approach that reflect major intellectual disagreements about the kind of information that researchers should be looking for and how they should go about obtaining it. The positivist philosophy underlies experiments, surveys, and other statistical studies and imitates the ways in which those in the natural sciences go about their work. If the topic is suitable, researchers can do high-quality work using the positivist model, but depending on what you want to learn, imitating the hard sciences is not always the best approach.

The interpretive constructionist approach guides observational and depth interviewing projects. We argue that for many research problems, this paradigm is more appropriate. In this chapter we describe these contrasting models and then indicate why and how we use an interpretive constructionist approach. We conclude the chapter by presenting the *responsive interviewing* model, which builds on an interpretive constructionist approach and frames the way we design research, collect data, and analyze our findings.

But why worry about the philosophy underpinning qualitative interviewing? One reason is that understanding the interpretive constructionist approach enables you to adapt to unexpected research problems and work out new solutions that enable you to collect information that is both thorough and credible. Another reason is to help you deal with the paradigm fights that sometimes create obstacles for qualitative researchers. In many academic disciplines, powerful individuals—often those who provide the grants or edit major journals—believe that only quantitative research, such as surveys, experiments, and statistical analysis of official data, is rigorous and systematic. To justify your research approach, you need to understand their assumptions and how the assumptions of your model differ.

In addition, in policy shops, research institutes, and universities, approval is required before doing research—from a boss, a dissertation chair, or increasingly from committees called institutional review boards (IRBs), which are set up to protect human subjects. Unfortunately, those whose approval is needed might be unfamiliar with interpretive constructionist paradigms and erroneously assume that all social research is undertaken in the positivist way. As a result, they may demand to see questionnaires composed of identical prepared-in-advance questions and assume that the questions will be asked by dispassionate researchers to a random selection of subjects. As a naturalist researcher, you must be able to explain why you are not asking all your interviewees the same question and why you cannot predict all the information you will be looking for prior to the interviewing. Being able to explain differences between positivist and naturalist philosophies enables you to convince bosses, thesis supervisors, and IRB members that your work is legitimate and that your methods are sound.

An Introduction to Philosophies of Research

A research philosophy, or paradigm, shapes how people study their world. According to LeCompte and Schensul, "[a] paradigm constitutes a way of looking at the world; interpreting what is seen; and deciding which of the things seen by researchers are real, valid, and important to document" (1999, p. 41). A research philosophy also indicates how research ought to be conducted, by whom, and with what degrees of involvement or dispassion. Research philosophies address four key questions that distinguish positivist from naturalist approaches.

FIRST, WHAT IS THE CORE GOAL OF RESEARCH?

Is it developing and testing theories and discovering general principles or is it describing and understanding complex situations? Is it documenting need and creating the basis for action or reform?

WHAT DOES TRUTH MEAN?

Is there truth out there that is independent of human perception? Or does truth differ from person to person, according to what individuals see and experience and how they interpret events, stories, and conversations? Do the findings of the research represent some objective truth, the understanding of the researcher, the various understandings of those being researched, or some combination?

WHAT TYPES OF RESEARCH INSTRUMENTS ARE APPROPRIATE?

Research instruments are built on assumptions that differ in each paradigm. A questionnaire presupposes that the questions asked make uniform sense to the people being surveyed and that the answers make sense. Positivists accept these assumptions. Naturalist researchers question the possibility of uniformly shared understandings. Instead, in naturalist research, the researchers themselves become the data-gathering instrument whose skills in listening, observing, and understanding are crucial.

HOW DOES AND SHOULD THE RESEARCHER AFFECT THE PROCESS OF DISCOVERY?

Is it possible for the researcher to be neutral and not affect what is seen or measured? Positivists say yes, but naturalists argue that since the researcher is human, not an automaton, the researcher inevitably affects what is learned.

COMPARING POSITIVIST AND
NATURALIST-INTERPRETIVE PARADIGMS

Let us assume you are employed by a nonprofit organization that has worked for years to provide poor people with affordable housing. To get more grants, your organization has to show the foundations and government agencies its prior accomplishments. Suppose the grant makers are pleased with the number of homes your organization has built but want to learn about the impact of those homes. To answer them, you might do a study to discover how many people your organization has helped find decent-quality, affordable housing in safe neighborhoods, and if, as a consequence, people need to move less frequently.

You begin with a survey on a random sample of households, both those your organization has helped and others in the same neighborhood. You ask each household the same questions: how much they earn, how much housing costs them now and how much it cost in the past, and how long they have lived where they now live. You also ascertain the age of the housing, its size, how many modern amenities it has, and similar indicators of housing quality.

This initial research follows many positivist assumptions. It assumes a shared understanding of what income and what housing costs mean to determine on average whether people in the homes the organization built are getting the same or better housing for fewer dollars than before. You are trying to measure the average impact of the program; if most people are better off, the program has been effective. To show impact, you should be able to compare the housing quality and cost between those your program has helped and those you have not reached.

You might decide, however, to continue the research and conduct in-depth interviews to hear from program beneficiaries how improved housing affected their lives. For instance, you could find out that children who are living in stable, affordable homes do better at school since they do not have to move so often. Or you might discover that those who bought homes from your organization gained self-confidence, joining neighborhood groups and setting up their own businesses. You might learn that people who feel better about themselves more often get involved in local politics, and you might then decide to extend your research to include the political reawakening of the neighborhood.

Naturalist researchers doing this evaluation project would proceed from the nuanced stories they hear from different people to construct a portrait of what improvements in housing have meant for individuals and their communities. Positivists would be more likely to go in a different direction. They would do a survey and ask if people feel empowered, asking each potential respondent the identical question and requiring answers of the "yes, a lot," "some," and "no, not at all" variety. The positivists would then count how many people answered "yes," "some," or "no." Naturalist researchers would retort that classifying responses into narrow categories such as *yes* and *no* obscures what empowerment means to the individuals and how it occurs. At this point, the contrast between research philosophies is stark.

POSITIVISM AND ITS CRITICS

Emulating physicists or biologists in their approach, positivist social researchers look for the uniform, precise rules that they claim organize social behavior. Positivists in the social and behavioral sciences examine simplified models of the social world to see how a small number of variables—gender and education, for instance—interact. The language of positivism is a numeric one; the goal is a series of statistical equations that explain and predict human behavior. Because positivists seek rules that apply uniformly, they extract simple relationships from a complex real world and examine them as if context did not matter and as if social life were stable rather than constantly changing (Denzin 1989; Lincoln and Guba 1985).

Positivists presuppose that knowledge is politically and socially neutral and is achieved by following a rigid plan for gathering information. They argue that a commitment to quantitative precision and an accumulation of facts is the way in which to build a close approximation to a reality that exists independently of human perception. They express what they learn through mathematical manipulation of variables they have predefined, often taking these definitions from an existing academic theory (Lincoln and Guba 1985). Because they assume that truth can and should be measured with statistical precision, positivists routinely reduce complex information to numbers and ignore that which is difficult to quantify; because they seek general rules, they often ignore subtleties or unusual cases.

Positivists assume that objects and events that researchers study exist independently of people's perceptions and hence there can be only one version that is true. The idea that there may be several different constructions of events by the participants, each of which is true in some sense, underlies much of qualitative interviewing but is unacceptable to positivists. For instance, survey researchers, following a positivist philosophy, develop standard questions to ask all their interviewees. With some questions—what is your age or for whom did you vote in the last election?—imposing a single, standard definition is not problematic, because most people agree on what each question means. But people may have different conceptions of fairness, happiness, or religious belief. Interpretivists would argue that trying to impose a standard definition of such terms across different people is misleading or confusing. Two respondents may answer "yes" to a question, but mean different things.

In gathering survey data, interviewers act in a uniform way with every research subject and do not get involved with the interviewees, so that the answers cannot be attributed to the personality of the interviewer. Survey researchers ask everyone the same questions and the respondents are allowed to answer only in categories that are designed in advance by the researcher. Respondents are treated as interchangeable parts, with no particular individuality, except on background characteristics that are defined by the researcher. Since the researcher words the questions in advance, the interview is intellectually dominated by the initial perceptions of the researcher rather than the understandings of the interviewees.

After they have gathered data, positivist researchers calculate the sums and averages of their measures. If one wants to know on average whether women are paid less than men for identical work or if some geographic areas receive fewer mortgages, statistical data are appropriate. The economic background of those imprisoned, the number of people laid off by the airlines after 9/11, and the number of homes built by community groups are all important objects to count and measure. You don't lose much, if anything, in translating these concepts to numbers, and sometimes you can see trends and relationships through statistical analysis that you cannot see with the naked eye.

However, if you stop the research at the counting stage, you miss a great deal. You know what people say they earn, but you do not know what that means or whether there are major differences in how people who have the same income live and feel, whether they feel poor or successful. You don't know how they live on their income, how they deal with gift-giving holidays such as Christmas, or what they do about unexpected medical bills. In short, the counting aspects of the research, though useful, tell only a small part of the story, and not always the most interesting or useful part.

A number of research philosophies, such as the critical, postmodern, feminist, and constructionist paradigms, oppose specific parts of positivism. Rather than looking for underlying and unchanging truths, the way positivists do, proponents of these other philosophies argue that the goal of research is learning about contingent truth, truth that seems to hold at a particular time under specified circumstances. Rather than assume a neutral researcher and impartial fact-based research, these paradigms assume that the researchers' ideas and personality affect the research and that the aim of research is to bolster a social or political agenda or give voice to those who have been silenced. We will limit our discussion to ideas from these alternative philosophies that point to some of the more serious criticisms of positivism and that have shaped the responsive interviewing model.

CRITICAL THEORY

Research that follows the *critical theory* (Kincheloe and McLaren 2000) paradigm emphasizes the importance of discovering and rectifying societal problems. Rather than advocating neutrality, critical researchers emphasize action research, arguing that research should redress past oppression, bring problems to light, and help minorities, the poor, the sidelined, and the silenced. In this model, knowledge does not exist outside the perceiver, waiting to be discovered by every researcher as an identical and universal truth. Instead knowledge is subjective, what you see depends on whose perspective you take, whose eyes view it. This insistence on subjectivity is sometimes called *standpoint theory* because the theory emphasizes whose standpoint or point of view you are taking. Most versions of feminist, queer,[1] and critical race theories emphasize the importance of *standpoint*.

Critical research is a means of empowering the oppressed. Critical researchers explicitly take sides by studying underdog groups, those facing oppression, suppression, and powerlessness, in order to give voice to the victims of crimes; migrant workers; the hospitalized ill; AIDS patients, their lovers, and their advocates; political and social minorities; and the handicapped. Critical researchers examine situations in which the accomplishments of the oppressed were ignored, defeats were prematurely accepted, or careers were waylaid or ruined and try to learn how and why these things occurred. For those who accept a critical paradigm, the truth they study is the reality of oppression. Research is about documenting how that oppression has been experienced and how ordinary people can understand the causes of the prejudice, poverty, or humiliation they have suffered. Research should lead to action to reduce the problems caused by oppression and try to "connect the everyday troubles individuals face to public issues of power, justice and democracy" (Kincheloe and McLaren 2000, p. 289).

FEMINIST THEORY

As part of the broader critical approach, *feminist theory* pays particularly close attention to issues of dominance and submission and how these issues affect understanding.[2] To feminist researchers, surveys are disempowering because they do not allow the interviewee to explain what he or she feels and because the pretense of neutrality ignores the cultural assumptions that shape the survey questions. Further, the reduction of information to summary numbers and the interchangeability of interviewees dehumanizes, while the stripping away of context obscures the structures that perpetuate unjust systems of dominance.

Feminist researchers have worked out a research methodology that is gentler and that humanizes both the researcher and the interviewee. Allowing people to "talk back" (hooks 1989) gives a voice through interviews to those who have been silenced; talking back becomes a political act. Feminist researchers argue that the interviewer and interviewee should try to build a relationship in which they share responsibility for finding the words and concepts in which ideas can be expressed and lives described, and by doing so emphasize the importance of issues in which women are deeply engaged. If positivists disempower interviewees, feminists intentionally empower them.

Feminist researchers argue that a more open, loosely structured research methodology is necessary to learn about women, to capture their words, their concepts, and the importance they place on the events in their world. An interview should not involve applying a sterile instrument to a passive object, but should resemble normal conversation in which the interviewee influences the exchanges. Further, in the course of time, the researcher may become a friend to the interviewee. Feminist research emphasizes the importance of cultural affinity between the researcher and the conversational partner, with some feminist researchers claiming not only that women should interview women but also that interviewers need to be in the same position as the interviewees; for example, adult students with children should interview other adult students with children.

Because the researcher is playing an active role in the interview, he or she needs to be aware of her own emotions. The interviewer's emotions affect what he or she can hear and understand. If the interviewer is anxious, it may be difficult to really hear what interviewees are saying; if the interviewer is angry at what is being said, he or she may change the direction of the questions or fail to hear positive things about the research question.

POSTMODERNIST THEORY

Researchers who identify themselves as *postmodernist* also reject much of positivism. Postmodernism assumes that reality is not fully knowable and that truth is impossible to define. At the extreme, some postmodernists worry that nothing at all can be known and claim that the best that can be accomplished is for researchers to allow people to share experiences and feelings with one another. Postmodernists argue that neutrality is impossible because everyone has interests and attitudes that influence how topics are selected, what questions are deemed appropriate, how they are asked, and what means of analysis are considered appropriate. Like snowflakes, no two researchers are exactly alike, so the conclusions reached by different researchers are unlikely to match. This lack of match is not problematic for postmodernists, because it is just recognition of the fact that knowledge is situational and contextual.

Rather than accepting that there is one correct view as the positivists do, postmodernists argue that the researcher's view is only one among many and has no more legitimacy than the views of the people being studied. It is important therefore to present a range of views and conclusions, in as nearly raw a fashion as possible, that is, in the words of the speakers, with little interpretive overlay. Among the positivists, the researcher is authoritative, what he or she finds is close to truth, and he or she is the voice of the written report. But because the author's voice is not privileged in the postmodernist paradigm, the postmodernists have created a dilemma about whose voice is and ought to be communicated. Some argue that only the interviewees' voices should be presented through unedited videotapes or transcripts of recordings of what was said (Atkinson 2001; Denzin 1997; Gergen 1999; Schwandt 1999, 2000).

INTERPRETIVE CONSTRUCTIONIST THEORY

To interpretive constructionist researchers, how people view an object or event and the meaning that they attribute to it is what is important. It matters less whether a chair is 36 inches high and 47 years old than that one person perceives it as an antique and another views it as junk. Constructionists expect people to see somewhat different things, examine them through distinct lenses, and come to somewhat different conclusions. In this sense, multiple and even conflicting versions of the same event or object can be true at the same time. The person who calls a wooden chair an antique is no more correct than the person who views it as junk; he or she just comes to the chair with different experiences, knowledge, and opinions, resulting in a different interpretation.

Constructionist researchers try to elicit the interviewee's views of their worlds, their work, and the events they have experienced or observed. Rather than looking for the average and ignoring the specific, as positivists often do, interpretive constructionists look for the specific and detailed and try to build an understanding based on those specifics (Berger and Luckmann 1967; Charmaz and Mitchell 2001; Gergen 1999; Gubrium and Holstein 1997; Hammersley 2001).

Some constructionists are concerned with the lenses through which people view events, the common expectations and meanings through which people interpret what they see and what happens to them. If those expectations and meanings shared by groups of people are passed from one generation of group members to the next, they then form part of a *culture*. If some people view an old chair as an antique, where did they get that idea? What definition of antique are they using? Is any object more than 40 years old an antique? Or does it have to be valuable to be an antique, for example, made by a particular furniture maker or made in a particular style? What determines whether a chair will be bought and resold by an antiques dealer or a used furniture store? Constructionists would say that groups of people create such definitions and share them with each other. Children may learn the meaning of antique from their parents or in a museum if they try to sit on a very old chair and the museum guard shoos them away. The meaning may be passed along in books with pictures of particular chairs and their prices. Constructionists would argue that *antique* is not an objective idea but a designation given by people to an object that makes it meaningful (and expensive) for them.

Constructionists often pay attention to the shared meanings held by those in a *cultural arena*—a setting in which people have in common matters such as religion, history, work tasks, confinement in prison, or political interests. By living and working together or even routinely interacting in a neighborhood or profession, people come to share some meanings, some ways of judging things (Gubrium and Holstein 1997, p. 172). For example, a professional group of budgeters might hold in common an idea of what budgetary balance means. Nurses in a cardiac rehabilitation unit may have a shared idea of a typical patient that includes eating unhealthy food and reluctance to exercise. Street vendors of magazines, many of whom are homeless, together form a cultural arena in which they understand meanings in a similar way. Though the city ordinances define the situation otherwise, the street vendors do not see it as theft when they take and resell the recyclables people have put out at the curb for municipal pickup (Duneier 1999). Interpretive constructionist researchers work to figure out what the shared meanings are in some particular group, recognizing that though each person interprets the events he or she encounters in a somewhat distinct manner, he or she is likely, at the same time, to bring to bear the understandings held by peers, family, friends, coreligionists, or members of other groups to which he or she belongs.

The cultural lenses that people use to judge situations are often taken for granted and as such are invisible (Schutz 1967, p. 74). As a consequence, it is difficult for researchers to directly ask about culture. Instead, researchers have to learn about culture by asking about ordinary events and deducing the underlying rules or definitions from these descriptions and pay particular attention to unusual usages of words and to the stories that convey cultural assumptions.

Those who follow the interpretive constructionist approach recognize that researchers also make cultural assumptions that influence what they ask and how they construe what they hear. Interpretive researchers do not need to drop their cultural assumptions and assume those of the conversational partners, but researchers do need to be cautious lest they fail to hear the meaning of what the interviewees have said because their own cultural assumptions get in the way. The ability to get into the world of someone who does not share one's own lenses requires an ability to first recognize and then suspend one's own cultural assumptions long enough to see and understand another's (Gergen 1999, p. 50).

Like those in the various critical schools of thinking and the postmodernists, interpretive constructionists reject many of the tenets of positivism. Positivists often seek to quantify what they study, but constructionists argue that the meaning of a number is socially constructed—not an absolute that exists outside of the meaning that people give it. Numbers do not speak for themselves. The president of a company might interpret recent economic indicators as signs of increased productivity, whereas workers may look at the same numbers and see longer hours without any pay increases. They each bring different constructions of what success is to the numbers and take away separate meaning and conclusions.

Positivists often look for the central tendency, some measure of what is average or typical. Interpretivists are usually not interested in averages but in syntheses of understandings that come about by combining different individuals' detailed reports of a particular event or cultural issue.

Interpretivist researchers try to sort through the experiences of different people as interpreted through the interviewees' own cultural lenses and then weigh different versions to put together a single explanation.

Excessive reliance on statistical measures strips away context, and hence meaning. An interpretivist might say, "I don't know or understand what someone means when he/she answers on a survey that abortion is wrong some of the time." Such an answer cries out for a follow-up question: When is it wrong and when is it okay? The constructivist would listen to stories and try to figure out how the interviewee determined if abortion was acceptable or wrong. Constructionists argue that positivists often ask questions that have complex answers using techniques that allow only simple responses.

Responsive Interviewing

Responsive interviewing is what we have termed our approach to depth interviewing research. The responsive interviewing model relies heavily on the interpretive constructionist philosophy, mixed with a bit of critical theory and then shaped by the practical needs of doing interviews. The model emphasizes that the interviewer and interviewee are both human beings, not recording machines, and that they form a relationship during the interview that generates ethical obligations for the interviewer. In the responsive interviewing model the goal of the research is to generate depth of understanding, rather than breadth. The third characteristic of responsive interviewing is that the design of the research remains flexible throughout the project.

TWO HUMAN BEINGS

The responsive interviewing model recognizes the fact that both the interviewer and the interviewee are people, with feelings, personality, interests, and experiences. Interviewers are not expected to be neutral or automatons, and who they are and how they present themselves affect the interview. Each interviewer develops his or her own style that he or she is comfortable with and that matches his or her personality. On the other hand, because the interviewer and interviewee interact and influence each other, the interviewer has to be self-aware, examining his or her own biases and expectations that might influence the interviewee.

STYLE

The responsive interviewing model accepts that researchers develop different styles. Some interviewers are most comfortable encouraging others to talk while minimizing their own involvement. They keep their opinions to themselves, not challenging, even when an interviewee contradicts him- or herself, exaggerates accomplishments, or engages in finger-pointing. This nonconfrontational style is best when an interviewer can reinterview the same person, so particular topics can be broached a second time. Other researchers are comfortable with a more direct approach. These interviewers like to challenge their conversational partners, point out possible contradictions or omissions, and mention conflicting interpretations. This more aggressive style is most useful in showing the interviewee that more is expected than pat answers.

Style shows itself in the way in which researchers prepare and conduct an interview. Some researchers like to introduce themselves and the topic, start the interview right away, ask their questions, and leave. Others prefer a more gradual approach, spending more time building up a relationship with chat on nonrelated matters before beginning to ask questions. In preparing for an interview, some simply write down the broad topics they want to cover, whereas others more carefully note possible follow-up questions, mentally or physically crossing them off if interviewees answer them before they get to ask them. Others rely on their memory and spontaneity to formulate the right questions as the interview goes on. Some interviewers take copious notes, whereas others rely on audio recorders almost exclusively, concentrating more on listening carefully and less on taking notes.

None of these stylistic variations is inherently right or wrong. What works is a style that makes the conversational partner feel comfortable, obtains needed information, and is compatible with the researcher's personality.

SELF-REFLECTION

Rather than pretend that interviewers come into the situation with no biases and can listen to answers without sifting them through their own experiences and cultural lenses, the responsive interviewing model argues that researchers need to continually examine their own understandings and reactions. Personal involvement is a great strength of the responsive interviewing model, because empathy encourages people to talk, and yet active involvement in the interview can also create problems, as your own emotions and biases can influence what you ask and how your interviewee responds.

To be a successful interviewer, you have to sensitize yourself to these biases and learn to compensate for your own slant.

During the pauses between your interviews, you should look over your interviews and see if your questions are inappropriately leading the interviewee to specific answers or if you are avoiding following up in places that warrant additional questioning because you do not want to hear what might be said. If you find that you are so strongly committed to your own perspective that you end up asking leading questions or avoid pursuing certain matters because you find them too stressful, you probably should pick a different research topic.

Self-reflection can help improve the quality of interviews in other ways as well. If you see yourself losing your temper or getting short with an interviewee when you suspect he or she may have lied to you, you may want to work out ways of avoiding asking questions that might elicit lies. Make sure you are not asking for personal information too early in an interview, be cautious about saying anything that sounds as if it might be an accusation or criticism, and be aware that if you ask questions about rule violations, you might cause your interviewees to evade your questions.

Also watch yourself as you increasingly identify with those whom you are researching. You do want to be empathetic, but some researchers get so enthralled with what they are learning that they forget to ask about the downside of the topic. If this applies to you, you might want to build into your pattern of questions ways of approaching topics to ensure some balance.

Self-awareness is not only useful for improving the quality of interviews, but is also necessary to protect yourself as you become more deeply involved in the world of those whom you are studying. In responsive interviewing, influence is a two-way street. Responsive interviewers run the risk of being overwhelmed when they recognize how little they really know about a topic they thought they understood and how much there is to learn. Anticipating that your understanding will grow can help you deal with feelings of insecurity.

Researchers may also be affected on a personal, political, or social level by what they are learning. You may become so angry that you decide activism is more important than research. Or, you could start out feeling sympathy for those who take the time and the risk to run for office but end up feeling skepticism about their motivations and effectiveness, making you feel alienated. These kinds of changes may affect your self-image in destabilizing ways.

In the extreme, the empathy that enables a person to be a skilled interviewer can cause the researcher to question his or her own values. If you find yourself sympathizing with interviewees who are killers, racists, or religiously intolerant, or who are abusing public trust, you might begin to have questions about yourself. If empathizing with views with which you strongly disagree makes you feel too hypocritical to function well, then you may have to redraw the boundaries of your research to avoid topics that you cannot handle well. If you cannot empathize with both management and labor, then just study management or just study labor. If you can persist with the study, though, you will find that the intense relationship that is necessary to learning will fade gradually after the study is done. You may end up with changed attitudes, but your basic values are likely to remain in place.

Be cautious, however, that your own confusion about where your loyalties lie does not motivate you to reject the interviewees and their world so strongly that you write about them with anger. One could imagine studying gay bars, for example, and empathizing with the patrons you are interviewing to such an extent that you come to wonder about your own convictions or beliefs. When you do the write-up, you may reject the interviewees and their stories as a way of telling yourself, and the world, that you are not gay and as such write a report that is not fully honest. If you are sufficiently self-aware, you will be able to see that what you are doing is biasing your report, and you put the project down and deal with the personal implications before resuming the writing.

IN A RESEARCH RELATIONSHIP

Central to the responsive interviewing model is the understanding that the interviewer and interviewee are in a relationship in which there is mutual influence, yet in which individuality needs to be recognized. Though the researcher initially establishes the general direction of the project, the conversational partners set the more specific path. Initial questions are expressed in a broad way to give the interviewees the opportunity to answer from their own experiences. The interviewees' answers then suggest to the researcher what to pursue and what to ignore. The low-key and open-ended way in which interviewing is conducted encourages the conversational partners to suggest topics, concerns, and meanings that are important to them.

During the extended conversations, the interviewer and conversational partner develop common understandings that differ from person to person. Responsive interviewers recognize that each conversational partner has a distinct set of experiences, a different construction of the meaning of those experiences, and different areas of expertise. As such, researchers create new questions for each interviewee because they need to tap this distinctive knowledge. In addition, interview questions change as the relationship between the researcher and the conversational partner evolves. Questions are worded differently depending on the level of closeness and trust, and ultimately friendship, that develops over time. What a researcher can ask during a first-time interview with a government official who has granted a one-time 30-minute time slot is dramatically different from what he or she can ask during a fourth interview that takes an entire afternoon with a person who has become a friend.

Because the responsive interviewing model assumes a mutual and personal relationship between interviewer and interviewee, the researcher is bound by the same norms of reciprocity that apply elsewhere in his or her life. What the researcher receives is the time, thoughtfulness, and openness of the interviewee. What does the researcher give back?

The project itself may benefit the conversational partners by helping them overcome problems they face or making those problems visible to the public and policy makers. Even if the researcher cannot help solve problems, he or she should ensure that the interviewing experience is pleasant and fun and perhaps helps the interviewee understand his or her own experiences better. The researcher should not be bullying, or pursue issues the interviewee is reluctant to discuss, or be demeaning or deceptive. A little humor, warmth, attention, and support can make the interview rewarding for the conversational partner. Ideally, the interview experience should leave interviewees better off.

Because the researcher is asking for openness from the interviewees, reciprocity suggests he or she reveal something of himself or herself. At the very least, interviews should not become power games in which you try to make the conversational partner reveal all while you yourself remain silent. You should not go after personal information you do not need. You should take the least intrusive route to what you do need, leaving the choice of whether and what to reveal to the interviewee after you have expressed an interest in a matter.

As part of the developing relationship with the conversational partner, the researcher takes on deep ethical obligations. These include the obligation to report the interviews accurately and fairly, the responsibility to keep any promises made in order to get the interview, and the commitment to not harm the interviewees. Although ethics requires kindness and gentleness toward your interviewee, as a researcher you are also obligated to be accurate in what you report. Sometimes there is a tension between reporting accurately and not harming interviewees, especially if you have found out something unflattering. Though you aim for balance in your presentation, you need not *always* present in your writings *everything* that you have learned. Ethical researchers decide whether the harm they might inflict in what they report is justified by the increased accuracy. Often presenting the negative things you learned will not be necessary to communicate the narrative you are putting together.

DEPTH OF UNDERSTANDING AND FLEXIBILITY OF DESIGN

The goal of responsive interviewing is a solid, deep understanding of what is being studied, rather than breadth. Depth is achieved by going after context; dealing with the complexity of multiple, overlapping, and sometimes conflicting themes; and paying attention to the specifics of meanings, situations, and history. To get that depth, the researcher has to follow up, asking more questions about what he or she initially heard. Research design and questioning must remain flexible to accommodate new information, to adapt to the actual experiences that people have had, and to adjust to unexpected situations. The researcher creates future questions based on what he or she has already heard, requiring the researcher to analyze interviews throughout the project rather than just at the end.

To get that depth of understanding, design must remain flexible. Each major new discovery may require a redesign, figuring anew whom to talk to, where to carry out the study, or what concepts and themes to focus on. The interview questions the researcher intends to ask may differ from the ones actually asked if the interviewee goes in an unexpected but relevant direction.

This flexibility contrasts sharply with survey research that often begins (and ends) with questions positivist researchers develop before they gather their data. In the responsive interviewing model, many of the questions asked emerge only during the course of the research and are then pursued to find detail or evidence that underlies the answers. Because the questions cannot be fully worked out in advance, responsive interviewers need a high tolerance for uncertainty, especially at the beginning of the project.

The box on the next page summarizes the key characteristics of the responsive interviewing model as both a philosophy of research and a set of data-gathering techniques.

Characteristics of the Responsive Interviewing Model

1. Interviewing is about obtaining interviewees' interpretations of their experiences and their understanding of the world in which they live and work.

2. The personality, style, and beliefs of the interviewer matter. Interviewing is an exchange, not a one-way street; the relationship between interviewer and interviewee is meaningful, even if temporary. Because the interviewer contributes actively to the conversation, he or she must be aware of his or her own opinions, experiences, cultural definitions, and even prejudices.

3. Because responsive interviews depend on a personal relationship between interviewer and interviewee and because that relationship may result in the exchange of private information or information dangerous to the interviewee, the interviewer incurs serious ethical obligations to protect the interviewee. Moreover, the interviewer is imposing on the time, energy, emotion, and creativity of the interviewee and therefore owes loyalty and protection in return.

4. Interviewers should not impose their views on interviewees. They should ask broad enough questions to avoid limiting what interviewees can answer, listen to what interviewees tell them, and modify their questions to explore what they are hearing, not what they thought before they began the interview.

5. Responsive interviewing design is flexible and adaptive. Because the interviewer must listen intently and follow up insights and new points during the interview, the interviewer must be able to change course based on what he or she learns. Interviewers may need to change whom they plan to talk to or where they plan to conduct an interview as they find out more about their research questions.

Responsive Interviewing: Guidance for Design

Our discussion of responsive interviewing should be taken in the spirit in which it is given: It is meant to be read, understood, and reacted to, not to be authoritatively implemented as some sort of revealed dogma. A philosophy should not be a list of commands or instructions to always do this, or never do that. Even the strongest advice may be offset in some situations by a broader good to be achieved. But, especially when you feel lost, having a compass—a research philosophy—is useful because it provides guidance, suggests what to pay attention to, and alerts you to problems that may arise. In addition, a guiding philosophy provides legitimacy by helping to explain and justify why you have picked a particular set of research tools and designed a project in a particular manner.

The responsive interviewing model affects the design of research, the plan that links the research problem to the questions to be asked, and the choice of people with whom to talk. Because responsive interviewing is about learning what people think about their experiences and what rules they operate under, the model implies finding people who have had particular experiences or are members of specific groups whose rules, traditions, and values are of interest.

Defining the topic in ways that allow the interviewees to share with you their experiences and then working out the question sequences that get you the depth you need take several iterations. You first try out topics and questions, and then change them based on the responses you get. The design must therefore be tolerant of mistakes and facilitate the correction of false steps. Pauses for reflection are built into the design, and during such pauses researchers compare what they asked with what they should have asked and what requires more depth, and alter questions accordingly. In the responsive interviewing model, analysis is an ongoing part of the research process, not just something that happens at the end.

The goal of interpretive constructionist research is to find out how the conversational partners understand what they have seen, heard, or experienced. Responsive interviewers elicit from the conversational partners examples, narratives, histories, stories, and explanations. Concrete illustrations help ground the answers in the experiences of the interviewees in ways that provide nuance and precision, context, and evidence all at the same time. Individual interpretations are not seen as right or wrong in themselves but rather as different slants on what happened, slants that the researcher puts together to construct his or her understanding of what has occurred. At the end, as Geertz pointed out, we are telling our version of their understandings (Geertz 2001).

In responsive interviewing, as in all naturalist research, the researcher is the instrument, the tool of discovery. The researcher's self-confidence, adaptability, and willingness to hear what is said and change direction to catch a wisp of insight or track down a new theme are what make responsive interviews work. At the same time, the researcher has to be cautious not to impose his or her views on the interviewee. If the interview questions stay close to what the interviewees know and are willing to talk about, the resulting report will be fresh and credible.

Notes

1. *Queer theory* is a term developed and used by gay, lesbian, and transsexual activists to describe their own research and theory; they pointedly use the word *queer* to defy the negative implications of the term. It is difficult for us to use a word that still carries so much negative baggage, but we understand their intent (Duberman 1997).

2. Synthesized from Anderson and Jack (1991), Devault (1990), Edwards and Ribbens (1998), Gluck and Patai (1991), Harding (1991), hooks (1989), Oakley (1981), Reinharz (1992), and Reissman (1987).

3

Design

Choosing Topics and Anticipating Data Analysis

To obtain convincing results from a responsive interviewing project, research has to be carefully designed. To design a project, you pick an appropriate topic, formulate your research question, select an initial site or sites, choose your interviewees, and decide with what questions to begin and how to ask them. As research continues, you respond to what you have already learned and alter what you ask and of whom in order to better pursue the new material.

The first step in qualitative design involves *choosing a topic*; that is, determining what is of sufficient interest and importance to research. Then with a topic in mind work out a *specific research question,* the puzzle about that topic you will try to resolve. You make sure that both the topic and the research question are best answered through depth interviewing, that what you are asking is important, and that what you propose to do is feasible.

At the very beginning of your research, you anticipate the analysis by asking yourself what you are seeking to accomplish. Are you trying to explain a political puzzle, work out cultural concepts or themes, create a narrative from a series of linked events, determine whether a program is working or not, portray personal histories, or make others aware of persisting problems? You have to anticipate the analysis to make sure that your questioning provides you with material rich in examples and evidence to support any conclusions you might reach. You also ask yourself *how far you want to generalize from what you have learned.* Are you interested only in the case you are studying, or do you expect your results to apply to cases you did not study?

With a research question in mind and an idea of how far you want to generalize results, you then choose where the study will occur, with whom you need to speak, and what organizations or groups you will need to include, and then map out roughly the type of questions you will ask. In this chapter we discuss how to choose a topic, translate it into a viable research question, and anticipate the later analysis. In Chapter 4 we discuss how to design the project to make the results convincing. In later chapters, we describe ways to structure the interviews and word questions to obtain the information needed for the planned analysis.

Choosing a Topic and Focusing the Research Question

You begin to design a project by picking a topic and then within that topic determining your research question. A *topic* refers to whatever it is that interests you: for example, how the police have adapted to a post-9/11 world, how divorcees find a mate, what rules guide corporate ethics. *Research questions* are the specific concerns that you want to answer through the project: Are local police taking advantage of post-9/11 insecurity to increase their power and budget? Do divorcees look for new mates in all the wrong places? Does the corporate culture differ from company to company in the same industry, or do industry-wide trends determine what is accepted as right and wrong?

Sometimes research questions are more formally presented as hypotheses, that is, statements that suggest how two or more concepts or underlying ideas are related. The following is a restatement of one of the example research questions just mentioned as a hypothesis: Industry trends determine what is considered right and wrong. In the hypothesis we are asking if one concept—industry trends—is related to another concept—perceptions of right and wrong—by questioning whether industry trends *determine* right and wrong.

In responsive interviewing projects, however, research questions are usually less formally stated. Research questions evolve as you pursue new themes that are suggested in the interviews, so you do not want to restrict yourself to examining only those hypotheses with which you begin. If you state your research question as a hypothesis, be prepared to drop it, modify it, or exchange it for a new one during the study. Depth-interviewing research requires openness to new ideas not anticipated at the beginning, and constructing formally stated hypotheses works against such openness.

Before starting a project you should be sure that depth interviewing is the best way to explore your topic and that the research question is important. You also need to be concerned with practical matters of feasibility, ensuring that you can complete the project with the time and resources available and can find people knowledgeable about the topic who can be persuaded to participate.

Choosing a good topic and formulating a viable research question can take weeks or months, as both the topic and question emerge iteratively. The following hypothetical but realistic example shows how a student experienced an aggravating situation and then iteratively turned it into a research project:

Example: Coming Up With a Topic and Research Question

Martha recently returned to the university for a degree after years of working. Through experience she learned that though the university advertised for adult students, it made insufficient provision for them. Day care was inadequate, parking was inconvenient and expensive, and faculty didn't take into account how long it had been since the returning students had taken courses such as math and statistics. She was frustrated and angry but thought she could turn her anger to good use if she could study the university's efforts to get adult learners enrolled (*topic*). She phrased the research puzzle as follows: Why would the university recruit a clientele they are not prepared to serve (*research question*)?

Martha had to think about what might cause this odd organizational behavior. After reading the student newspaper's archives and talking to some of her professors, who acted as general informants, she decided on a number of possibilities. Maybe the enrollment dropped and the school was desperate for students and tuition revenues but lacked the money to add services for new clientele. Or maybe the faculty were traditionalists who continued to do the same thing from year to year, regardless of the changes in the background of their students. Or maybe the university culture was one of sink or swim, providing educational opportunities but leaving it to the students whether to avail themselves of those opportunities. A fourth possibility was that there is no communication between the admissions office and the faculty so that faculty did not know how their students were changing or what their backgrounds were until after students floundered in classes.

Examining the possible explanations with interviewees seemed to Martha to make a fine research project, but in initial, informal conversations to test out her ideas, interviewees denied that the university was ignoring the needs of returning students and seemed

---

(Continued)

(Continued)

unwilling to pursue the matter. Martha had to back up and rethink the project and modify it to mesh with the understandings of her potential interviewees.

She modified the topic to ask about a broader question of how the university was adapting to a shortfall in enrollments (*topic*), since the recruitment of adult learners was likely to be only one of several thrusts. She thought interviewees would be more aware of the enrollment decline and its financial threat than they were of implied promises to newly recruited students and they would be more willing to talk about this newer focus because it seemed less critical of them and the university. She also thought of another approach, that of interviewing the adult learners themselves, to see how they coped with the university without adequate support (*topic*), whether they protested, whether they banded together with each other or other student constituencies, and whether they persisted or dropped out, overwhelmed by the difficulties (*research questions*).

Again, she needed to do some preliminary interviews to see which topic would be most feasible. She talked with some of the returning students and found herself becoming interested in the stories of those who persisted regardless of the difficulties. She saw their reactions to the problems they confronted—child care, time conflicts with jobs, out-of-date courses—as reflective of their ability to adapt to life problems more generally and began to formulate an idea about personal resources and social capital (of the returned student), what help they can get, how they cope with problems, and how they learn and grow (*topic*). In talking with university officials she found that they were interested in the problems of enrollment decline (*topic*). She reasoned that this topic had practical importance, and that when she was done with the project she would be able to tell university administrators what factors were most important in causing adult learners to drop out (*importance of the research question*), helping both the university and the adult learners.

She was intrigued by the adult learners and how they responded, but she could see that the topic about the university's adaptations to enrollment declines was potentially more important for policy and was much easier to design and carry out. For the adult learners project, she would first have to figure out what personal resources and social capital consisted of, itself a major project. She chose the project that was more feasible. Later, Martha might attempt the more difficult project.

WHERE DO TOPICS COME FROM?

Sometimes the research topic is assigned to you by a professor or a supervisor or as part of an applied research contract. For example, on one consulting assignment, Irene was asked to explore why communications in a probation and parole office had broken down and how they could be fixed. Working as a consultant for the U.S. Agency for International Development, Herb did an evaluation project on economic development in the Philippines to find out if recipients spent foreign aid wisely. Asked by a friend who had a grant, Irene worked on an oral history project about the relationship between a small college and the community in which it was located. But if a topic is not assigned to you, you have to work out one on your own.

Most of us are bombarded with possible research topics all the time, but we tend to ignore them rather than see their possibilities. Often, finding a topic means paying attention to ordinary events and then asking which of these interests you the most. You can begin by thinking about what you do, your paid and volunteer work, your hobbies and relaxations, or your religious and family life, each sphere of activity suggesting something worth researching. Maybe you attended a family reunion and would like to figure out what happens at family gatherings, or you just came back from a bird-watching trip and would like to explain to those who have never been on one what goes on: the language, the goals, explicit and implicit, the competition, and the status orderings of a typical bird-watching trip. Reflecting on your own experience often suggests research ideas. For instance, you have probably had many experiences of meeting new people or groups of people. From these social interactions you might come up with the following possible research ideas: How do people function in groups of strangers? How much of themselves do they reveal? What kinds of things are inappropriate to discuss? How are newcomers socialized into the group?

Experienced researchers come across topics by seeing ordinary things through social-science lenses. Mitchell Duneier had been ignoring the tables set up by vendors in Greenwich Village in New York City to sell books and magazines. One day, though, he noticed a book he had written on one of these tables and struck up a conversation with the vendor. Because he was a sociologist, Duneier found himself intrigued by the answers, starting a multiyear study that examined how people living in poverty, often homeless, managed to create, maintain, and protect a business on the sidewalk (Duneier 1999).

Another way to start is to think about issues that concern you politically or socially. You might be interested in violence against women or gays, computer dating, adoption, guerrilla warfare, or corporate intrigue; you might want to know why people lie or why they join model airplane clubs or church choirs. You could be fascinated by the role of lobby groups in government or how people know if they are doing a good job in their work. You might be interested in self-help groups for the chronically ill. With the right twist, any of these personal concerns could become a research topic.

Social anger motivates many qualitative studies. William Wilson observed increasing joblessness in the inner-city neighborhood near where he lived and set out to document why it was happening (Wilson 1996). Having friends with AIDS motivated Lather and Smithies (1997) to document their anguish. Sometimes when you see a social problem, you want to influence public policy. You might want to study ways to redesign and fund apartments to accommodate people with disabilities or look at programs in which tenants help manage public housing to see if increased responsibility leads to more success on the job market.

Topics often grow out of personal experiences that leave you puzzled or frustrated. One researcher who spent his life in the military was fed up with congressional micromanagement, so he wanted to study congressional oversight of executive-branch agencies (Merritt 1998). A student who ran into opposition from the city council when he tried to get a speed bump built on a neighborhood street was curious why council members resist citizen input and why some citizens persist in trying to make an impact (Berg 2002).

Topics reflect one's personality. Herb, who in university matters is often opposed to the majority position in meetings, is deeply interested in how people dominate others. A colleague who works most of the night, sleeps late, and owns only one sports coat is deeply interested in what behavior gets labeled deviant. Irene is curious about how organizations, political candidates, and individuals deal with defeat and decline in a society that emphasizes success and growth. These interests can be turned into research questions by asking why people are afraid to complain, how law enforcement agencies treat those whose actions they don't understand, and how bureaucratic agencies respond to budgetary cutbacks.

Sometimes topics develop out of the researcher's ethnic identity. African American researchers may be especially interested in how the civil rights movement of the 1960s shaped current politics. Jewish researchers might feel drawn to studying the political movement that denies the murder of 6 million Jews in Europe during World War II. Those of Mexican or Caribbean ancestry might be especially interested in the impact of current immigration policies. Felix Padilla wondered why he was able to succeed academically when others of his ethnic group did not and began a study on the culture of Puerto Rican Chicago (Padilla 1992).

Research topics also emerge out of experiences in school and from readings in your field. Part of Herb's graduate education focused on countries in Southeast Asia. With the exception of Thailand, each country had been a colony, and Herb wondered how the lack of colonial experience affected government in Thailand, a question that turned into his dissertation research. In an undergraduate class, Jay MacLeod learned about "blocked aspirations and mobility" as reasons why the poor do not move into the middle classes. He had at that time been doing volunteer work with teenagers in a low-income area and started interviewing them (as well as observing them) to figure out what they wanted to do with their lives, what preparations they were making for jobs, and what obstacles they faced (MacLeod 1995).

MOVING FROM TOPIC TO RESEARCHABLE PUZZLE

For the topic to turn into a research project, you need to find a puzzle or a problem that you can solve or answer. This puzzle is your research question. A single topic may yield dozens of research questions, in which case you pick one or two for your study.

One approach to working out the researchable puzzle is to think about your topic and ask about what appears to be wrong and then question why. Suppose you are interested in children's sports and observe parents fighting with referees at children's hockey games. This appears foolish, as these are little kids learning to play a sport; no one, least of all the adults, should come to blows about it. From this odd behavior a researchable question emerges: How do parents view their children's games? Or, suppose you recognize that government programs to interdict drug supplies are not working, but government continues to throw money at these programs. Surely that is puzzling; why does that occur? You would then formulate research questions such as who advocates continuing existing government programs, or ask how drug control programs have worked in other countries.

Another way to come up with research questions is to read published reports and ask yourself if it is possible that the author got the direction of the causal arrows wrong. If a report says weather causes road deterioration, it is not likely that the reverse holds, that road deterioration causes weather. But, what if the report suggests that students who study hard get good grades? Might it not be the case that good grades cause or encourage more studying? For your research question you might want to ask how students react to low grades on exams, whether such grades stimulate more or less studying.

Sometimes recognizing contradictions in ordinary events opens up both a topic and a research question. For example, diners in a restaurant often continue to talk about very private things when a server is putting food on the table. The diners treat servers as if they were invisible or deaf or completely uninterested. The overall research topic might be finding out what privacy is, and when and how is it achieved. Research questions might deal with situations in which people believe that what they are doing is private even when there are other people around, such as when they use cell phones.

When the research topic concerns the culture of an organization or group, figuring out the research problem can take awhile. The first step is to examine the overall culture, the rules, meanings, and values that underlie and guide behavior. You may need to start off with some participant observation, joining the group and learning its ways, or you may need to collect stories and analyze them. From this preliminary work you learn about the taken-for-granted assumptions and rules and you ask yourself what about these assumptions seems most important or intriguing. For example, do several norms or values that you have seen seem contradictory? If an organization has strictly enforced rules against open conflict, how is competition for promotion handled or how are conflicts between divisions for resources resolved? These concerns become your research questions.

Research puzzles also emerge if you think about the opposites of what you are hearing or seeing. Suppose you were interested in decisions on whether to take someone who is in a coma off life support. What is the opposite of being in a coma? Being alive? Being mobile? Being conscious? Such a topic can suggest research questions on what it means to be alive and whether there is a continuum of life (or death) rather than just two end points with a sharp distinction between them. If you are studying economic development, and you hear advocates say that the community must give incentives to lure in new businesses, you can ask what the opposite of a financial incentive might be, and look for businesses that located in the community without the benefit of taxpayer-funded subsidies and study them. You can also look for options between ignoring new businesses and subsidizing them, and create research questions around these intermediate options.

Another way to come up with a research puzzle is to think about what has not occurred when you would have expected it to have happened. Suppose you are interested in comparative government and wonder how stability is maintained. One of the features of the United States, in comparison to other countries, is that there have been no military attempts to overthrow the government. Your research question could be similar to the following: Why has the military never made a coup attempt against presidents who didn't follow its wishes? Learning to see what is not happening, that could or should happen, that is warranted, provoked, and occurs elsewhere, but is not happening in the research setting, can suggest research puzzles.

To translate a topic into a research question requires some initial interviews in which you discuss your ideas with general informants or potential conversational partners. In these informal interviews, you find out if the question you have in mind resonates with the interviewees, if they think it is important, if they are willing to talk about it, or if they think you are on the wrong track. For example, Herb had done a lot of reading on community groups that used protest tactics to pressure government but noticed that there was not much written on community development organizations that built homes, opened stores, and created jobs in poor neighborhoods. He thought that contrasting the two approaches might make an interesting research question. When he talked to interviewees about his idea, they argued that it was passé, and suggested that he instead focus on how development groups accomplished projects against overwhelming odds. Herb pursued that research question for the next several years.

DETERMINING IF A TOPIC IS SUITABLE
FOR QUALITATIVE INTERVIEWING

Once you have a suitable research topic, you need to make sure it is suitable for depth interviewing. To do so, answer the following questions:

Are You Looking for Nuance and Subtlety?

You might want to conduct a counting study to determine how the size of a prison population has changed, but undertake depth interviewing if you are interested in finding out how prisoners learn to survive in a brutal situation. You need depth interviews if you want to illuminate concepts such as *privacy*, *pain*, *dominance*, *deference*, and *loyalty* that collectively help define prison culture.

Does Answering the Research Question Require You
to Trace How Present Situations Resulted From Prior Events?

Why are unions striking? How did the state get into such an incredible financial mess? How did that person get to be mayor? Each of these questions requires determining what past events brought about the current situation.

Is an Entirely Fresh View Required?

If existing literature does not explain your research problem or if the current approach is not working, you may need to look at your problem in a different way. Depth interviewing studies encourage considerable departures from current understanding. To gain new perspectives on problems such as why public housing policies have failed, you would want to listen carefully as residents, managers, and government officials described their experiences. If what you are looking for is a new approach to a practical problem or a new or considerably amended theory, depth interviewing is appropriate.

Are You Trying to Explain the Unexpected?

Why did one father beat up another boy's father at his son's hockey game? Why did France oppose the U.S. policy of attacking Iraq if Hussein didn't disarm? Puzzling out problems that you would consider unusual or unexpected often requires responsive interviewing because you do not have prior experience from which to draw hypotheses to test.

Does Puzzling Out the Research Question Necessitate Layers of Discovery in Which Initial Questions Are Asked to Discover Alternatives That Are Then Explored in Turn?

Quantitative studies have shown that women are more likely to die after an initial heart attack than are men, suggesting that a suitable research question for depth interviewing might be to determine why. In the first round of interviewing, you could ask about differences in behavior and discover that women do not get as much exercise as men. That's important and does suggest needed changes in behavior. But it also poses another question: Why do women get less exercise than do men? Are women more fearful after a heart attack than men and so limit their activity? Do women feel social pressures that curtail their behaviors? Are women more depressed and withdrawn after suffering a heart attack than are men? Or perhaps there is a combination of reasons. A second set of conversations is required, precisely the approach taken in responsive interviewing.

CHOOSING A TOPIC FOR IMPORTANCE

Topics need to be important to the interviewer, the interviewee, and a broader public. A topic the researcher thinks is unimportant is not likely to be investigated thoroughly. At the same time, if the interviewees find the topic trivial, they will provide only superficial answers. You certainly do not want to spend many months or years researching a topic only to confront the "who cares?" question from readers when the study is done.

Sometimes showing the importance of a topic is simple. The research may be on matters that affect hundreds or thousands of lives, cost billions of dollars, or explain major historical events. If you can put your results in the middle of a policy debate, no one is likely to question its importance. For example, Irene is working on a project on government contracting out, that is, hiring private firms to do government work. For several years the president has been pushing for more contracting out at the national level, which has become highly controversial, as unions protest the loss of public-sector jobs and legislators question whether some jobs are inherently governmental and therefore should not be contracted out. Regardless of the content of her findings, the results are likely to inform an ongoing policy argument.

However, it may be more difficult to justify the importance of studying some relatively common cultural process. You may need to explain that ordinary events routinely have major impacts not only on the participants but also on the society. Routine decisions at work may empower employees or repress them, creating either a model of democracy or a hotbed of unionism and conflict. The (unfortunately routine) physical danger of some inner-city neighborhoods contributes to the formation of gangs and probably contributes to higher occurrences of high blood pressure and strokes. Working together in unions with people from different ethnic backgrounds can help forge a class consciousness with far-reaching social effects.

Another way of showing the importance of a cultural research topic is to argue that if you can track down how particular norms are learned, you may be able to intervene, to make needed changes. If you understand how children get hooked on drugs, maybe you can design a more effective program to prevent them from starting. If you can trace out where some police officers pick up the norms that justify violence against suspects, maybe you can adjust training to minimize that violence.

Sometimes the important impact of a cultural study is to help bring about change to solve problems. When managers first enter an organization, they come with their solutions to long-term problems only to find that many of the projects they launch die quickly, whereas others take off with a velocity that startles them. Without an understanding of the organizational culture and the ways in which these projects threaten or reinforce that culture, a manager may have a hard time predicting what solutions are likely to work. Obtaining this kind of knowledge can save time and frustration.

You can justify the importance of a narrowly defined study if you can show that what you are studying represents a larger problem. If you are examining corruption in a small city, you can make the case that what you learn applies to corruption in general. If you want to study the meaning of tattoos in one prison, you would argue that though tattoos might not seem important, what they represent more broadly is. Tattoos might symbolize defiance, group affiliation, self-expression, or responses to limitations of freedom, all of which are issues that go far beyond body markings. To justify a project, you should be able to demonstrate what broadly applicable principles are involved.

Sometimes self-reflection suggests the ways in which a research question addresses broader issues. Suppose you want to study life histories of middle-age women. What do you hope to find out? How did you get interested in this topic? Your answer could be something like this: "I am interested in the lives of middle-age women because our society focuses so much attention on the young that some middle-age women feel invisible. I wonder what it is like to feel invisible. I am interested in invisibility more broadly, and this could be an example." Explaining invisibility is the broader issue that gives intellectual importance to the life histories you are gathering.

Sometimes a topic is important because it makes a problem clear or gives a voice to people ignored by society or too cowed to protest what is happening to them. Interviews with imprisoned adults and their spouses about how they deal with their children may help give voice to the unintended victims of the public policy of incarcerating people for possession of small amounts of illegal drugs—the children. By giving voice to the voiceless, cultural studies help balance the record. If a study gives dignity to work that has traditionally been invisible and thankless, by explaining the work that women do in caring for their parents or preparing meals, for example, the study becomes important. Similarly, a study may be important if you can lead readers to understand and accept a group that society has stereotyped or stigmatized. For example, Angrosino's *Opportunity House* (1998) looks at the lives of a handful of mentally disabled adults, and in doing so substitutes engaging portraits of individuals for seemingly inexorable social stereotypes.

Cultural studies are important when they pass along the values, norms, and beliefs of one generation to another, so grandchildren know what their grandparents or parents lived through. What was it like to live through the Great Depression or World War II at home or in the field? What was it like to be a coal miner in West Virginia a generation ago? Or to be an African American before the Civil Rights movement?

There are, in short, many ways to justify the importance of a research question. If you are having trouble finding a way of doing so, maybe you are really not interested in that topic and should find another.

THE FEASIBILITY OF THE RESEARCH

Feasibility requires that you conduct a project with the financial resources available, that you have sufficient time and energy to complete the work, and that you are emotionally up to researching the matter. Sometimes limitations are practical: Can you travel away from home? Do you have the money? Can you get someone to take care of your children? Can you arrange a place to stay overnight? If the project interests you but appears to be too large, ask yourself if the scope can be reduced, perhaps by breaking it up into smaller pieces that can be done sequentially.

A project might be within your financial and time constraints but be too emotionally draining as depth interviewing exposes crushing problems that the researcher might find stressful. Talking with people who work in day-care centers caring for babies with AIDS might be an important project, but the stories volunteers tell might be too heartbreaking to pursue. The researcher's feelings about some subjects might be so intense that hearing certain examples or narratives would be difficult. Someone who has been raped may not be able to pay proper attention to the narratives of rapists. If you feel that bankers and lawyers are parasites, you may conduct superficial interviews with them or goad them into angry responses.

Can you interview people of whom you disapprove? Our colleague Jim found it difficult to interview some prison staff because he found them hostile and racist, but he had to learn to curb his antagonism because to understand prison life he really needed to hear their side. Strong positive bias can also create interviewing problems. Herb, whose writings advocate for the indigent, has trouble listening when his interviewees express frustration at the self-defeating behaviors of the poor.

A feasible project requires you to have access to appropriate interviewees. You might have a wonderful topic to study, for instance, how judges make their decisions, but cannot get permission to carry out the study because judges refuse to talk to you. Years ago, Irene tried to conduct a study comparing budgets in private and public universities, but was not allowed access at the private universities and had to change the research design to focus only on the public institutions.

Research questions and approaches can be adjusted to make the work more feasible. Though community development is a national movement, to reduce expenses, Herb limited the scope of his study of the subject to organizations no farther than a day's drive from home. When Irene was picking a topic for her dissertation, she decided to study problems of failure, decline, and losing. Her first thought was to talk with individuals who had failed at something, such as political candidates who lost elections or students who did not pass comprehensive examinations. Finding students after they failed comprehensive exams was difficult, if not impossible, and politicians who lose elections often disappear from sight. Instead, she formulated her research question to examine organizations that were suffering financial declines. Organizations cannot hide easily and individuals inside the organization were less likely to blame themselves for the decline and be more willing to talk about what was happening to the organization (I. S. Rubin 1977).

Sometimes access is easiest to gain at a place where researchers work or have close friends. In such situations, you work out a research question appropriate for the setting, rather than pick a setting to investigate your research question. If you have access to prisons, you might think about research questions that deal with freedom, privacy, sex, status, protection, or violence. A hospital setting suggests interviewing about pain management, family support of patients, the occupational hierarchy, the sick role, status among medical personnel, or even the role of humor in reducing tension. Among less obvious topics might be the practice of working two shifts back to back with resulting fatigue and fear of mistakes, hospitals' adaptation to governmental regulations, and romances between nursing staff and patients. You still want to be sure that the topic is important, but within that constraint, why not do your research where you have good access?

Design With Analysis and Theory Development in Mind

Once you choose an important and feasible research question that is appropriate for a depth interviewing project, the next stage of design involves looking to the end of your research. You ask yourself now, as you begin, what type of analysis you plan to do and what kind of theory you hope to build. Only by anticipating what you plan to do with the data early on can you ensure that you obtain the needed information. If you anticipate analyzing how people use particular concepts—the underlying ideas through which people understand and explain their world—you need to plan questions to elicit those concepts, refine them, and get examples of how they are used. If you want to create a narrative—a rendition of events that reconciles various accounts you have received—you need to be sure that you have built into your questions inquiries about specific events you are interested in, as well as ways of checking the truth value of different versions.

ANTICIPATING THE ANALYSIS

Suppose your study is about how people respond in arguments. In your first few interviews, you learn that people respond differently when they are contradicted. Some people report that they get angry, others say that contradictions make them think, and a few say they do not mind. You analyze these preliminary interviews and decide that you are working toward a theory focused on how people handle being contradicted rather than the more general topic of arguing.

Anticipating what information you will need in your final analysis, you redesign your questioning to ask for detailed examples of how individuals respond to being contradicted, paying close attention to the specific circumstances. Are some contradictions made in ways that are embarrassing or rude? Do people react differently to gentler contradictions? You also ask yourself how people might differ in how they handle contradictions. To answer this question, you need to plan with whom to talk so you have enough variation to make interesting comparisons. Do men and women differ? Do bosses and workers handle contradictions differently? Does educational background affect how people respond? You might also wonder if the situation in which the contradiction occurred affects how people respond. Are contradictions made in private more acceptable than public ones? Do contradictions that occur in conversations between couples at home elicit a different response from those that occur at work? You now have reformulated your research question to focus on a theory about what makes a contradiction embarrassing and when. In anticipating this theory, you have modified the questions you will ask, figured out what groups of people you need to talk to, and determined the kind of sites you need to include in the study.

In cultural studies, you begin with a less formulated idea of where you are going, so early analysis is vital. At the beginning, your interviewing involves general questioning because you often start out with little idea about the content of the culture. You ask people to talk about their typical days or what happened at some ceremonies. By itself, however, such information leads nowhere unless you anticipate its theoretical significance by noting what core cultural concepts and themes are mentioned that explain how the people you are studying understand their world. With this goal in mind, you redesign your interviews to elicit examples of the concepts and themes that are central to the interviewees' understanding, ask about each, and then follow up for detailed examples. Doing so provides you with the data needed to draw nuanced conclusions about the content of the culture.

In topical studies, you are trying to explain events that have happened, in the order in which they occurred, and what it all means. You begin to interview with a set of initial research questions: for example, how the opposition won the mayoralty or what happened when the new computer system was introduced. Based on your analysis of these preliminary interviews, you focus the research questions to mesh with what you have discovered: If the mayoral election was won because of neighborhood organizing, you concentrate on learning who organized the neighborhoods, the issues that rallied the neighbors, and the nature of the organization that was built. In the second example, if you find out that yes, the new computer system changed a lot, but it was just part of the move into a more centralized business model, you may now want to explain how that approach came about.

As you reformulate your research question, you also think about what broader implications will be apparent and interview to obtain information on these larger concerns. In the previous examples you may ask questions such as the following: Where does opposition to the mayor come from? Who has the ability to mobilize sufficient support to topple an incumbent? Did the mayor make some important mistake that the opposition was able to capitalize on? Did he or she just go too far, get greedy or extreme in his or her policies? With these ideas in mind, you may also ask in other places if the mayor took his or her policies to extremes or if an effective opposition arose and wrested the mayoralty out of his or her hands.

In our other example, you may have learned about how computer change came about in one organization, but what are the broader implications of this study? One possible implication might be that to be successful, technical innovations that also create a lot of chaotic change need support from the top; another is that integrated changes, where three or four related changes are made at the same time, are less likely to be successful, because any part that doesn't work will seriously damage other parts that are working. You continue to ask about the computer changes but you focus more on questions concerning support from the top or integrated changes because these are the themes that have implications beyond the research setting.

In a topical study, as you build toward your final analysis, you require answers to specific questions, such as what efforts were made to bring down the mayor or reduce his or her power and why were they not successful, or what happened when a second or third management reform was introduced after the new computer system was put into place. You want to be reasonably sure that what you learn is right, so you will build into the interviews checks on what people know, how good their memories are, and what biases they may have, so that you can figure out which interviews to lean on more heavily when you put the results together later. When events are controversial, you want to make sure that you have interviewed people who can provide the various sides. In addition, you need to work out some time to try out your new ideas on your interviewees, see what they think of them and how they might modify them, or whether they have evidence contradicting your tentative conclusions.

ANTICIPATING THE TYPE (NOT THE CONTENT) OF CONCLUSION YOU WANT

In your design, you ask yourself about the purposes of the research and the types of conclusions you want to obtain. For instance, in a study of the delivery of medical services, you might be looking for general statements about how hospitals deal with pain or you might be more interested in narrower findings that describe the battles in a specific hospital between those who want to alleviate suffering (through the use of pain medicine) and those who want to aggressively and continuously attack symptoms even if they result in pain. Depending on where you see your work going, you would pick different research sites and interviewees while asking somewhat different questions.

You analyze your individual interviews while the project is underway to look for core concepts and themes that ultimately will be used in structuring a theory, and after doing so, you work out follow-up questions about them. However, you may have heard many concepts and themes in any given interview. How do you choose which ones to follow up? One answer is to look ahead to what kind of report you want to produce and pick the concepts and themes that are the most relevant for that kind of report.

Suppose you were interviewing in a retirement community, and in one interview heard the term *growing old*, which you assume is a basic concept summarizing how residents see their experience. You then follow up on this concept to learn what it means to the retirees and hear a variety of component ideas, including fear of illness, loss of physical strength, reduction of sex drive, loss of good looks, financial insecurity, and loneliness. In the same interviews you also hear some upbeat concepts, including fewer responsibilities, less concern for how people view them, more realistic expectations of people, and the pleasures of grandchildren.

Each of these components is itself a concept that might warrant additional exploration, but which ones you explore depend on the goal of your research. If you intend to create an academic theory on the life course, moving from childhood to adulthood to maturity and finally old age, you might explore how the loss of good looks relates to self-esteem, or how the types of loneliness people feel affect the types of new relationships, if any, they form. A researcher with a more psychological bent might examine how people balance the negatives—fear of illness, loss of physical strength, loneliness—with the positive aspects of aging—fewer responsibilities, less concern for how people view them, more realistic expectations of people, the pleasures of grandchildren. In contrast, a policy person working for the retirement home might focus more on the physical and financial well-being of those living there and spend time following up on matters such as loss of physical strength and financial insecurity.

ANTICIPATING THE THEORY BUILDING
AND GENERALIZING OF RESULTS

In the responsive interviewing model, theories are induced from the data to discover how different concepts and themes mentioned in the interviews relate to one another. To successfully work out such a theory, you have to recognize the concepts and themes central to your research while you are still collecting data and then modify your questions to make sure you obtain more detail on what each of the concepts and themes mean, get examples of each, and learn how they relate to one another.

Concepts are core ideas that can be summarized as nouns, noun phrases, or gerunds. Though any interview is replete with different concepts, you focus only on those that help you move toward the theory you are developing. You become sensitive to concepts by listening to recorded interviews or reading over transcripts and noting the words or phrases that interviewees use to explain their examples or describe their work or their personal lives. Some of these words might sound unusual to you, as the technical jargon within a field often does. Or a concept may just be an ordinary term that interviewees repeat a lot because it is important to them. Community developers describe their work using terms such as *empowerment*, *social equity*, and *housing affordability*; budgeters use terms such as *cash balance*, *earmarked revenues*, and *off-budget expenditures*. Among the police, terms such as *perp* (perpetrator), *mark* (victim of a fraud), and *scumbag* (a person of low moral character) are labels for underlying concepts. These terms often convey goals or values, perceptions or attitudes toward the work or the customers, clients, or victims, or represent strategies that frame action. They are the clues to what is going on in the setting.

Sometimes the interviewees do not actually name the idea; they just describe its characteristics, and the researcher has to provide the label for the concept. Frequently used symbols and stories are often indicative of important underlying concepts. In the famous Uncle Remus stories, Br'er

Rabbit prevailed against opponents by outwitting them without open defiance. A researcher could label the underlying concept *wiliness* or possibly *safe defiance*. The first term emphasizes the cleverness, the second the success of the tactic.

Sometimes interviewees use one concept and name it, and refer to other concepts without naming them. For instance, in discussions on budgets, Irene heard frequent mention of earmarked money, money in a budget that has to be spent on a particular item and cannot be spent on anything else. She also heard interviewees talk about money that could be spent on any range of items. This second kind of money was highly valued, because it was more flexible and could solve a wider range of problems. The interviewees did not explicitly label this second type of money, so Irene called it *nonearmarked money*. She then explored this second concept, asking where the nonearmarked money came from, who controlled it, and how it was spent.

You can listen for concepts, and then ask questions that will help you understand what they mean and how they are used and gradually weave the concepts together into themes, that is, longer explanatory phrases or statements. Sometimes the interviewees state the themes themselves to explain why things occur, and by doing so move you rapidly toward an inductive theory. Herb's interviewees might say, for example, "The bankers don't respect community groups, so we have to compromise sometimes to get funds." The two concepts are respect and compromise, and they are linked to form a theme, that lack of respect results in forced compromises.

Themes are statements that explain why something happened or what something means and are built up from the concepts. As part of an iterative design, the researcher constructs theories of how and why things happen, doing so by combining separate themes that together explain related issues. The implications of the emerging theory are then examined with further questions that explore the themes in more detail and are asked both of the original conversational partners and of additional interviewees whose insights now seem relevant.

To illustrate how the researcher moves from identifying and modifying concepts to hearing themes and linking them into possible theories, suppose you were interviewing professors about problems they have had with students. In the first set of interviewees, professors complained about students who missed deadlines and students who submit the same paper to several different professors. You summarize the material initially as illustrating two concepts, lateness and cheating. You continue to interview asking about other problems and learn that professors complain about students making up wild excuses for not coming to class or failure to get assignments in on time. You expand your idea of what professors are talking about beyond cheating to ways of getting out of work, a different underlying concept. Handing in the same paper to several instructors may be less cheating than just another form of getting out of work.

In the interviews, you also heard professors explain that they feel put upon when the students do not treat the faculty with the respect that their intellectual achievements deserve. In the same interviews professors condemned the students for spending too much time drinking and partying. These answers introduce two more concepts, *lack of respect* and *time spent partying*.

The next step in building a theory on professor-student interaction might be working out integrative themes to explain how the professors interpret what is going on with the students. You do so by combining separate ideas that you have heard to see if they seem to make sense. One theme to investigate might be that students try to get out of work because they lack respect for professors as intellectuals, whereas another might be that students try to find ways of getting out of work because they are caught up in a culture that emphasizes partying. In subsequent interviews, you then ask for examples that support or fail to support these possible thematic connections.

The next phase of the work therefore would be to interview some students to obtain their perspectives on your emerging theory by asking for examples. You ask students if they sometimes failed to get their assignments in on time, and if so, what the reasons were. You question further about what acceptable excuses are (as well as the real reasons) and what it means when a student gives an off-the-wall excuse to a professor. You would ask and then listen carefully to hear if and how student interviewees relate the concepts of respect, getting out of work, and partying. You would discuss with them whether they respect their professors and what partying entails. When students describe a professor whom they really respect, you follow up to learn if they work more in his or her course than in others. If these ideas do pan out, you then explore them in more detail asking students what respect means, who they respect, who they don't respect, and how they behave in the classes of professors they respect. You would also look at partying, what it means, whether it is an antidote to loneliness and boredom, whether it is just a time-out from studying, or whether partying represents an anti-academic attitude. From these evolving questions, you might get a very different picture than from the professors about how your themes relate to each other, but both the interviews with the professors and those with the students are geared toward developing a theory on student-professor relations.

The cycle of theory building and redesign can take you in a number of different directions, depending on your interests, the audience for the report, and the theoretical or policy purposes of your research. If you are concerned with pedagogical matters, you would want to know what happens to the quality of teaching when professors perceive that many students are trying to get out of work. Do some professors become demoralized and reduce the effort they put into teaching, or do they become angry at administrators for admitting students who are not interested in learning? Do the professors try to sort out the students who are interested in learning and give them special attention and invest their egos in the success of these students?

A different avenue might be followed if you were focusing on student life, in which case you would want to inquire if the culture of excuses that grows up in the university affects other student actions. Do students think such excuses are okay? Did they make such excuses when they were in high school? Do they offer similar excuses in their jobs? Each possible avenue of inquiry suggests further concepts to look for, questions to design, and a choice of whom to interview.

If you have the time and resources, you can continue theory building by picking different sites to see how well your initial theory fits. In doing so, you may change your mind about what the important themes are and how they relate to one another.

Suppose as part of a policy study you examined a prison that had a riot, and the guards, the prisoners, and the warden all argued that bad food precipitated the riot. The emerging theme linking having a riot to quality of food is what you want to explore and test. As part of the ongoing design, you now pick two sites in which the pattern discovered does not hold and examine them to figure out why. One site is a prison noted for having bad food but relative social calm and the other reputedly has decent food but did have a riot. If your tentative theory is correct, bad food should lead to riots and good food should lead to the absence of riots. These exceptions should make you wonder if there are conditions that lead to social calm even when the food is bad and whether there are conditions that lead to riots even when the food is good. In each of the new settings, you interview guards, prisoners, and the warden about both food and social order. You also ask about prison life in general. You want to test the importance of the quality of food but not exclude other reasons why riots happen.

You now have three settings to compare. Suppose that in both prisons that had riots you learn that guards and prisoners referred to each other in ways that showed mutual racial disdain. In one, the riot was triggered as the guards yelled out, "You [racial epithet] deserve to eat this slop," whereas in the other, the guards locked up the prisoners and yelled

You [racial epithet] should be kept in cages like the animals you are." The prisoners retorted, "F***ing [racial epithets]." You start to suspect that the riot stemmed from racial tension rather than food; the food was simply an excuse. This conclusion is strengthened as you learn that in the second prison that also had a riot, the food improved because of an advocacy effort of the Good Prison Association, though little effort was made to improve the racial climate. Your conclusion is given further credence as you learn that in the prison that avoided a riot, the food was miserable, but the guards spent time commiserating with the prisoners over the terrible food and racial antagonism seemed relatively low.

Example: Selecting Sites to Build a Theory

When Irene began to study how budget processes change in cities, she started in one city where she had good contacts, and then chose additional initial case studies from across the country, knowing that administrative practices in budgeting varied in different regions of the country. After initial interviewing, as she compared the cases, she also discovered that the legal form of government affected how budgeting was done. Whether the mayor (an elected official) or the city manager (an appointed professional) had real power seemed to have important implications for the budget process, an unanticipated finding. With that tentative new theme in mind, she redesigned her work and added two more cases that reflected clear examples of different governmental structures, a strong mayor form in Boston, Massachusetts, and an effective council-manager form in Dayton, Ohio. This redesign now included two cases with powerful managers, two with powerful mayors, and two in-between. When she was doing the final analysis, she looked to see if the cities (cases) with powerful managers budgeted alike, and whether cities with powerful mayors were similar to each other but different from the cities with powerful managers. The choice of cases allowed for the development and testing of a theory that came about from what she had discovered during the research: that the structure of the government and distribution of power strongly affected how budgeting was done.

As Irene's budgeting study and the prison example indicate, designing qualitative interviewing to build a theory involves not only thinking about what ideas you will test and questions you will ask, but also where you do the study and whom you interview. Further, the process of theory building is continuous, as you test your initial ideas, modify them, and retest them until fewer and fewer changes are made with each analysis-theory cycle.

For instance, from an analysis of his early interviews in a few cities, Herb learned that community development organizations feared that if they directly pressured city government for additional support, officials would retaliate and cut off all their funds. Instead of directly pressuring funding agencies, community developers formed advocacy coalitions that did not themselves rely on government funds (and so could take some risks), and these coalitions worked aggressively to get cities to pay for community projects. To test the emerging theme that coalitions buffered financially dependent community organizations from retribution, Herb chose other cities in which to interview, some with stronger coalitions and others with weaker ones. In each site, Herb asked about how the city government and community development organizations worked with one another. In the cities with weaker coalitions, interviewees told Herb that the government ignored the development organizations. By contrast, in cities with strong coalitions, interviewees gleefully described campaigns that changed governmental agendas. The emerging theory of the importance of coalitions was strengthened by the interviews from the comparative sites.

At some point, you decide that you have created the theory that best fits your case or cases, and begin to think about how far you want to extend it. Do the results apply only to the research site in which you collected your data, or can you generalize more broadly? To generalize, you design your project to include interviewing in a variety of settings, some quite similar on background characteristics to those in which you initially interviewed and others quite dissimilar. *Similarity-dissimilarity* sampling helps you decide how far your results extend.

If your theory is right, the similar sites should produce findings close to what you learned initially. If you do not come up with similar results in the similar site, you have to question whether the site really was similar or whether your theory was wrong. Suppose you are doing an oral history to learn about the obstacles Latino organizers face and have interviewed those who worked with César Chávez, an organizer in California, and noted certain consistent themes. You might want to conduct a comparative study, this time interviewing those who worked with Ernesto Cortes, a community organizer in Texas, in many ways similar to Chávez, to see if similar themes turn up. If you find similar themes, then you can have more confidence in your conclusions. They *should* hold in this new setting and they do. In fact, studies that have been done on the topic confirm that the results hold up well (Levy 1975; Rogers 1990; Warren 2001).

Another way to extend your results further is to choose a setting that is very different in background or site characteristics or both and then ask the interviewees in that setting the same questions you asked before. If you find the same themes in this very dissimilar setting, you gain confidence that your findings hold more generally.

Suppose you are studying how students understand the purpose of college. In your initial cases you interviewed white male fraternity brothers (a background characteristic) on academic probation (a background characteristic) from Playboy Private U. (a site characteristic) and heard the theme that "going to school is just buying a degree." To test out how far this theme extends, you look for interviewees who differ greatly in background characteristics. For instance, you would interview African American females (background characteristic) who are graduating Summa Cum Laude (background characteristics) from Prestige Tech U. (site characteristic). If in this very different setting you hear the identical theme, you can reason that buying a degree might be a broader theme in student culture, though of course you would check it out in more than these two cases.

Central to extending your results through dissimilarity sampling is learning how to choose interviewees in ways that best vary background features. Assume you are researching how married faculty women combine career and family and have worked out an initial theme that the women feel so pressured to spend more time with their children that they feel guilty for every minute they are not at home with the children. To test out the generality of this theme, you vary the background characteristics of the academic women that you subsequently interview—how oriented they are to research and publication, the willingness of their husbands to spend time with the kids, and the income level of the family (the ability to pay for good-quality day care). In picking the background features to vary, you need to work out for yourself how each one might influence the theme of guilt about child care and include only those characteristics that have a logical connection. Having varied the backgrounds of the interviewees, if you find that each one expresses guilt in a similar way, you gain confidence that the themes you found initially are descriptive of academic women in general.

Conclusion

Design in qualitative interviews at first seems unsystematic, but what appears chaotic is merely a continuous redesign. With continuous design, you keep building on your new findings, while gathering evidence for, testing, and changing your emerging theory. You modify questions to test emerging ideas and then choose new sites and interviewees to see how far you can generalize your theory. This approach to design ensures that when you finish gathering data, you will have answered your research question and have sufficient material to produce a rich and nuanced report. The design also ensures that when the project is done, the results will be on target, convincing, and important. Ideally, the results will also be generalizable.

4

Continuing the Design

Making the Research Credible

Through careful design you ensure that your results are credible to the reader of your research. To enhance credibility, you choose interviewees who are knowledgeable, whose combined views present a balanced perspective, and who can help you test your emerging theory. You investigate your research problem thoroughly, accurately present what the interviewees have said, and carefully check apparent contradictions and inconsistencies. You write up your report transparently, so readers can see how systematically and accurately you collected, recorded, and analyzed the data.

Choosing Interviewees

Your interviews gain credibility when your conversational partners are experienced and have first-hand knowledge about the research problem. To convince readers that your research does not have an unintended slant, you select interviewees whose views reflect different, even contending, perspectives. Once you have formulated your tentative theory, you choose interviewees who can help you flesh out the theory, modify it based on their experiences, or steer you away from a nonproductive avenue of inquiry.

FINDING INTERVIEWEES WHO
WILL PROVIDE USEFUL INFORMATION

Interviewees should be *experienced* and *knowledgeable* in the area you are interviewing about. Finding them may take skill and time, sometimes including a bit of detective work. Picking the low-hanging fruit—that is, talking only to interviewees who are easy to find and talk to—may not give you a balanced or accurate picture.

Experienced

Finding interviewees with the relevant, first-hand experience is critical in making your results convincing. A report from someone who was kidnapped is better than one from a journalist who interviewed the victim. If you want to learn about student culture, talk to students who have participated in that culture, not to their parents, guidance counselors, teachers, or even resident assistants.

Finding students to talk to may not be difficult, but finding the person who attended a particular meeting that occurred years ago may be more problematic. Your search for particular individuals may be hit or miss in the beginning, but once you find one person who was involved in the matter, he or she can usually tell you who else to talk to or where you might find documents that list the names of others who were involved.

One way to begin is to ask for help from general informants who have already observed the scene. Social workers and even the police might be able to point out informed gang leaders. Political lobbyists can tell you which congressional staffers were most involved in drafting particular pieces of legislation.

When you are examining a specific issue such as a political dispute or a successful protest, you can look in newspapers, on Web sites, or in newsletters for the names of people who were involved. If you are studying a historic or political event, you can often find out who did what by looking in court records, libraries, or archives (including newspaper archives). Sometimes a bit of detective work and preliminary inquiry is required to get started. In an oral-history project about a black musicians' union, for example, Diane Turner (1997) had to ask around to find consultants in the field who could tell her the names of performers who had been in the union.

Knowledgeable

It seems obvious enough that the people you want to talk to should be knowledgeable about the research problem. To learn about computer viruses, you do not interview graphic artists but instead track down specialists in computer security. The problem is that not everyone who *should* know about something is necessarily well informed.

Assuming that a police specialist in computer crime will know something about hacking is reasonable; a mayor ought to know about making political deals with council members; an executive director of a social-service agency should know what that agency accomplished. But a person's position is not always a good proxy for what he or she knows. New city-council members are often ill-informed about governance. New police officers will be able to cite rules and regulations but may not know how things are actually done. One health-policy analyst may have spent a lifetime studying health care, whereas another may have squeaked by learning the minimum necessary to stay employed.

Sometimes you cannot figure out in advance how much someone knows. The best you can do is choose a person who is in the appropriate position and then after interviewing him or her decide if you have obtained the information you needed. More often, however, your preliminary research suggests who is knowledgeable. When Herb first started studying growth issues, he knew of the importance of city officials, housing developers, and environmentalists. After a while he figured out that those who controlled the sewers were also crucial, as sewer capacity limited growth, so he added the sanitary engineers to his list of people to interview, and when they were interviewed they suggested including road planners.

When you have little to go on in figuring out who might be informed, one approach is to first find people whose job it is to monitor that arena, and ask them with whom to speak. For example, reporters follow specific beats, such as the art world, city hall, or immigration; those in charge of computer bulletin boards normally pay attention to developments in cyberspace; editors of newsletters for religious groups, environmental groups, or model-airplane clubs can guide you about current activities in their respective fields. People who run professional organizations or trade associations or who act as consultants keep tabs on what is going on and can point out to you who is likely to have the specific knowledge that you want to obtain.

In cultural studies, almost any member of the group should be able to provide you with examples of common practices, beliefs, and values, but few are experienced in communicating what they take for granted to outsiders. So you look for "encultured informants," individuals who know the culture well and take it as their responsibility to explain what it means (Spradley 1979, p. 47). The server at the restaurant with several years experience, the sergeant in the police district, and the full professor at the university are often knowledgeable about their respective settings and able to describe the culture to you.

In both topical and cultural studies, rarely can you find a single individual who has all the information that you seek. Instead, you look for people who know about particular parts of a problem and then piece together what they collectively know. If you are studying how a corn field became a strip mall, there may have been many people involved along the way, each of whom knows a part of the story, and you want to talk to all of them.

With a Variety of Perspectives

The credibility of your findings is enhanced if you make sure you have interviewed individuals who reflect a variety of perspectives. The philosophy of responsive interviewing suggests that reality is complex; to accurately portray that complexity, you need to gather contradictory or overlapping perceptions and nuanced understandings that different individuals hold.

Sometimes you are simply after complementary understandings. If you are researching for a biography, you would want to include the person's spouse, children, friends, other relatives, and work associates, because each one would know the subject of your biography in a specific context, would see him or her a little differently. If you are studying religious values, you should seek the views of both clergy and congregants, because how seriously they take the values will differ.

In cultural studies you note from your early interviews or observations the distinguishing characteristics in the group and then interview people who differ on these specific characteristics. Key distinctions may be between the old-timers and the new recruits, between PC users and Macintosh advocates, or between those who want to fight back and those who prefer to accept the status quo. If you are examining what *courtesy* means, the relevant distinctions might be between those who are higher or lower in a bureaucratic hierarchy or those with higher or lower status in a group. You are not looking for any differences at all but looking for those that are related to the concepts and themes you are working out. As you continue to interview people from each of the relevant categories, each new conversation should add less and less to what you already know, until all you start hearing are the same matters over and over again. At that point, you have reached what Glaser and Strauss term the "saturation point" (Glaser and Strauss 1967), and you stop.

In topical studies, you picture the research arena as a theater in the round and try to locate interviewees with different vantage points on what is going on at center stage. You then talk to individuals from each of those vantage points. In studying an educational system, school board members, principals, teachers, parents' associations, and students all have their own slants. When Pushkala Prasad (1991) studied the founding of the clerical union at Yale, to obtain these distinct perspectives, she conducted semistructured interviews with union organizers, clerical and technical workers, faculty, students, representatives of the Yale administration, and members of the New Haven community.

When you are studying controversial issues, you want to obtain all sides. A police officer and a speeder are likely to have very different views on why a ticket was given. Our experience is that when we solicit alternative views and our interviewees are aware that we are doing so, interview quality and credibility improves. In a business dispute, you might want to speak to union members first, and then, armed with the union perspective, ask to talk to upper-level management to get their version. Upper-level managers may be irritated enough at the things the union is saying to want to set the record straight. Herb's experience is that people from one side of a dispute will suggest what to ask the other side and even provide needed documents. Interviewing both sides not only helps ensure balance but also ensures considerable depth, as people want to make sure you really understand their views.

You do not need a vast number of interviewees to increase the credibility of your findings; instead, you have to be able to convince readers that you have interviewed to obtain different points of views and that when brought together these understandings provide a complete picture. You might want to double-check certain key conclusions, but once your double-checking verifies your initial findings, you can stop.

To Build and Test Theory

Though you want to be able to describe what you have heard and in doing so answer your specific research question, you also hope to be able to build a theory that has broader implications. With this goal in mind, you select interviewees in ways that give you confidence in extending what you find beyond the immediate research setting.

For instance, suppose you are studying a bureaucratic squabble about whether to reduce funding for day care and increase funding for highway repairs in a municipal budget as a step in building a theory that might explain the source of municipal conflicts. To begin, you need to figure out what this squabble is really about. Is this an argument over priorities, whether the city should reduce funding for day care and increase funding for highway repair? Or does it reflect a quarrel between the public works department and the city manager, suggesting that the theory will be about contests over power in a bureaucracy? Or is it symbolic of deeper schisms in the community and resulting disagreements over who should be involved and how political decisions should be made? Testing each of these ideas requires asking specific questions from a different set of interviewees, and you have to do so to see which provides the best explanation.

If the argument is really about tradeoffs between specific types of expenditures, there should be plenty of evidence of other quarrels over budget tradeoffs that you can learn about by interviewing other department heads concerning the frequency and intensity of budget quarrels, perhaps on the tradeoffs between having more police on the street or better road repair, or between more spending for downtown improvements in parking or neighborhood spending for improved drainage. To examine if the quarrel is more about the city manager asserting control over the director of public works, a different approach is required. If the battle is over control and not really about a budget item, you should find evidence of conflicts over nonbudgetary items between the city manager and the public works director, perhaps over staffing or issues of management style. To test this out, you might want to talk to both the city manager and the public works director about prior conflicts, what started them and how they were resolved, and then compare their answers to those of the other department heads and see if their answers differ in tone or content. If this battle is between the manager and the public works director, the public works director is likely to be more emotional, angrier, or more frustrated than his peers in other departments. To explore the third possibility, that you observed only the edge of a social cleavage that goes beyond City Hall, you would interview council members, the mayor, interest group representatives, and homeowners' association activists and organized groups representing the poor, and ask them in general what types of issues cause clashes and the role the different groups played. In this way you can determine if what you initially saw at City Hall reflected larger social issues rather than narrow bureaucratic concerns.

In building theory you combine several themes and then test them to see if they hold. Next, you try to figure out the mechanisms that link cause with effect and conduct interviews to explore if these mechanisms hold. If you suspect that family income and educational background affect how unmarried teenage girls cope with pregnancy, you interview unmarried teenagers who differ in terms of income and education and work out a series of questions that encourage them to discuss ways in which income or education influenced their decisions and their strategies. If you find no differences between your interviewees, you would then reject the idea that income and education explain how teenagers cope with pregnancy.

Searching out mechanisms is easier when you include considerable relevant variation in your choice of interviewees. In her study of pregnant black teens, for example, Elaine Kaplan tried to include as much diversity as she could, seeking out older women who had been teenage mothers, as well as current teenage mothers, and teenage mothers from middle-class backgrounds as well as those from poor backgrounds (1997). Kaplan also talked to teachers, counselors, and black and white teenage girls who did not get pregnant. By interviewing a broad range of people, she was able to describe the context of teenage pregnancy; by looking at older and younger women, she was able to examine the effects of teenage pregnancy over time; by looking at teens from middle-class as well as working and poorer families, she could determine what the results of poverty and other factors were; by interviewing white as well as black teens, she could see the impact of race. Kaplan built into the selection of interviewees sufficient variation to suggest different mechanisms for her theory on how pregnant teenagers coped.

To summarize, how you choose your interviewees is central to building confidence in your results. You do not necessarily have to talk to a lot of people, but you have to talk to people who have had the appropriate experience, are knowledgeable, and are able to explain to you what they know. You need to select interviewees who collectively present an overall view of your topic, while at the same time choosing them with sufficiently different backgrounds to provide convincing evidence for the theory you are trying to build.

Thoroughness and Accuracy

An appropriate choice of interviewees helps make your arguments credible, but you also need to show that your questioning and sampling have been thorough and that what you report is accurate.

Thoroughness means investigating all the relevant options with care and completeness, checking out facts and tracking down discrepancies. Thoroughness means choosing interviews to obtain disparate views and carefully piecing together the separate parts of a puzzle. Thoroughness requires preparing follow-up questions when evidence is missing or thin, or when you hear something that sounds puzzling. Thoroughness involves carefully backing up each explanation you offer with evidence from your interviews. If you cannot find evidence, or if the results do not hold up in a variety of situations, you do not report them.

Thoroughness means investigating new paths as they crop up, redesigning the study as often as necessary to pursue these new directions. It entails testing out alternative explanations, talking about them with interviewees who have different backgrounds and perspectives. Sometimes thoroughness means digging back in time to tell a story from the beginning or looking for missing parts of narratives. It might involve your tracking down promising leads that introduce new ideas or identifying and then interviewing knowledgeable interviewees who might change your interpretation. If you find a gap in logic when you get to the write-up, you go back to the interviewing to fill in the missing links.

Accuracy requires that you be careful in how you obtain, record, and report what you have heard. Accuracy includes representing what the interviewees have said exactly as spoken. At the most technical level, that means not making mistakes as you transcribe and when possible asking the conversational partners to check your transcription. When writing reports, an accurate researcher does not rely on memory about what people said but instead examines each interview transcript.

Accuracy and honesty of presentation also mean that the interviewer does not put words in the mouth of the interviewee, substituting his or her opinions or experiences for those of the interviewee or selectively choosing (and hence biasing) what the person said. Sometimes accuracy means getting across the meaning of what interviewees have said rather than quoting them exactly, especially if the quote is convoluted or says two or more things at the same time. To be doubly sure you are right, draw up a summary and ask your interviewees if this is what they meant.

Most importantly, accuracy means creating a description and explanation of the research setting or laying out a process with such clarity and understanding that participants in the research recognize and acknowledge your description of their world. You may want to run your interpretations by your interviewees to make sure they see themselves and their world in what you have written. Your description and analysis should be good enough that strangers armed with your work would be able to understand the researched culture well enough to navigate the setting.

Believability

Believability means demonstrating that what you have been told is on the mark and that you have not been deceived by your interviewees. In conversational partnerships, most people try to be honest and open; lies are rare and easily discovered in a qualitative project. Over the course of a long, depth interview, and better yet several, you can usually figure out where a person is exaggerating and what areas he or she is ignoring.

Your interviewees should know that they do not have to talk to you, that you are not trying to catch them out, and that there is generally no need to lie. In addition, in many projects you get to know your interviewees well, and they get to know you well enough to be forthcoming. Because people know you are talking to others who might tell you the whole story, there is a tendency to be reasonably truthful. Still, if you should catch someone in a lie, try not to get upset over being deceived. Instead, back off and rethink why the lie occurred and then change what you later ask so you are not pressuring interviewees to tell you something untruthful.

Oddly enough, when they do occur, lies can be useful clues to what is going on in your data. For example, criminologist David Luckenbill wanted to find out the income of young male prostitutes he was studying but felt they were exaggerating how much they earned. Toward the close of the conversation, Luckenbill asked his interviewees if they could give him change for a $10 bill and learned they did not have enough cash to do so. Luckenbill realized that his interviewees were lying about their income, but rather than discounting what the interviewees said, concluded that these young men so wanted to justify their occupation that they greatly exaggerated their earnings.

Even though lying is not a major problem, you still need to choose interviewees and design questioning patterns to minimize distortions, calculated omissions, and exaggerations. You question in ways that enable you to verify what the interviewees tell you, reconcile contradictory or inconsistent information, and fill in gaps of missing material. Try to make sure you do not push interviewees beyond what they know and are willing to talk about. You make your results more believable by using multiple sources of information and building some redundancy into the design. You can often check out what people are saying by observation and background work. A leader of one organization will probably not distort the fact that he or she has had or is having a fight with another organization when you have witnessed public disagreements and are known to read the newsletters of each organization.

Interviews are more believable when it is clear that the interviewees have had direct access to the information requested. If you are talking about the president, and you interview a guard at the Capitol, readers are likely to ask themselves how a guard could know this type of information. You design your questions and choose your interviewees so that you establish not only what they know, but how they know it. Do they have first-hand experience? Have they studied the matter themselves? If you are after a technical point, do they have the requisite expertise? Irene always starts her interviews with a few questions on the conversational partner's experience base—how long they have worked in their current job, what work they did before, and if she doesn't know, she asks some details about the work.

   To help you recognize distortions, fabrications, and omissions, you build redundancy into the design by asking the same question in different ways to check out the results. If you encounter inconsistencies, you can ask about them politely. You might broach the subject with the following: "I noticed that you mentioned earlier that you did not like the planning aspect of the budget process, but now you are talking about the importance of planning in revenue projection. That sounds contradictory...." Then let the conversational partner explain the apparent contradiction. Keep in mind, though, that people can hold two contradictory views simultaneously, and both may be true in the sense that the interviewees believe them both. A person can believe in environmentalism, because clean air is good, yet drive a large car because it is safer. You need to check out the inconsistency and find resolutions where they exist, but you do not have to force people to an unrealistic level of consistency or embarrass them about the compromises they have made.

   Redundancy also means asking at least some of the same questions to different people in separate roles in ways that allow you to check your interviews for consistency. Suppose you were conducting a study of street people and discovered that though there were widespread norms of food sharing, street people felt that it was okay to steal from each other. Such a finding appears somewhat inconsistent, and to make your report believable, you need to show that you explored these differences. You could do so by asking people when it is okay to steal and when it is not, hoping to obtain more nuanced answers, for instance, that it is okay to steal but not so much that people end up with nothing to eat. If you cannot resolve an inconsistency between interviewees, you may have to pick between different versions. To make your choice of versions more believable, you need to show how you evaluated the interviewees' memory, the quality of the evidence, and the bias or slant in each version. Sometimes rather than pick one version, you present two or more different versions and use the sharp differences to explain why a conflict was so severe.

   When you are checking out inconsistencies or omissions, if possible, compare your findings with other sources of information, such as documents, newspaper stories, court depositions, or testimony. When asked about how he knew that interviewees were telling the truth, an investigator with the National Transportation Safety Board (NTSB) argued that on the one hand people wanted to be helpful, to figure out what had caused a plane to crash, and on the other hand, the agency checked all the facts against a broader context. The NTSB interviewer reported that all the information they get from interviews is cross-checked, not only between interviews, but also between interviews and evidence from the debris of the airplane, and between the answers in the interviews and radar and weather data recorded over the planes' flight path (personal interview with David Bowling, June 22, 2001).

In research projects where lying, distortion, or exaggeration may be a problem, such as when someone has done something wrong or embarrassing, you may need to make extra efforts to get past fronts, images, or self-serving versions of a story or event. Suppose you were interviewing students who dropped out of college and asking them why they left. This is a sufficiently embarrassing problem that some interviewees might not tell you the whole truth. They might say they dropped out because they lacked money, but perhaps there were other reasons as well that they failed to report. Normally, you would only ask people about their own experiences, but if the self-reports are suspect, to encourage your interviewees to explain more fully the reasons for dropping out, you might take a different tack and ask the interviewees to provide examples from other people they know. In most answers, the interviewee will be drawing on his or her own experiences as well as those of friends and acquaintances, and may point out which examples are personal. Giving the interviewees the option of talking about other people helps avoid embarrassment while still keeping the discussion grounded in real examples.

Sometimes distortions reflect an obligation the interviewees feel to provide a formalistic reply because of their work role. Electric-company spokespersons may insist that the nuclear plant accident never put citizens in any health danger, because to admit otherwise might force costly repairs and invite lawsuits for health damage. Police and court employees are particularly likely to give formalistic answers, because if they admit they do not follow appropriate procedures, their evidence is suspect when presented in court. Similarly, scientists might give normative answers about how they do their research, because actual procedures may seem too casual and threaten their credibility and possibly their funding (Thomas and Marquart 1988). Even qualitative interviewers might sometimes tell you how something *should* be done rather than the way they *actually* do things because they are afraid of losing your respect.

Ideally, you work to phrase questions in ways that avoid formalistic replies. If what you are asking about might involve violation of rules, laws, or norms, you should probably work out an indirect way of approaching the matter. One way people provide indirect answers is through telling stories that contain the answer but without saying so in so many words; rather than asking a question directly you might want to ask for stories on the topic and then analyze them for themes they contain. Another approach to use if the initial answer seems vague is to follow up by presenting a concrete incident of the type under discussion and ask for comments about it. Conversely, if a person has detailed a specific project in harmonious terms and you suspect that you are getting an overly optimistic report, later in the interview you can ask about stresses more generally.

Overall, try to avoid asking questions that might evoke formalistic answers. When our colleague Jim was asking court officials to discuss how they carried out hearings on parole requests, all he got back were descriptions of the formal procedures. About to give up, Jim switched his line of questioning to topics he knew were not covered in the manuals and asked the officials how they felt about the convicts. To this question, the interviewees responded directly and openly. The officials elaborated and indicated how their negative feelings toward the prisoners influenced the way they conducted hearings. Another approach is to base your questions on what you and the interviewee have both observed. The interviewee is unlikely to give you an idealized answer because he or she knows you just saw what actually happened.

Only if these more polite and indirect approaches fail and you really need the information would you want to risk a more challenging approach. "I really want to talk to you about the role of faulty welds in the coolant system in the recent shutdown of the plant, and whether officials knew about the welds. That is what some folks are saying, and I would like to get your side." That is pretty challenging wording, but it may be necessary if the interviewee has been giving nothing but bland statements. He or she may respond to find out how much you know, and in doing so confirm or disprove your suspicions. Or you may get a detailed rebuttal of the charges. Once conversational partners start to explain, the tendency is for them to get it right, especially if you have already shown that you are sympathetic and trustworthy. If you are concerned that interviewees might distort or omit information, for example, in an evaluation project, avoid boxing them into conclusions that make them uncomfortable. It is better to ask what obstacles a program has run into than to word the question to ask why something in particular failed. Asking about obstacles avoids the implication that the problems were not addressed or that the interviewees were at fault.

Be cautious about asking questions before the interviewing relationship is fairly solid and the interviewee knows that you are informed enough to test the answers you get. Irene almost always talks with subordinates and technical staff before interviewing bosses and political appointees, and then from what she learns, words her questions to send signals that say, "I already know quite a bit; if you say something that sounds a bit off, I will pick it up." You can ask a ranking official about layoffs in a federal agency by saying something like the following: "The unions have argued that there was no need for a reduction in force, but that it was carried out anyway. What could they mean by that? What was the reason for the reduction in force?" By mentioning that you have talked to union representatives and implying access to their documents, you suggest that you are not ignorant and reduce the likelihood of getting a misleading answer. Being seen around as a patient observer is another way to encourage people not to distort. If it is even remotely possible that you could have seen and heard some event or discussion, interviewees are unlikely to claim those things never happened and are less likely to omit them from the discussion.

Unfortunately, though people often try to tell the truth, sometimes their memories have faded or they have blurred two or more events or characters together, or not remembered exactly what was said. Oral historians often tell their interviewees what period of time they will be covering and ask their conversational partners to look for documentation they may have kept of those days, such as diaries, appointment calendars, or old newspaper clippings that might refresh their memories. The National Transportation Safety Board investigator mentioned previously often encounters crash survivors who cannot remember what happened. To deal with this problem, he carefully leads them up from earlier events before the flight and well before the crash, going step by step until they cannot remember any more. Other interviewers learn how to link what they are asking with events they are pretty sure the interviewees can recall. When Irene was interviewing about how cities changed their budget process, she sometimes asked questions about events 20 years earlier. Instead of asking for dates when something occurred, she asked the interviewees if they remembered who the mayor was at that time. A change in mayor is a big event, and workers at City Hall tend to remember it. Once Irene knew who the mayor was, she could check on the dates of that mayor from other sources.

Demonstrating Credibility Through Transparency

Transparency means that a reader of a qualitative research report is able to see the process by which the data were collected and analyzed. A transparent report allows the reader to assess the thoroughness of the design of the work as well as the conscientiousness, sensitivity, and biases of the researcher. Interviewers maintain careful records of what they did, saw, and felt and include portions of this record in their final write-ups so the reader can determine where and how the researcher went beyond what the interviewees said.

To ensure that data is transparent, you should keep notes or recordings that others can read or play back, so long as confidentiality and anonymity are protected. Keep in a log how the transcript was made, whether directly from tape, from notes, or from memory; how it was verified; and the level of detail it contains. If the transcripts are edited versions of the audio recordings, the log should note the kind of material that was left out. Your path of analysis should also be transparent, with a record kept showing the coding categories you used, that is, how you sorted out what people said.

Be as precise as you can in your records. On notes that you reconstructed from memory, include details such as "this is my term, not his" or "I am not sure of the order here; the point about her mother may have preceded this." If you have paraphrased a question or response, mark that too, so you know later that you cannot use it as a direct quotation. Also include a record of your feelings about the whole interview, such as "this interview was filled with tension" or "the group was friendly and teasing, and it was hard to get past the small talk."

Both for your own records and to make it clear to others what you did, keep a separate notebook, almost a diary, of your project. If you did participant observation, describe what occurred, when it took place, how long it lasted, and provide a summary of what you learned. You can keep a running file of ideas as they emerge and in it also note what was happening in the research—how you felt, with whom you were speaking—when you made major decisions, such as determining to follow a particular theme or explore a specific concept. You are making your own biases, slants, and reactions transparent to others. You may want to refer to this log when you write up the report, and it should be made available to others in the unlikely event that they want to examine it.

The requirement that the research process be transparent encourages the researcher to stay close to the data in writing up a report, including summary statements only when they can be backed up with the words of the interviewees. Flights of imaginative fancy are controlled when the original interviews are publicly available and quotes from the interviews are presented in the report to support each major conclusion.

Conclusion

In this chapter we have shown how to design an interviewing project to ensure the thoroughness, accuracy, and believability of the research. In doing so, you let the reader see, to the extent he or she wishes, how you arrived at your conclusions without overwhelming him or her with unimportant details. In your write-up, make your research process visible but not intrusive. Quote generously from your interview transcripts to back up key points. The reader should be able to follow the logic of the analysis, hear the voices of your interviewees, and distinguish the voice of the researcher from those of the interviewees.

Good design prevents twin nightmares from becoming reality. The first nightmare is getting to the end of the data gathering and not having anything significant to tell. The second is coming up with sparkling findings only to have their importance, representativeness, or truth value questioned. Design guides the choice of interviewees and the lines of questioning to help build understanding, verify ideas, and provide evidence for emerging themes. It keeps the study on track, even if in an iterative approach to research you do not know exactly where the final destination will be when the train first leaves the station.

5

Conversational Partnerships

I n responsive interviewing, the researcher and the interviewee develop
a relationship within a *conversational partnership* that influences the
interviewing process. In this chapter we examine what affects this interviewing relationship, beginning with how the personality and emotions
of the researcher affect the conversational exchange. We discuss ways in
which interactions differ depending on gender, ethnicity, and social class
and how the interview situation changes depending on the shared understanding of the research role of the interviewer. We then describe how
to encourage potential interviewees to participate and share their experiences. In a conversational partnership, the researcher is obligated to behave
in a courteous and ethical way. We end the chapter by examining the
rigidly rule-bound approach to ethics imposed by many institutional
review boards and offer suggestions on how qualitative researchers can
respond to these rules.

Emotions and Personality of the Interviewer

How you feel and how you act in an interview can greatly affect the
quality of the exchange. Interviewers, especially those just starting out,
are likely to be anxious, find the intense concentration of the interviews
exhausting, and react emotionally to the personalities, circumstances, and
opinions of their conversational partners.

HANDLING ANXIETY AND FATIGUE

An interviewer who is tense often has trouble paying close attention and
misses important points on which to follow up. In addition, nervousness

might upset conversational partners who then become eager to conclude the interview and respond quickly and with inadequate depth. Being relaxed creates an environment for a thoughtful, rich interview.

Plan ways to make yourself comfortable during the interview so that you will be able to relax. Before the interview gain confidence by taking time to learn something about the interviewee and the research setting. Better yet, when possible start with someone you already know and with whom you are comfortable, rather than beginning with the nerve-wracking effort of building a new relationship before you are certain about what you want to ask and how. If you find yourself getting panicky before an interview, take a walk or do some exercises, and take a few deep breaths.

Keep in mind that you will make mistakes—everyone does—but they are rarely important. If your questions indicate that you misunderstood something, conversational partners usually correct you. We have found that when our conversational partners know what it is that interests us, if we ask the wrong questions, the interviewees rephrase what we have said and answer the questions we should have posed.

During an interview, your level of concentration is high, you are listening hard, trying to extract themes, deciding what to follow up and how, and asking for explanations and examples. This effort can leave you wound up, more so if the interview is particularly emotional or exciting. Before interviewing others, you need time to calm down. If possible, rest between interviews and try to avoid back-to-back interviews, lest you show up for the next interview looking as if you are on some mood-altering substance. We build in buffer time between interviews, doubling our estimates of transportation time, and, when possible, scheduling ourselves for a meal between the interviews. If someone runs late, you can always skip the meal. When interviews must be scheduled close together, work out a way of creating a psychological space to separate one interview from another. Read a newspaper or a few pages of a novel, or do some window shopping or some bird watching for a few minutes.

You cannot keep up a pace of two to three interviews a day, looking them over, transcribing them, and preparing for the next one, and still have time or energy to think about what you are doing. Ultimately, to stay calm, you need to take periodic time-outs.

UNDERSTANDING AND ACCOMMODATING TO YOUR OWN PERSONALITY

Personality influences interviewing style, affecting how comfortable you are in chatting, how persistently you hunt down missing information or contradictions, and how closely you stick to the initial set of questions. Aggressive personalities might scare interviewees by demanding evidence rather than pursuing controversial issues in a less threatening manner. On the other hand, some interviewers are too passive, failing to pursue ideas that need clarification. You need to balance your personality with the interviewing situation. If you are too aggressive for the situation, back off a bit; if you are too passive, force yourself to follow up a bit more. You also have to accommodate to the interviewee; for example, if you are interviewing people who are treated by others as marginal or voiceless, avoid asking questions in a demanding way.

If you are too intense, lighten up by introducing a little chat. Or, conversely, if you are too gregarious and have too much polite banter at the beginning of an interview, work out a shorter introduction and stick to it. If you are anxious and find yourself asking only the questions that you have written out in advance regardless of what the interviewees are saying, accommodate by writing out only a few questions and force yourself to wing the rest by listening and responding to what you hear.

Another crucial personality attribute that affects interviewing is how empathetic you are, that is, your ability to show caring interest in the content of what the interviewee is saying and the emotion expressed. You show empathy by asking questions to obtain the details that allow you to imagine what your interviewees have experienced, even if the questions are slightly off your topic. Suppose you are trying to figure out how well a cardiac rehabilitation program is working and have never had a heart attack. In an effort to develop and show empathy, consider taking some time to ask about the episode that landed the interviewee in cardiac rehab before focusing on the evaluation questions: "Can you tell me what happened to you? What did the heart attack feel like?" Listening to the answer can help you build understanding of what cardiac rehab means to your interviewees.

Being too empathetic can be problematic. If you identify too closely with those you study, you may only ask follow-up questions that show your interviewees in a favorable light; you may fail to question about the whole matter. Empathizing with those who have faced great personal losses or endured debilitating diseases can be draining, whereas empathizing with someone who has done something terrible can be confusing and upsetting, as you wonder about your own values. You may need to back off a bit.

One solution is to intentionally schedule interviews with others who can provide balance with those to whom you usually speak. If you have been talking with convicted felons, consider switching for a while to interviewing victims or their families. Or you may find that keeping diaries, jotting notes on interview transcripts, or exploring your interviewing experiences with your colleagues can help you avoid overly identifying with those you study. Remember that you are a scholar, a student, or an evaluator, not a planner, a community developer, or a city budgeter. The distance provided by taking notes also makes it easier to end a study and withdraw from the conversational partnerships when the project is over.

EXPRESSING YOUR POINT OF VIEW AND UNDERSTANDING YOUR BIASES

Researchers often have strong feelings on their topics and wonder if it is okay to express those views during the interviews. You should resist the urge to make strong statements of your morality in the middle of an interview; if you cannot refrain from expressing sharp disapproval at the mention of abortion, alcoholism, or child abuse, you probably should not interview on these topics. In less extreme cases, if your interviewee asks your opinions, you can give them briefly. Though it is tempting to agree with the interviewee regardless of your own beliefs, it is better to present your opinions honestly, but in a nonjudgmental way. For instance, if you are opposed to handgun ownership and are interviewing a gun hobbyist who asks what you think, you could say the following: "I grew up in a household where guns were considered evil, so I just accepted some negative ideas about hunting. This is the first time I am really hearing the other side." Honesty, however, does not require you to blurt out everything you think or feel. You are not lying if you fail to immediately reject blatant racism, anti-Semitism, or sexism that may be revealed in interviews. If pressed, you can take evasive action with some innocuous-sounding statement such as, "I am not sure I agree with you on that, but that is neither here nor there. I would like to hear what you think about . . ."

A related problem occurs if strong personal feelings or biases cause you to distort what you are hearing. You may not follow up on leads that contradict your preconceptions, and in doing so may not get subtleties, evidence, or details that might lead you to question your beliefs. If, for instance, you have a tendency to blame men for the problems women experience in their lives, you may find yourself systematically ignoring evidence to the contrary. Rather than pretend to have no biases, it makes more sense to examine your preconceptions and work out how your feelings might slant the research and then with this understanding in mind, work to formulate questions to offset your biases.

RECIPROCITY AND SELF-REVELATION

Conversational partnerships, like all relationships, involve and create obligations. One obligation is to help the interviewee feel protected and comfortable during and after the interview. When interviewees tell you in detail about their experiences, they expose themselves to you and trust that you will not violate their confidence or criticize them. They deposit a part of themselves, an image of who they are, into your safekeeping and in doing so end up feeling vulnerable. You have an obligation to show concern with the emotional impact of the interview, perhaps by making the interviewee more comfortable about revelations by exposing what you feel in turn (see Harrison et al. 2001).

Rather than just asking and listening, sometimes researchers may need to answer some of the same questions about themselves that they have posed to the conversational partner. As Jaquie Aston put it, "I believe that a certain amount of disclosure is essential. It facilitates a sense of trust and mutuality and it increases the comfort level of the narrator" (Aston 2001, p. 147). If an interviewee asked how you handled the holidays, you could respond in a way that shows empathy with how your interviewee feels about the holidays: "My own brother died a year and a half ago, and I know the holidays are still hard for me."

Openness on the part of the interviewer not only helps the interviewee feel more protected, less exposed, but also helps build empathy. If the interviewer finds these questions painful or difficult, he or she is likely to be more aware of how difficult these questions are for the interviewee and work to buffer the interviewee from the emotions of the interview. On the other hand, the interviewer needs to be cautious not to hijack the interview and turn it into a self-examination.

THE RESEARCH RELATIONSHIP
DEEPLY AFFECTS THE INTERVIEWER

Listening intensely to details of someone else's life is an involving and nearly addictive experience. The excitement of discovery and the need to be continually alert to puzzles is thoroughly involving and becomes central to the researcher's identity. Further, over time, interviewees may become closer and be more real to researchers than their own families so that ending the project can be painful. When the research is done, there is not only a loss of intimacy, but also an end to the excitement of discovery. At the conclusion of the research, the temporariness of the conversational partnerships may make interviewees feel abandoned or even deceived, as when a close friend or intimate suddenly breaks off a relationship. In turn, interviewers may feel depressed and unfinished, as if something that was part of them is now gone.

Throwing yourself into the analysis and write-up can help you retain some of the excitement of discovery and keep you feeling close to the interviewees. You can continue to maintain research relationships after you formally exit the field by sending drafts of your writings to the interviewees for comment while keeping up a personal snail mail or e-mail correspondence or phone relationship. Some of the interview relationships you make will become more normal friendships, continuing to enrich your life for many years.

Research Roles and Social Boundaries

As you begin a conversational relationship, you have to figure out how to present yourself in ways that are nonthreatening, that reflect who you are, but that still enable you to ask in-depth questions. How should you present yourself when conducting the research; what role do you take? How do you interview across social boundaries of class, ethnicity, or education?

DEFINING RESEARCH ROLES

People relate to one another through culturally understood roles in which obligations and responsibilities are known to both parties. Wives and husbands form an interactive pair of roles, as do parents and children, bosses and workers, teachers and students. In responsive interviewing, the two roles are the researcher and those being researched, but simply calling yourself a researcher explains little because the meaning of academic research is not widely understood.

If you fail to spell out what your role is in ways interviewees can understand, they may assign a role to you that makes interviewing difficult (Gorden 1987; Gurney 1985). For instance, Pauline Bart, who studied Jane, the abortion cooperative, reported that the women whom she wanted to interview initially refused to speak with her because they cast her in the role of the hostile academic, and "they were antiacademic and antiprofessional" (Bart 1987, p. 340). In poor neighborhoods, people who come around asking questions are often social workers, landlords, undercover police, or repossession agents, rather than supportive researchers.

In establishing an acceptable research role, you have to show who you are in ways that the interviewees accept and understand. Bart had to demonstrate that she was sympathetic with the prochoice women and not part of the establishment they rejected by explaining that she had been a feminist activist in Chicago, that is, she was part of their movement. She added that she did not have a grant, reassuring her interviewees that she had not been bought off by the establishment. When setting up appointments, Irene tries to distinguish herself from reporters whom people might not trust by saying, "I am not looking for scandals or conflicts; I am trying to understand how this process has changed over time" or "I am looking to see how the change of government form has affected the budgeting process." These are not questions a reporter would be interested in. In addition, Irene shares her formal credentials as a teacher, scholar, and consultant to make it clear that she is not a reporter.

Fortunately, there are a large variety of research roles that interviewees generally accept, including that of student, professor, and author. For example, as a college undergraduate, Jay MacLeod became well acquainted with gang members by tutoring them in academic subjects and joining them in basketball games. When he began his research, he played on his known role as a student. "I needed to explain to both groups the proposed study, my role as researcher, and their role as subjects. This I did in a casual way before initiating a conversation on their aspirations. I simply explained that to graduate from college, I must write a lengthy paper and that instead of doing a lot of research in a library, 'I'm gonna write it on you guys down here and what kinds of jobs you want to go into after school and stuff like that'" (MacLeod 1987, p. 174). People understand that students prepare papers.

Being seen as a professor has plusses and minuses. On the plus side, professors are known for asking questions, so the role justifies your doing a lot of investigation, but on the down side, professors evaluate people and judge what they do not know, and that way are seen as threatening. When we present ourselves in the role of professor, we emphasize that the purpose of doing research is to learn about the real world in detail so that we can teach students what the interviewees' lives are like. This formulation helps cast the interviewee as expert, which helps reduce the threat value.

A more general research role is that of author. An author, like a professor, is granted freedom to ask questions, yet is not seen as an evaluator in the way a teacher is. Further, authors put the words and experiences of those they study into print in ways that provide publicity to interviewees. To encourage people to see him as an author, Herb sends his conversational partners a book he has written based on a prior project. Irene gives her conversational partners lists of books she has published.

In cultural research, the most effective role may be as novice, someone who is ignorant of the most basic things, almost a child, who has to be taught what everyone else already knows. To be seen as a novice, you have to show that you are willing to accept the culture and want to learn about it. You may have to spend considerable time before the interviews learning the specialized vocabulary of the group you are studying and sometimes you literally learn a foreign language, as we did for our Thailand experience. As part of his research in a working-class Italian community, William Whyte moved there and began to learn Italian. As he explained, "My effort to learn the language probably did more to establish the sincerity of my interest in the people than anything I could have told them of myself and · my work. How could a researcher be planning to 'criticize our people' if he went to the lengths of learning the language?" (Whyte 1955, p. 296). Sometimes you demonstrate acceptance by becoming one of the group, a member of the choir, a football player, or a police officer. John Van Maanen (1978) understood that police often viewed outsiders as "assholes" or "know-nothings," that is, people who cannot possibly understand their world, so there is no point in trying to explain it. To overcome this barrier, Van Maanen went through a police academy so that he was no longer an untrustworthy outsider to the officers he wanted to study.

In topical research, you cannot assume the role of ignorant novice, because you have to know enough to pose meaningful questions. Instead, in your research role, you want to be seen as a person who can be trusted to report fairly what you hear and informed enough to make the conversation worthwhile. To take on the role of someone who is knowledgeable about a field, you have to do background work; observe; read books, articles, and hearings; scrutinize newsletters; and examine archival documents.

Choosing between different research roles does not mean that you distort who you are, but rather that you select those aspects of yourself that make sense in the world of the interviewee (see Snow et al. 1986; Reinharz 1997). You may be a medical sociologist, but also a daughter, and can use either role in exploring the pill-taking experiences of your elderly interviewees. Though you can focus on one role or another, you are not play-acting; the role in which you present yourself is, and should be, part of who you actually are. You cannot pretend to be knowledgeable if you are a novice, or a Hispanic if you are an Anglo. Deception is ethically wrong, manipulative, disrespectful to interviewees, and usually will not work.

CROSSING BOUNDARIES

In creating a relationship with interviewees, researchers often have to cross the boundary from being an outsider to being an insider. Historically, some qualitative researchers claimed that taking the role of an outsider would produce better research because the interviewer would not be caught up in the cross-currents of a group or an organization. Other scholars have taken the opposite position, that the role of an insider is better because interviewees assume that the researcher is sympathetic and understands their language, concepts, and experiences. The insider-outsider issue is still being debated (cf. Gorden 1987; Horowitz 1986; Naples 1997).

Being an insider can make you seem less threatening, in part because you know the rules and are as bound by them as the interviewees are. Also, locating yourself in the social space that the interviewees know and can control may be helpful. For example, if interviewees know your boss or the president of your organization, or even your dissertation director, they may feel that they have some influence over you. Just giving them the name and phone number of someone who is responsible for you may reassure them that, if they have a problem with you, they can control your behavior by talking to your superior.

Insider and outsider statuses are frequently defined in terms of class, sex, race, or ethnic lines that some think are hard to cross. For instance, Maxine Baca Zinn quotes a study by Americo Paredes that argues that Anglo researchers misrepresent Chicano behavior because they don't understand the "performance" element of the culture. Not only do Anglos have stereotypes of Chicanos, the Chicanos have stereotypes of the Anglo interviewers, both of which make it more difficult to conduct an accurate study. Moreover, many Chicanos go out of their way to tell the researcher what he or she wants to hear (Paredes 1977; Zinn 2001).

Some researchers handle the insider-outsider question by building research teams that combine both. For example, one recent study at two state psychiatric hospitals created a research team that brought together university faculty as the outsiders and nurses from that hospital as the insiders (Thomas et al. 2000). The nurses made sure that the questions asked made sense in context, that the identities of patients were protected, that the data sought were legal and available, and that the research was not too time-consuming.

The border between insiders and outsiders is not always clear, as you might feel that you are part of a cultural or ethnic group you are studying, but your interviewees may treat you as an outsider (DeAndrade 2000). Researchers almost always have characteristics that set them apart from those being studied. You might be a black woman interviewing black women, only to find that class, income, education, or diction separate you from your interviewees. Moreover, being viewed as an outsider is not necessarily bad for the research because interviewing across class, gender, or ethnic barriers produces better results in some areas than when the backgrounds of interviewer and interviewee are matched (Cannon et al. 1988).

Cross-ethnic interviewing seems to work best when the interviewees are motivated to explain their ethnic experiences to others. For instance, researchers investigating how ethnic differences between interviewer and interviewee affected conversations on sensitive topics compared the content of conversations between Chicana women and Anglo interviewers and Chicana women and Chicana interviewers and found that

> [i]n terms of both the quantity and quality of references to sex-related topics . . . the women did speak more, and more freely, to the Anglo about sex-related matters. It was also predicted that this pattern would reverse itself when the topic was switched to discrimination as it was assumed that the speakers would be more inclined to discuss their feelings about prejudice with another Chicana and would be apt to avoid or minimize such discussions with an Anglo. This did not prove to be the case. (Tixier y Vigil and Elasser 1978, p. 95)

Herb, who is white, found he could talk comfortably about race with African Americans so long as he introduced the topic first. Afterward the conversational partners readily became the teachers and instructed Herb on the consequences of racism in American society. The conversation (probably) was different than would have occurred between two African Americans, but important information was shared nonetheless.

Though most topics can be discussed across social boundaries, differences in style of presentation can sometimes make it difficult. Such communication gaps are apparent in many male-female conversations. Deborah Tannen (1990) has argued that women understand messages as part of an established pattern of communications, not as isolated utterances. In addition, women may be more likely to give multiple messages at the same time, requiring the interviewer "to listen in stereo, receiving both the dominant and muted channels clearly" (Anderson and Jack 1991, p. 11). A male interviewer not used to listening in stereo might miss much of the message.

Another difference in gender styles is that women develop conversational patterns that allow them to get around male dominance. Devault argues, "While much feminist research in linguistics is designed to show how language and the organization of talk contribute to the subordination of women, it also shows, often, how skillfully and creatively women speakers circumvent and subvert the processes of social control," whether they do so by "talking back" (hooks 1989) or "telling it slant" (Devault 1990, p. 112). Further, women may be more likely than men to hesitate before answering. A woman's hesitation should not necessarily be interpreted as showing ignorance or fear; rather, women may be thinking of ways to express themselves that avoid [male] dominant vocabularies (Devault 1990, p. 100). The researcher should be patient with such hesitations and not jump in with a suggested word or phrase.

Other problems in communications may arise in cross-gender interviews. A blunt question from a male to a female may get a less detailed and thoughtful response than a more indirect question. When a woman is interviewing a man, the male conversational partner may be troubled if the interviewer seems too assertive, being used to women's more indirect language. Female interviewers may need to work out a style that combines being nonthreatening and professional (Gurney 1985, p. 43).

Encouraging Participation and Initiating Contact

The conversational partnership is what makes responsive interviewing work. You know why you participate in that relationship, but why should the interviewees? How do you encourage someone to describe his/her experiences in an open manner?

WHY PEOPLE AGREE TO BE INTERVIEWED AND TALK OPENLY

People are usually more willing to talk to you if they know you— know where you live, where you work, who your boss is, and what your project is about. If you immerse yourself in a research setting, you can usually talk comfortably to the people in that setting. You might want to live in a neighborhood or housing development when you are studying that community, meeting neighbors on the street as you come and go, attending street parties, going to baseball games, or doing your wash at the laundromat. Or you may want to go to the professional meetings attended by the people with whom you want to talk. You can frequent the places where the people you are trying to meet hang out. It may take a while before people know you and accept you, but after a while you can call them for lunch or a beer and talk about your project.

Qualitative interviewers also gain access to experienced, knowledgeable interviewees along social networks. In cultural studies, it is common to start with a personal acquaintance who is a member of the group being studied. Felix Padilla began his interviewing of Puerto Rican gang members after being introduced by a student of his who was a member of the gang (Padilla 1992). Both William Whyte (1955) and Elliot Liebow (1967), whose studies are widely read for their vivid descriptions of inner-city life, gained access only after they befriended local leaders who introduced them to other people in the community. Mitchell Duneier (1999) in his study of sidewalk book venders picked up a conversation with one vender who was selling a book Duneier had written. This individual, who befriended Duneier, introduced him to others involved in the same occupation.

If the people you are looking for are considered vulnerable, they may be particularly hard to reach and then to convince to participate in your study. In one study about black teenage single moms, finding conversational partners and getting them to trust the researcher enough to talk was a major part of the work. The researcher negotiated access in two nearby communities, volunteering in a social-service center to make contacts and using the network of social-service providers and counselors she met through this participation to help introduce her to teenage mothers (Kaplan 1997).

Once contact has been made, most people like to talk about themselves, enjoy the sociability and sense of accomplishment, and are pleased that somebody is interested in what they have to say. On the other hand, they may be busy, feel incompetent, or fear exposure, in which case you may need to persuade them to participate. Once you understand what motivates people to talk to interviewers, you can often build on those motivations to gain cooperation.

The interviewer can offer to help memorialize a vanishing way of life, a skill, a religious practice, or a long-gone set of events. Your questions communicate to the interviewee that what he or she knows is valuable, should not be lost, and could be taught to you, and through you, to others. Similarly, an interviewer provides the conversational partner with attention and recognition. You can encourage participation by mentioning what the interviewee has accomplished; for instance, in a study of crafts, you could say, "I came to you because people thought you were the most skillful weaver," or in a conversation about fiscal management you could begin with "I wanted to talk to you because I thought the budgeting system you worked out was very impressive." Being interviewed can confirm the interviewee's status, as the conversational partner learns he or she is important enough to be included in the group of those being interviewed. "Who else are you talking to?" the interviewee might ask. By letting your interviewee know that you think of him or her as part of a distinguished group of individuals, he or she may be more willing to talk to you: "I have an appointment with the city manager tomorrow, and I saw the mayor yesterday and will speak with the budget director this afternoon."

Sometimes people grant interviews because they want to be helpful in solving a problem. A professional interviewer for the National Transportation Safety Board explained to us that people were willing to talk in great detail about what they saw in plane crashes because they wanted to make air traffic safer. In an introductory letter or at the beginning of an interview, you can explain how the answers provided will be used to solve a problem that the interviewees care about.

People often need to talk about terrible experiences they have had; expressing how they feel can help ease grief and reduce terror. Support groups of bereaved parents complain that friends and relatives tell them to get on with their lives, to forget the dead child, but they do not want to, they want an opportunity to talk and remember the child, to grieve openly. The researcher offers recognition of the pain and loss and an opportunity to reflect back on an important period in their lives and, by doing so, helps make suffering meaningful. For example, researchers conducting oral histories of the Holocaust gave survivors an opportunity to remember and honor the dead.

One researcher explained why those suffering from AIDS talked so openly: "[M]any of my respondents explicitly refer to their interviews as 'legacies.' They are participating in this project despite the pain it might cause them because they believe I will use their stories to help others. Thus they shoulder me with the responsibility of giving meaning to their lives and their deaths" (Weitz 1987, p. 21). The researcher may be able to offer one kind of memorial.

People also participate in interviews to gain favorable publicity for their political or social concerns, occupational or ethnic group, or with whatever they identify. Librarians might want to talk about efforts to combat censorship; historical preservationists might want to make a case for restoring an old building; members of a religious group might be eager to explain how they celebrate particular holidays. In each case, interviewees want their activities to be viewed in a favorable light. Interviewees whom others look down on, such as prostitutes, illegal aliens, or homeless people, might hope that the researcher can gather their hurt and angry voices to call attention to their suffering.

In contentious situations, people talk to get out their side of a story. Management might control how newspapers describe labor disputes, so spokespeople for the unions might be eager to be interviewed by someone who might get their perspective across. On one occasion, Herb had failed to get an appointment with a funder of community groups, though he had made many attempts. Finally, Herb wrote again, including a paper that explained the community group's side of a dispute with the funder. The funder then agreed to explain why the community groups were wrong.

Sometimes people participate in an interview simply because you have been recommended by their friends or colleagues. Once, Irene was trying in person to get an appointment at a distant city hall, and was not getting anywhere, when a gentleman walked up behind her and asked her where she was from. "DeKalb, Illinois," she said, thinking the person would never have heard of it. "Oh," he said, "your mayor is Greg Sparrow; do you know him?" "Yes," she said, "I know him well; he was a student of mine, and he appointed me to the budget review committee." "Okay," her new friend said, "I know Greg well. I will get the appointment for you." Irene not only got the appointment, she also got a lesson in what she was supposed to have done to get appointments at distant city halls, namely, use her mayor as part of a network. When she returned home and told her mayor the story, he said, "Irene, you should have told me what you were doing; I could have arranged the interviews for you."

Sometimes such network recommendations occur without your asking for them. People whom you interview are likely to share with each other their experiences in talking to you. Recently, Herb called up people he did not know to set up appointments. Each woman readily set up an appointment, and when interviewed each one was open and informative. Though pleased, Herb was puzzled about the instant rapport until the interviewees explained that in a previous project Herb had talked with their husbands (who had totally different surnames) and their husbands had enjoyed the conversations.

BUILDING TRUST

Although there is no simple formula for building trust, there are a number of things you can do to facilitate it and a few things to avoid that can destroy it. Trust increases as people see that you share a common background with them. Having gone to the same school or religious institution, having grown up in the same neighborhood, or having shared friends are forms of linkage that initiate trust. Having someone vouch for you is another important way of building trust. You may make network connections and then use them when making an appointment: "Bob Albertson suggested I call you; he said you were the most knowledgeable about what happened and that you might be willing to talk to me." Finding that you share a mutual friend may make you seem more responsible; mentioning that you have had some relevant job experience may make interviewees more confident that you will understand their answers. If you have family nearby, have friends in common, or work some place they know, you fit into their social structure in a way that they can understand. You are not a rootless stranger.

You can create a shared background prior to interviewing if you conduct participant observation during which the potential conversational partners have a chance to see you and how you behave. At meetings, potential interviewees may observe you talking to those whom you have already befriended, which makes you less of a rootless stranger. In his current study, Herb participates in phone conferences that involve many of the activists he is studying. In the introductory part of one of the phone conferences, a leading activist indicated that he knew Herb and Herb was one of the group. Later when Herb called up others involved in that phone conference, he was not treated as an outsider.

Being seen as honest, open, fair, and accepting helps build trust. As a demonstration of good faith and a promise of fairness, Herb shares with potential conversational partners what he has already written about their world. Many read this material and comment on it. Further they can see from what he has written that Herb is sympathetic to them, protects confidentiality in interviews, and presents a full and balanced account.

MAKING THE INITIAL CONTACT
AND SETTING UP APPOINTMENTS

You have already chosen people who should be knowledgeable about the topic and now you want to persuade them to talk with you. Doing so involves far more than finding them and setting up an appointment, although these two tasks are important. You also want them to understand what your research is about and to be willing to participate in a meaningful and open way. People do not have to speak to you. You have to ask, explain to them what your research is about, and assure them that their involvement is voluntary, while convincing them to be helpful.

Sometimes people say no, mostly because they are too busy. At times, you can make an appointment weeks or months ahead to get on someone's calendar, or you can call back weeks after his or her busy season. Herb once wondered why a person with whom he already had a good conversation did not return his calls when Herb was asking for another interview. Herb had forgotten that he was calling at the peak of grant-writing season when his conversational partner was overwhelmed by deadlines. When the grant writing was over, she called Herb and chided him for not getting back to her for a second interview.

The two hardest groups to reach are economic and political elites and the extremely downtrodden. Elites may be too busy to talk or want to control what is said about them, and they have staff who buffer them. To persuade such a person to grant an interview requires you to show that they or their organization will benefit from your research. Our experience is that meaningful contact with elites often occurs only after you have been referred to them by their own subordinates or by their friends or colleagues. Individuals from neglected and exploited groups have also been reluctant to be involved in research. Too often they find that they are the objects of research, spend a lot of time for someone else's benefit, and get nothing out of it. Research just repeats the exploitation they have experienced. Getting interviews with individuals from these groups usually requires a period of participant observation or perhaps activist work in which you prove your mettle and demonstrate your concern.

When you are already engaged in a participant observation study, setting up an initial interview is usually straightforward. You have probably asked people questions already, such as "What's happening at that ceremony?" or "What's this meeting going to be about?" The shift to an interview mode may be as casual as an invitation to join you for a cup of coffee and chat. Later you may want to ask for a more formal interview.

Most of our recent work involves people whom it would be difficult to meet in informal situations (sometimes because they are employed in cities far from where we live). We have worked out a system of letter writing and phone calls that has been successful in gaining initial appointments. The letter requesting an interview should be reasonably brief yet include information describing the project, why the person has been chosen to be in the study, and why he or she should participate. The letter should radiate professionalism, indicate concern and interest in the life or work of those to be interviewed, and reassure interviewees that the information will be used in accordance with their wishes. An example of a request for an interview might read as follows:

Dear Ms. Lobbyist:

I am a student working on my dissertation at Northern Illinois University on the topic of what makes health care legislation politically feasible. As you have been a key actor in developing and pressing for health care proposals over the last few years, I wanted to talk to you about how you judge feasibility, and how you think others judge it. I will be talking to a number of other people active in trying to shape health care legislation, beginning on March 17, in Washington. Would you be willing to see me sometime that week? Ideally, I would need about an hour. Any time at your convenience, morning, noon, or night, would be fine. I will give your secretary a call next week.

If you have any questions about the project or about me, please give me a call at 815-753-xxxx.

Sincerely,
Marilyn Wantstoknow

In this example, the researcher is assuming the role of a student. The material will be part of a dissertation, so presumably will not be widely circulated. The topic is delineated, as is the reason why the interviewee was picked to be in the study. The letter could be improved by adding a sentence that shows why the researcher is somewhat informed about the topic and sympathetic to those whom she will interview. "Before I began my PhD research, I was a health planner, so I am sensitive to the technical aspects of these proposals, but I never fully understood why some of the best technical proposals did not make it through Congress." Such an addition establishes the interviewer's background and sympathies and states the research problem in an engaging fashion.

In his current project with well-educated, highly literate, committed social activists, Herb tries to word his cover letters to communicate that he is knowledgeable about the field, wants to get the interviewee's perspective across to others, and supports the work his potential conversational partners do. He includes with his introductory letter a book he has written on a topic close to the one he is interviewing about. The book helps establish that Herb is a legitimate scholar and that his work will be published, so he can be a useful voice. Those who actually read the book (and a surprising number of his interviewees do) can see that Herb has protected the identity of those interviewed, and that, though the book presents a realistic portrait, it is sympathetic to those studied. One part of his letter emphasizes that he is an active member of the same groups as the interviewee and is familiar with the interviewee's world and work; the other part encourages the potential conversational partner to become involved and help shape the project.

Department of Sociology
Northern Illinois University
DeKalb, Illinois 60115
815-753-xxxx
hrubin@niu.edu

Sept. 23, 2002

xxxx
Executive Director
State Activist Organization
Address

Dear Name:

I'm Herb Rubin, a sociologist who has been studying and writing about community-based renewal efforts (as well as on organizing and protest) for quite some time. I don't think you know me, though we did meet very briefly at the NCRC[1] conference. I've been following your work closely, especially the recent actions against BrickYard Bank, and I have been listening to, and occasionally participating in, the NCRC conference calls during which you offer your insights on direct action.

In my current research, I've been studying a variety of organizations that support community rebuilding, including trade associations such as NCCED, activist coalitions such as NCRC, NLHIC, and other similar national groups. In addition, I have been looking at the Rehab Network, Woodstock, and until its recent demise, CANDO in Chicago. As the work now stands, I am asking three core questions: (1) how support organizations and their coalitions, through training and advocacy, give definition and direction to the community-rebuilding movement; (2) how support organizations and their coalitions frame a public policy agenda in support of community renewal; and (3) what changes occur within the support organizations and the coalitions as they attempt the first two tasks.

From my current work, especially with Woodstock in Chicago, I have learned how local organizations help shape the national agenda. It certainly appears that STATE ACTIVIST ORGANIZATION is an example for other organizations and through its coalitional work, especially within NCRC, has had a profound national impact. As such, I would like to ask from you a two-fold favor.

First, I am wondering if you would be willing to chat with me about the efforts of STATE ACTIVIST ORGANIZATION by itself and as an active member of NCRC to support CRA, oppose predatory lending, and work for economic justice. Second, I would like to discuss with you the possibility of including STATE ACTIVIST ORGANIZATION in the study as an illustration of an organization that has had an important impact nationally.

I am requesting to set up a phone conversation in which I will answer any questions you might have about the project, and then if you are willing, schedule a later appointment to talk with you about how STATE ACTIVIST ORGANIZATION helps shape national public policy.

My interviews are unstructured and informal, as I'm primarily interested in learning the insights of people engaged in renewal work in their own words. To give you a flavor of how I present research (as well as to illustrate my support for the community renewal movement), I've included a copy for your personal library of *Renewing Hope within Neighborhoods of Despair: The Community-Based Development Model,* the book that came out of my last study on the CDC movement.

I'll allow for mail time and then give you a call to see if it is possible to set up a phone interview.

Thanks in advance.
Herb Rubin

Rather than awaiting Herb's call, on receipt of the letter this particular individual immediately called Herb and set up a time for a telephone interview.

Depending on the circumstances, Irene sometimes encloses a resumé with the letter requesting an interview. She has found that many public officials become interested after they see she does consulting, because to them the consulting is real world and indicates Irene might know something of interest to them. City officials want to know how they stand compared to Phoenix or Boston. Finding out gives the interviewee a reason to participate.

Other variations of the introductory letter are sometimes appropriate. You can include a list of the specific topics to be covered. For example, in the health care proposal study, you could say, "I am particularly interested in the contribution your office made to changing House Bill 75." If you are representing yourself as someone who supports a movement and wants to publicize its successes, then your credentials that back up these claims should be offered. "I spent three years in ACT-UP (a radical gay rights group) from 1985 to 1988." To support the claim that you are working on a book, you might mention what you have published related to this topic, especially material that is supportive of the agency, program, or movement.

After writing the letter, we usually wait an appropriate amount of time for it to be delivered and read. We then call up the interviewee to answer any questions that the person might have, see if he or she is willing to be interviewed, and if so work out the scheduling. In his last two projects, in which several hundred interviews were set up in this manner, Herb has been turned down only twice.

Ethical Responsibilities
Toward the Conversational Partner

Central to the responsive interviewing model is the importance of obtaining rich data in ways that do not harm those being studied. On occasion, researchers have behaved unethically, sometimes disguising what they are doing, violating confidentiality, exposing research subjects to sanctions from governmental authority, or disturbing subjects emotionally. In response to these ethical lapses (and far worse ones in the medical and biological sciences), professional societies have established codes of ethics and universities, as well as other organizations that conduct research, are required by the federal government to set up institutional review boards (IRBs) to ensure that research does not harm those being studied.

Responsive interviewers have an obligation going beyond any rules set up by IRBs to deal ethically with their conversational partners, respect interviewees, and honor any promises made. Respecting interviewees normally means not deceiving them, not pretending to be someone you are not, and not leading interviewees into thinking that some benefit will come to them from the research that you cannot deliver. You should not lie about your sponsorship. You should not tell them you are writing a book or an article about them unless that really is your purpose. Wasting their time is disrespectful.

Respect is shown in how you act toward your interviewees. Be unfailingly polite and make it clear that you appreciate your conversational partners' help. Avoid mockery or sarcasm, not just while interviewing, but also in the write-up of the research results. Show you care what the interviewee is saying by not interrupting a story, even if it is not on your research target. Show that you understand the interviewee owns his or her own words. Ask permission to record and be responsive to requests to turn the recorder off. If you feel that certain answers are worth quoting, ask permission right then to use those quotes.

Even after you have received permission to record your interviewees, you may still have to periodically remind interviewees that your notes and recordings will be used in the study. When your project involves both participant observation and interviewing, and you are socializing with those you study, they might forget that you are a researcher and blurt out something that they would not do in a more formal setting. You should ask them if that comment is for quotation or is off the record, reminding them that you are studying them. Herb attends conferences of groups that he studies and occasionally drops into meal-time conversations that he is a professor writing a book on the organization to remind people what he is about. Another approach is to write up the notes of the informal conversations and run them by the interviewees before using that material, allowing them to veto its use.

When you promise interviewees that you will not reveal their identity or link their comments with their names, it is imperative to keep that promise, and if there might be situations in which the promise becomes impossible to keep, you should warn your interviewees. For example, if you are interviewing in a prison, you may not be able to guarantee confidentiality, because notes or recordings may be seized.

In some studies, protecting confidentiality is simple. If you are interviewing students at a large university, you can use made-up names in both the notes and the publications. But in many situations using such pseudonyms is not enough to provide confidentiality. Those who work in the same field or share common interests may recognize one another through the background information you do provide in your report. In tracing out the behind-the-scenes tactics to change a federal regulation or promote a governmental bill, a researcher might not use names, but those who lobby on that issue know which organization did what and do not need the names to identify the actors. In this case, you may need to disguise the issue itself.

When Irene was doing her dissertation research, she multiplied the numbers in key tables by an undisclosed number, so the statistics would still tell the same story, but experts in the field would not be able to figure out from enrollment or budget data which universities were studied or who was being quoted. In another study, she gave the city she was studying a pseudonym, so that no one could figure out when she talked about the city manager, who that might be, and then further made sure that when she used a quote, even anonymously, that the information could have been provided by at least several other people or documentary sources. Herb warns his interviewees that even when he leaves out their names, others in their field will recognize them and in his writing often withholds part of his story if that part will uniquely identify an organization or individual.

Protecting confidentiality may mean collecting and maintaining data in such a way that they cannot be used in a court of law if your notes were subpoenaed. It means keeping the interviews in a secure place, so that others cannot run across the interviews by chance. Sometimes it means destroying any evidence that links the information in the interviews to specific individuals. In the extreme, if you are called on to provide evidence in court, you must decide whether to risk contempt of court and refuse to testify. In rare circumstances and with much procedural hassle, academic researchers can get a certification from the federal government that allows them to shelter their interviews from the courts. But for the most part, researchers are not immune from court sentences if they keep silent. Because of this threat that hangs over research, researchers need to be very clear about what they will do if they somehow become embroiled in such legal proceedings. If you cannot imagine yourself going to jail for contempt of court for refusing to turn over interview notes, then you should not promise confidentiality to an interviewee who might be engaged in some unlawful activity.

In some extreme cases, qualitative researchers have gone to jail to protect their interviewees and keep their promises of confidentiality. When Mario Brajuha interviewed restaurant workers for his dissertation in the early 1980s, he had no reason to suspect that his data would ultimately land him in jail; he was only studying the social construction of the workplace (Brajuha and Hallowell 1986; Hollowell 1985). Brajuha promised his interviewees confidentiality because some of them feared what they said might be used against them by coworkers or supervisors. However, when a fire occurred in the restaurant, police suspected arson and subpoenaed Brajuha's interview notes as part of their investigation. Brajuha was in a difficult ethical position: He could surrender his data to police and break his vow of confidentiality or he could keep his promise and go to jail. He chose to honor his promise and went to jail.

Most of the time, you will not encounter situations that are as difficult as Brajuha's, but you should keep your data in such a way that if such a situation should arise, no harm would come of it. For example, people's real names are often not important in your research, and by leaving them out or giving people pseudonyms, you protect conversational partners in case your notes end up in the wrong hands. You should be prepared to destroy your notes rather than allow access to them by people who would hurt your conversational partners. If you carry a recorder into a prison to conduct interviews, be prepared to quickly destroy the recordings. If you think you might be stopped and searched and your notes confiscated, do not take notes; memorize the conversation as best you can. At worst, you lose part or all of one interview, which is a lot better than harming a conversational partner.

However, when you learn about something illegal or that could get someone into trouble, you may have mixed feelings about your role and responsibilities (Magolda 2000). If you report the person to the authorities, you will most likely ruin the research, having proved yourself unreliable, not only to that interviewee, but to other potential interviewees. If you do not report such behavior, you may feel guilty if someone else is later hurt or victimized. To prevent this from occurring, you might ask your interviewees not to tell you about illegal behavior and remind them if they seem to be telling you something illegal that you may not be able to keep it confidential.

At times, though, you may feel that learning about the illegal behavior is central to the project, such as when our colleague Jim Thomas was studying computer hackers. Then you have to consider whether learning about the hackers, their world, their motives, and some of their techniques, without reporting on individuals, may ultimately be more useful to the society than reporting one individual's illegal activity to the authorities and ruining the rest of the research, not only for yourself, but for any other researchers who may want to study this area.

You have an obligation to warn interviewees if something they are saying may get them in trouble and give them an opportunity to retract what they have said or be quoted anonymously. If they do not give you permission to use some story or quotation, do not use it, even if you have to leave out exciting material from the final report. You may have to make some tradeoffs between the accuracy and punch of your report and protecting your interviewees, but with some thought you can usually protect individuals and still get your findings across.

Problems You May Run Into

When Irene was an assistant professor and needed publications to build a base for promotion, a journal editor told her he would accept a piece if she would name the city in which the study took place. She had promised her interviewees confidentiality and felt that revealing the name of the city would not only compromise that confidentiality, but would also embarrass the city, for no compensating intellectual gain. Irene withdrew the piece from the journal, knowing that her promise to interviewees took precedence over publication.

Another way of protecting interviewees is to provide them with the rights to look over their interviews, edit them, and examine the final manuscript before publication. Irene offers the ranking government officials she interviews not only the right to review and correct or change their own interviews, but also the opportunity to read in advance and comment on, but not the right to alter, chapters in which their agency appears. Her interviewees need to know how their agencies will appear in print and in what context and are afraid that what they say might put their agencies in a bad light. You need not promise interviewees a veto over what you conclude, but you should assure your interviewees that you will be fair and proceed in a balanced way.

Protecting interviewees also means not exploiting them. Studying any victimized group only for the purposes of professional advancement has overtones of exploitation. What you learn should somehow not only result in your own benefit but also help those who gave you so generously of their time and shared their experiences with you. At the least, you should make their problems more visible, raising the level of public discussion; at best, you can come up with policy proposals that will ameliorate your interviewees' problems and try to get those solutions adopted.

Some researchers try to compensate interviewees by paying them, especially if they have a grant that includes funds for this purpose. If they publish a book based on interviews, they may share the royalties. This strategy is limited, however, because most academic books do not make much money, and, when Mitchell Duneier shared the royalties from his study of street venders, he discovered that his conversational partners had neither expectation nor understanding of what he was doing (Duneier 1999).

Our feeling is that responsive interviewing projects can be designed to provide a more immediate reward to the interviewees. The conversational partners should find the interview itself enjoyable and a time to reflect and draw their thoughts together. They should get a sense of being a crucial part of an important project that provides them with an opportunity to create and frame a legacy of some sort. After long interviews with very busy people, we often feel guilty about the time we have taken. Yet, when we begin to thank them for participating, they interrupt and thank us for providing them with an opportunity to reflect and clarify their ideas.

When you are interviewing elites, they know they have the upper hand, that you come with a request that they can grant or deny, but when you interview people who rely on public programs, who are marginal to society, or who are in any position of dependence on you, they may see you as important, official, or having power over them. If you do not take appropriate steps to disabuse them, they might feel that they have no choice but to submit to an interview. Potential interviewees might need to be reminded that they can refuse to participate in a study and nothing untoward will happen to them. You may want to avoid doing research with those over whom you have some bureaucratic, financial, or social power, because it might be difficult to convince them that they really are free to say no.

In addition, you should not pressure interviewees into responding to specific questions if they do not want to answer them because doing so causes stress. Interviewing people about painful periods in their lives, such as divorces, rapes, or abandonments, might evoke more emotion than they can handle. It should not be the purpose of qualitative research to go after some piece of information so doggedly that the pain of the interviewee is ignored.

An interview is not an interrogation. It is unethical to browbeat your interviewees or imply they are lying or hiding something. Police in an interrogation may try to trick a suspect into confessing or call attention to inconsistencies in an effort to force a damaging admission, but interviewing this way intimidates people, is not courteous or fun, and puts people on the defensive, encouraging lies. Responsive interviewing requires a gentler, more respectful style that often gets better results, does not hurt interviewees, and is more comfortable for both sides.

Sometimes researchers intimidate their interviewees without intending to do so. Be cautious about asking questions that convey expected answers in the way the question is worded. For example, asking a female professor how she trades off career ambitions and family assumes too much and might force an answer that would parallel those of male colleagues, when her ambition might be to have a career that blends with her family.

A less dominating approach leaves room for the invention of common vocabulary that allows a better expression of what the interviewee feels. Devault describes how this is accomplished in feminist interviewing: "[W]e often need to go beyond standard vocabulary. . . . By speaking in ways that open the boundaries of standard topics, we can create space for respondents to provide accounts rooted in the realities of their lives" (Devault 1990, p. 99). Encouraging long and undirected answers provides such space, but developing a shared vocabulary can also do so. For example, Irene heard a conversational partner report on a meeting, claiming that he was "mushroomed." "Mushroomed," she asked, "what does that mean?" "They kept me in the dark and dumped shit on me." After an appropriate grin she asked for the details of that event, and then asked about other occasions on which the interviewee felt "mushroomed." This term was now shared and allowed them both to talk about a feeling, a status, and response to a situation that was not previously discussable without asking intimidating questions about a lack of status.

If you are in a situation where ethically you are wary of pressing for information, you can use a nondirective questioning style that allows the conversational partners the scope to determine the boundaries of what they discuss. For instance, you can explicitly present the interviewee the choice of whether or not to answer: "If this question is still too stressful, don't answer; we can talk about it another time, but you mentioned coming home to an empty house. Do you feel like talking about that?" Herb often questions people about controversial issues, such as conflicts between organizations. Rather than ask directly about the conflict, a matter of potential stress, he approaches the problem obliquely. When he is interviewing a person from one organization in the fight, he mentions the other organization in passing, though without indicating knowledge of the battle, providing the conversational partner with the opportunity to talk about the conflict if he or she chooses.

At times, efforts to protect interviewees are controversial, because they have the potential to clash with writing up a full, honest, and balanced report. Some researchers argue that writing is not complete or accurate if it leaves out negative parts of the story, and that it is not the researcher's responsibility to ensure that no harm occurs from what they have written. From our point of view, that statement is too extreme. If you can anticipate that some particular piece of information you present will be used by opponents to harm a program or to hurt those you have studied, maybe that piece of information should be withheld. On the other hand, if that information is vital to understanding those you have studied and it can be presented without harming identifiable individuals, then it probably should be included.

Fortunately, such problems are not common. Negative findings are usually not central to the narrative, and omitting them does not distort the truth value of what you have discovered. Also, at times reporting the negative findings is seen as helpful rather than harmful. Herb has been criticized by his interviewees for being too reticent about pointing out problems in the world of community development. His conversational partners want these problems to be known so they can be fixed.

Writers need to be aware of the tension between accuracy and balance on one hand, and protecting interviewees on the other, and perhaps not automatically come down on the side of literal truth. Some truths are not worth the pain that they cause. Others might be necessary for the pain they can prevent.

INSTITUTIONAL REVIEW BOARDS
AND PROFESSIONAL CODES OF ETHICS

A number of federal agencies have imposed a requirement that before research is eligible for funding, researchers must demonstrate that they will not harm their subjects. They also require that universities have policies in place to police research and ensure that human subjects are not being hurt. These universities have set up institutional review boards (IRBs) to which researchers, including students writing theses and dissertations, must submit their research plans and demonstrate how they will protect interviewees before they are permitted to begin their work. IRBs, which are usually composed of professionals from the researcher's organization and informed community members, review research proposals and can request changes that protect the subjects of the research before approving the proposal.

IRBs, as well as many professional societies, encourage researchers to obtain signed *informed consent* statements from people they are studying. An informed consent statement describes the purposes of the research, provides background on the researcher, and points out the benefits and possible risks to those involved. It usually promises to share results with those being studied, indicates the degree of confidentiality of the findings, and, most important, emphasizes that participation is voluntary. Participants in a study sign these forms to show they understand the risks described in the statement and agree to be in the study.

Codes of professional societies as well as IRB requirements force researchers to carefully think out the possible harm their work might cause. They encourage researchers to determine if information can be obtained in ways that are less disruptive for those being studied. These codes and requirements make it quite clear that those being researched are told they are being researched and have the option to refuse to participate.

This formal and rule-bound approach is intended to prevent harm to research subjects by preventing noncompliant research from going forward, but it can create serious (and unnecessary) difficulties for qualitative researchers. One problem is that before approving research, institutional review boards want to see written questionnaires and precise descriptions of those to be studied, but in qualitative research who you are studying and the questions you ask evolve during the course of the study. Another problem is that whipping out an informed consent statement and asking for a signature can be awkward at best.

To handle the problem of an IRB's insistence on knowing the design of the project before the research can begin, you can do one of two things. One possibility is to offer the IRB examples of the type of question and typical wording of questions, while making it clear that questions may evolve. Many IRBs will accept this procedure, although they may ask that if the study changes substantially that you then resubmit your application. Another approach is to conduct a substantial amount of preliminary research first, which is defined as unsystematic and exploratory, not intended for publication or dissemination, and hence not required to go through the IRB process. Based on this preliminary research, you can usually put together a research design that will be a fair guide to the rest of the work, and then submit this proposal to the IRB.

The signed informed consent forms are even more problematic. To the extent that interviews are an extension of a conversation and part of a relationship, the legal appearance and formality of a consent form may be puzzling to the conversational partner and disruptive to the research. You have already offered conversational partners anonymity and confidentiality, and yet now you are asking them to sign a legal form saying they are participating in the study. How can they later deny they spoke to you—which they may need to do to protect themselves—if you have a signed form saying they were willing to participate in the study?

You may have known someone in your research arena as a cooperative and helpful partner, orienting you to the field, before you decide to interview him or her. The transition from general informant to interviewee should be as natural as possible; pulling out a legal consent form to sign is an abrupt departure that says something has changed and now the conversation will be somehow risky. Moreover, with its flavor of medical experiments and hospital informed-consent rules, the form suggests a much more manipulative kind of research in which the interviewee is the passive recipient of some kind of treatment rather than an active partner. Because signed informed consent forms make the research look more risky than it is, they may discourage participation for no compensating increase in safety for interviewees. These problems arise because institutional review boards are not really geared for qualitative research.

If written informed consent is awkward, misleading, or unlikely to be understood or accepted by interviewees, and your research is not particularly dangerous to interviewees, you may be able to ask the review board to exempt the research from this requirement. If you have demonstrated that you have conveyed to the interviewees that their participation is voluntary and if you can explain clearly why written informed consent is inappropriate, they should be willing to grant a waiver of this kind of requirement.

Overall, qualitative researchers should not expect to achieve ethical research by following a set of preestablished procedures established by IRBs. You should deal with the IRB set of checklist requirements as best you can, explaining how you will protect the anonymity of responses if interviewees request anonymity, assuring the Human Subjects committees that you are asking for permission to record the interviews, and that you have let your interviewees know that their participation is voluntary. If you are dealing with interviewees who are particularly vulnerable, you should specify what consent means in those cases and how you have explained the project and how you know that they understand and have participated voluntarily. But you ought to keep in mind that mindlessly following the rules of the IRB can lead to conducting poor and inadequate research without increasing any protection to those being studied.

Be aware that research review boards may feel more comfortable with blanket promises, such as the provision of confidentiality to everyone in the study, but the researcher may not be in a position to guarantee that confidentiality, so a more modest promise would be in order. Your interviewees might want to be identified and want publicity for their group. In that case, ethical concerns require you to identify your interviewees, not keep their identities confidential. You need to protect your interviewees but do so in ways that might not fit the standard procedures designed by IRBs for medical or laboratory research. Generally, IRBs will accept procedures that protect human subjects, even if they are not the procedures they outline for all researchers to follow, but you might have to leave extra time for a longer review, especially if your research presents problems to them that they have not confronted before.

As federal rules and university interpretations of these rules remain in flux, we can only echo the thoughts of the Loflands: "In the face of this complexity, the only advice we can give is to suggest that before beginning your research, you acquaint yourself both with your campus's IRB policies and with the extent to which local researchers take them seriously" (Lofland and Lofland 1995, p. 43).

The requirements for ethical research go beyond the pro forma concerns of institutional review boards. You should study codes of ethics and read case studies of unethical behavior to sensitize yourself to possible harm you could cause. You need to weigh the impact of the hoped-for research outcomes with the possibility that someone will be harmed and the extent to which they might be harmed. IRBs may routinely demand that no one be hurt by the research, but your research may call attention to those who do need to be "hurt," such as illegal polluters or landlords who stint on heat and delay on necessary repairs or inappropriately keep damage deposits. You should not be paralyzed by this possibility but instead determine whether the aggregate good to be achieved exceeds the harm done.

Note

1. National Community Reinvestment Coalition, a coalition of groups working for economic justice.

6

The Responsive Interview as an Extended Conversation

If you know how to carry on a normal conversation, you can build on that knowledge to become a good interviewer, but there are nevertheless major differences between ordinary conversations and depth interviews. Qualitative interviews are more focused, more in-depth, and more detailed than ordinary conversations, and also less balanced, because one person does most of the questioning and the other does most of the answering.

Similarities Between Responsive Interviews and Ordinary Conversations

In both ordinary conversations and interviews, questions and answers follow one another logically. Participants work out ways to acknowledge when they understand, ask questions or look puzzled when they don't, and clarify ambiguities on request. In both cases, when participants want more detail they ask for stories or narratives.

MAINTAIN CONTINUITY

Both conversations and interviews need to maintain a continuous flow. If two people begin talking about a sporting event, they elaborate on what happened at the game and do not suddenly turn to politics. In an interview, you do not hop from one disconnected topic to another. Instead questions are carefully linked to one another, and when topics are changed, you use an explicit transition.

CLARIFY MEANING AND INDICATE UNDERSTANDING

Both ordinary conversations and interviews rely on similar ways of clearing up misunderstandings using *conversational repairs* (Schegloff 1992) through which ambiguous, vague, or otherwise unclear statements are corrected (Moerman 1988, p. 52). Suppose someone is telling a story and says, "She told me she wanted to run for office." Who is the first she, and who is the second she? The listener would ask for clarification: "Who told you that?" or "You mean Bella said that Edna wanted to run for office?" In both interviews and conversations, if the other party has misunderstood one of your questions, you politely listen to the mistaken reply, and then, without reference to the mistake, rephrase the question so it is clearer. In both polite conversations as well as interviews you indicate understanding through a nod of the head or an intent expression or by summarizing what you just heard before continuing the dialogue.

ASKING FOR NARRATIVES AND STORIES

In ordinary conversations, as well as in depth interviews, people want to find out the details. "Someone broke into your house? Tell me, what happened?" "What happened at the meeting this morning?" The answers provided in ordinary conversations and in interviews are often either narratives or stories. In a *narrative,* the speakers put together what they believe actually occurred, recognizing that what they say might be incomplete because they only saw part of what happened or only remember a piece of what went on. In contrast, a *story* is told to make a point or present a theme, either stated or implicit, irrespective of the accuracy of the details. In telling a story, events may be edited or reordered, and exaggeration may be added for effect.

When Irene, who was not overweight (not much overweight—Herb) (*not* overweight!—Irene), exercised regularly, and ate carefully, had a heart attack, friends and acquaintances were amazed and wanted to know what happened. Irene had to answer the same question over and over, so that her narrative of events describing the heart attack gradually became a smooth story that contained a lesson. The point of the story was "this is what a heart attack feels like for a woman; if it happens to you or someone you know, don't delay—get medical help." A story remains ready to use, like a jack-in-the-box, ready to spring when someone opens the lid by asking "what happened?"

ENDING THE CONVERSATION

In a normal conversation, when you are done, you signal that the conversation is over, but often leave the door open for some future contact, perhaps by saying, "I'll call you" or "Let's do lunch real soon." Similarly, you signal the end of an interview by thanking your interviewee and suggesting some future contact, such as "I may have questions when I look over my notes, would it be okay to call you?" or "I will get back to you with the transcript for you to look over."

Differences Between Interviews and Conversations

Thinking about how you carry out a long discussion with a friend is a good way to start becoming a skilled interviewer, but you also need to be alert to and master the differences between normal conversations and interviews. Depth interviews are about obtaining specific information that later will be analyzed. To ensure accuracy, the entire interview is recorded one way or another. A normal conversation may drift along with little goal other than sociability, but in interviews, the researcher is seeking particular information and so gently guides the discussion, leading it through stages, asking focused questions, and encouraging the interviewee to answer in depth and at length.

RECORDING

An obvious difference between interviews and normal conversations is that the researcher needs to keep a record of what was said for later analysis. Sometimes the record is informal, as when the researcher interviews for a while, and then leaves and jots down summary notes of what was said. When the situation permits, however, researchers take detailed notes during the interview, and/or use a tape or digital recorder, or even a video recorder. This record becomes the data that you analyze, first to figure out what follow-up questions to ask and later to develop the themes and theories that will be the product of the study.

Some interviewees become shy or hesitant when they know they are being electronically recorded; many, however, appreciate being recorded because recording ensures that you will get their message out accurately. Some begin to grandstand for the recorder, but, at least in our experience, most quickly forget about the presence of the recording machine. Situations differ as to whether it is better to take notes or to record electronically. Herb routinely records his interviews so that he can better concentrate on listening to the interviewees and plan his follow-up questions, though he does jot down the main ideas. Irene takes notes by hand when the material is at all sensitive, in part to give her interviewees deniability; they can always say "I never said that" if they feel they need to, and there is no proof that they did. In nonsensitive interviews, she too uses an electronic recorder (see Werner 1998).

Even when you are recording electronically, you should still take some notes. Doing so forces you to listen carefully enough to get down the main points, and also provides backup in case a machine fails. Note taking also allows the researcher to scribble down possible questions to use later in the interview while keeping track of what was being said if the interviewee is momentarily interrupted and then asks you, "Where were we?" Further, note taking helps pace the answers of the conversational partner as the interviewee is likely to slow down until you finish writing.

Taking notes requires practice and skill. Irene uses alphabetic shorthand and supplements it with a trained memory. Immediately after each interview, she rereads her notes and writes down in full any points that were only briefly sketched. Reading your notes immediately and then promptly typing them out in full improves subsequent questioning. Doing so helps you find those areas where you need to follow up and get more detail, where you need to ask about special terms or words, and where you can link future interviews to the ones just done so they all fit together at the end.

Electronic recording can distract both interviewer and interviewee and influence what people say, so you want to make the recording as smooth and unobtrusive as possible. If you are videotaping, try to do so without klieg lights. Make sure you have fresh batteries in your recorders and test them before the interview begins so you do not have to pause during the interview to tend the recorder. Similarly, if you are using a tape recorder, you may want relatively longer tapes, so you don't have to watch continually for the end of the tape. Better yet, switch to the newer digital recorders that are smaller, operate without tapes, and record for hours without any attention. Better digital recorders download sound files directly into your computer allowing you to listen to the interviews over and over and make copies with ease.

Electronic recording does have some disadvantages, though. In any situation that is intentionally informal, the recorder looks out of place. Moreover, you should not record a secret informant. Another problem is that people who rely heavily on recordings tend to lose their ability to recall conversations and events from memory. As a result, in those situations in which they cannot record and taking notes is too obtrusive, they may be unable to remember a lot of valuable information.

Transcribing, that is, typing out what was recorded, should be done as soon as possible after the interview is complete. If there is something unclear on the recording, you will still remember what was said and be able to fill in the missing material (indicating on the transcript that you are adding what you remember). If you are taking rough handwritten notes, you have to transcribe them quickly; if you wait a while before looking at them, they will appear to have deteriorated into unreadable hen scratchings. Especially when you are interviewing when traveling and hotel expenses are piling up, you may try to do several interviews in a day, without taking time to transcribe, figuring the recordings will keep. The problem with this approach is that you do not carefully review each interview before doing the next one, losing possible opportunities to follow up on wonderful material. And, of course, you end up with a huge task of transcription all at once. When really pressed for time, at least listen to the recording once before beginning the next interview.

We strongly feel (as do state attorneys) that you must receive permission before recording. Permission is legally required in most states when taping a telephone conversation, and whether legally required or not, you should always ask permission to record. If you are not clear about the ethics of recording, err on the side of caution. If a third person walks into the room when you are recording an interview, point out that the recorder is on and offer to turn it off. If an interviewee seems to forget the recorder is on and says things you think he or she would not want recorded, you might say, "Some of that was pretty open; I will send you the transcript, in case you want to edit out some of it."

KEEPING ON TOPIC WHILE OBTAINING DEPTH AND CLARITY

In an interview, as opposed to a normal conversation, one person, the researcher, asks most of the questions and in doing so tries to keep the interview primarily focused on the research question, though without aggressively controlling the conversation. The interviewer guides the conversation by asking follow-up questions that pursue the topic of research.

Such follow-up questions are intended to obtain depth, detail, and subtlety, while clarifying answers that are vague or superficial. It is the interviewer's responsibility to signal the interviewee about the level of depth that is wanted. In normal conversation, people customarily answer questions briefly: "How are you?" "Fine, thanks" is a perfectly acceptable exchange. But in an interview, you want something much richer. One way to alert interviewees that you are interested in depth is by not interrupting a long rendition of events and listening intently to the answers.

To signify that you want more depth, you follow up by asking the interviewee to expand on a response. In a casual conversation, one person may ask another, "How's business?" and the second person responds, "It's been great." That is not much of an answer, but it is acceptable in chitchat. In an interview, however, if you ask, "How is your project coming along?" and the conversational partner answers, "Fine," you would have to follow up with questions such as the following: "Did you get the financing you were expecting?" "Have you started construction yet?" or "What problems have you run into?" The interviewee will get the idea that you expect more depth.

Your wording should suggest that you are not looking for textbook-type answers. Irene once asked a budget officer how the city decided between allocations for the downtown area and the various neighborhoods. The interviewee got tense and said, "That sounds like a question we had in our ethics course in graduate school." Irene had asked the wrong question; she didn't want an ethics course answer. A better approach would be (and Irene used this in other cities) to ask about what kind of problems come to the budget officer for resolution, and which ones he or she passes along to the mayor. This more open-ended question assumes less, and encourages the budget officers interviewed to describe specific events and decisions that they have experienced.

In normal conversations people often answer formalistically, providing little detail. For example, families may answer questions from friends and relatives about a family member's health in a vague way: "He is doing as well as can be expected." In depth interviews, you have to word questions to avoid evoking such formalistic responses and can do so in many ways.

One approach is when asking the question to provide specific details signaling that you already know something about the situation and are interested in elaboration. Rather than asking, as you would in a passing conversation, "How is your dad?" (inviting the answer, "As well as can be expected"), it might be better to say the following: "I heard from Marty that your dad was up and around yesterday. How is his mood?"

Another way of getting depth in your answers is to ask a double-barreled question, that is, by asking two related questions at the same time to provide broad scope for an answer. "What do you like most and least about your job?" Framed this way, you indicate that you expect that there is both good and bad and that in answering it is appropriate to mix it all up and tell it whatever way it occurs.

You can also signal interest in depth by asking about specific words or terms you do not understand, something that is rarely done in casual chat. These may be technical terms that seem important, or they may be common words but used in an unusual way by the interviewee. For example, in a conversation with professional staff in government agencies, we have often heard the complaint that legislators micromanage them. Asking what micromanagement means, rather than assuming you know, as you would in an ordinary conversation, opens up a new line of questioning to obtain detail on how bureaucrats and elected officials relate.

Perhaps most helpful in encouraging people to provide depth and detail is to indicate your familiarity with the interviewee's world so that the person knows that superficial answers won't teach you all that much. Herb usually mentions that he routinely attends the conferences of organizations that he studies, showing that he is part of the group while signaling that he is aware of what is going on. Irene tries to use technical language familiar to the interviewees, even in her broad initial questions, as a clue that she wants nonsuperficial answers: "Could you walk me through the process of contracting, from the circulation of the initial RFP or RFQ to the final disposition, the termination, extension, or renewal of the contract?" The terminology, RFP (request for proposal) and RFQ (request for qualifications), signals a familiarity with the field, even while requesting a general orientation.

Interview Relationships Are Intentionally Guided Through a Series of Linked Stages

Ordinary conversations just happen; in contrast, depth interviews are structured around stages that differ in terms of what is asked and how. In the first phase of the interview, the researcher introduces him- or herself and the topic and makes an effort to build the confidence of the interviewee and establish some trust. In the middle of the interview, the researcher presents the more emotionally or intellectually difficult questions. Toward the end, the researcher reduces the intensity of the discussion. In practice, these stages might take place over several different interviews and often blur into one another.

INTRODUCING YOURSELF AND THE TOPIC

Interviews often begin with a few minutes of casual chat that can be about almost anything, from stores that have recently closed (or just opened) to shopping and food, to sports events, to your travel adventures. Sometimes a mild joke might be included to relax yourself and your interviewee. When Irene interviewed in Phoenix, city staff were holding a fair outside City Hall and had rented a snow-making machine. Her comment that it was funny that they welcomed her with snow when she had come from the north to the sunny south in the deep of winter set a tone that said this should be fun, relax.

If you have seen the interviewee before, early in the interview you should reestablish the connection: "You know, when I took my vacation this year, I thought of you, because I remembered that your wife was a tour guide." Or "When I spoke to you last, you were really stressed; how have you been doing?" On one occasion, Herb was interviewing someone in her home and noted three young children. He commented that he thought a year and half ago during an interview she said she had two kids. The interviewee smiled, complimented Herb on his memory, and indicated one was a neighbor's child. The interview then progressed smoothly.

Some interviewees are nervous and may lack confidence that they can answer your questions. In this first stage, you may want to spend a little time tactfully reassuring the conversational partners that they are competent, that what they say is of great interest to you. You might mention that other people identified them to you as knowledgeable people or you can refer to their experiences: "I've been told you've been making wooden chairs for over a decade." Or "I know you have been a senior manager for 20 years." By asking questions about the interviewees' personal experiences early in the interview, you signal that their personal experiences will frame the discussion. Herb will often begin an interview discussing a document the person has written (found on the Web or in newsletters) or a speech the person has given. People gain confidence to talk as they realize much of what will be asked is about their own lives and things they have already thought about.

Some interviewees fear that you will be judging them on the quality of their answers. It is important to remind the interviewees that there is no right or wrong answer, that you are interested in their experiences, what they saw or what they think. If you have a lot of formal education and the interviewee does not, you might want to say something that indicates your respect for people on the front line, who live their values, who, in the terms of one of Irene's interviewees, "keep their feet to the fire." When Irene is interviewing budget directors, she makes it clear as part of her introduction that practitioners dealing with real problems, not academics, have been the ones to come up with innovations and reforms, that it is the job of the academics to learn about the reforms and publicize those that seem to be working. That introduction not only establishes a role but also sets up the interviewee as an expert who has done something notable and worthy of study.

Next, you introduce yourself, suggesting your research role, and repeat the purpose of the research: "I am a professor from Northern Illinois University conducting a study on the evolution of municipal budgeting" or "I am doing research for a book on the history of community renewal in the United States" or "I have a grant to evaluate how well Head Start is working." In this introduction, you explain how you plan to use the information, if it will be a book, an article, a conference paper, or an evaluation report to a funding agency or to the legislature, or whether you are planning to use the information in some kind of campaign. You thank the interviewee for agreeing to talk to you, and discuss whether the interviewee wishes to be identified and whether he or she wants the opportunity to review and edit his or her remarks.

During the introduction, you normally mention experiences that you have had that made you interested in the topic or that show some commonality or connection with the interviewees. If you are interviewing in a prison, mental ward, or an intensive care ward, you can describe how you felt when you heard the door snap shut behind you. The people who work there hear that door shut every day. You have just acknowledged a piece of their everyday life. You can talk about jobs you have held as a health planner or as a housing administrator if you are interviewing health planners or housing directors. You can talk about people you both know, maybe the person who recommended that you talk to the interviewee.

Interviewees often want to know how you found them and why you want to speak to them in particular. They want to know that you are on their side, or at the least, they want evidence that you are not a loose cannon, an unpredictable person who can do them damage. A referral from someone they know and trust helps establish this accountability. If you don't have a suitable referral, you need to establish this accountability in some other manner. A letter from the interviewee's bureaucratic superior giving you permission to conduct the study may be helpful. The interviewer may not know you, but his or her superior clearly does.

The following example from Irene's field notes will give you some idea what an introduction sounds like in a first interview. She had already spent a few minutes chatting.

Irene: Good morning, Mr. Sette, it's good of you to agree to talk to me. As I mentioned in my letter, I am writing a book on municipal budgeting that focuses on how it has changed over the last 20 years. I will be studying six case-study cities, and Rochester is one of my cases.

Sette: Can I ask why you picked Rochester?

Irene: I looked at the budget and was struck by the level of openness in it. It's a good clear budget. Also, I was fascinated that Rochester gave up the city manager system a few years ago and wondered what impact that had, if any, on budgeting.

Mr. Sette asked the key thing he needed to know, why Irene picked Rochester. By indicating that she found the budget a very open document, she was telling him that she was not out to vilify the city or make it look bad. By explaining that she was also interested in the shift away from the city manager government, she was saying, "I have done my homework, I know the specifics of your political environment, and I picked your city because it is a laboratory with an important experiment going on." This answer calmed Mr. Sette's anxiety and began the interview relationship.

ASKING SOME EASY QUESTIONS, SHOWING EMPATHY

As you end your introduction, you begin the questioning by asking matters that provide the interviewee with a comfort level. Choose questions that are central to your research but not threatening and that deal with matters the interviewee almost certainly knows about, and ideally, feels good about. Herb finds out in advance about the successful projects community developers being interviewed have completed and begins the questioning by asking about these projects. Further, he casts the question in ways that show he knows about the difficulties the person had to overcome to complete the project. "As the director of a new organization, how did you *ever* get so much funding for your first project?" The question allows the interviewee to show competence and triumph, a good way to begin. Similarly, in Irene's municipal budgeting project, she asked a budget director to explain how he managed to reorganize the departments and programs so that he could create a program budget without the programs sprawling across two or more departments. She was awed that he had been able to carry out this task from the budget director's office, and she conveyed her respect for this accomplishment to the interviewee in the tone of the question.

You also help make interviewees comfortable when you empathize with the emotional implications of what they tell you and in doing so help set the tone for the entire discussion. Sometimes you show concern by the posturing of your body and expression on your face; at other times, you offer a brief statement of sympathy: "That sounds so bad. That must have been horrible for you" or just "Oh, my." Another way of showing emotional understanding is to briefly offer incidents in which you had similar experiences: "That is nerve-racking, isn't it; the one time I had to take over the switchboard, I cut off the boss in the middle of a call." Or "I know about that call from the hospital at 5:00 A.M." Be cautious, though, that the experience you describe does not minimize the interviewee's suffering by presenting a false analogy.

Conveying emotional understanding is easy when you do understand, but what about those situations in which you do not empathize with the interviewees? If you communicate disgust or disapproval, you will not get good interviews, but if you pretend to accept behaviors that are shocking to you, you might come across as hypocritical or deceptive. What you want to communicate is that you are interested in what they are saying and trying to learn from them. A researcher might not approve of sinking whaling boats as a political protest against killing whales but can still honestly say that people who live their values and actively try to protect species are doing something important that should be recorded and broadly understood. You can be understanding yet be yourself in an interview relationship, agreeing with some things and disagreeing with other things.

ASKING THE TOUGH QUESTIONS

After discussing some easier topics, you can usually ask more sensitive or difficult questions. If you are fairly sure that you will be able to interview the same person several times, you may want to ask only nonthreatening questions during the first interview and save the tougher ones for later. In his study of advocacy organizations, Herb asks about the background of successful campaigns during the first interview. Such material speaks to Herb's research question but is not threatening or difficult. In subsequent interviewees, Herb asks why other organizations failed to join in these campaigns or about missteps, far more threatening topics. Ethically, stressful questions should be asked only if the answers are central to the research question. For example, finding out about the compromises people make on the job can explain a great deal about how organizations work, but exploring why someone was fired might not be crucial to the research and may be highly stressful.

A sensitive question might concern a cultural taboo, such as plagiarism among professors or corruption among accountants, or it might deal with failures, losses, or defeats. If the subject is marital break-up, you may be able to ask about infidelity at this stage in the interview. You can explore compromises interviewees have made between what they think is right and what they feel they had to do to survive. Now is when you ask about issues that the conversational partner seemed hesitant about or avoided earlier in the interview.

However, sometimes you mistakenly ask sensitive questions too early because you did not know that the interviewee would consider them problematic. When Irene was interviewing in Rochester about the budget process, she asked about the technical issue of fund account surpluses and only later learned that it was highly sensitive because the press had been using the surpluses as a cudgel to beat up on the city. Irene never imagined that budget officials would get upset about questions concerning the size of positive fund balances that normally mean good financial management. Herb recently stepped into a sensitive area by accident when he asked about the internal politics of an organization, only to find out that there was an embarrassing battle going on involving racial and gender issues. Fortunately, it was his fourth discussion with a cooperative partner, who chided Herb, but then answered the question. If you accidentally raise a stressful issue that interviewees seem hesitant to answer, you should back off, and if it seems important, raise it again later, maybe in an indirect fashion that gives interviewees the option of discussing it or not.

Sometimes it is not the emotional or political sensitivity of an issue that causes stress, but the conceptual difficulty of the question you pose. Many interviewees can answer hard questions, but they sometimes need some help in beginning. One student of Irene's became flummoxed when he interviewed a classmate and asked her what she meant by feminist studies. The interviewee found the question too abstract to answer and the interviewer did not know how to proceed to make the question easier to answer. To make a question easier, rephrase it so that it relates more directly to the interviewee's experience. What Irene's student could have done was to ask the interviewee about her experiences in class: Was the interaction between the students and the teacher different in her women's studies classes than in her other classes? Were the relationships between the students different? What were her expectations when she first signed up for a women's studies class? Were they partly or fully met? If you reduce something broad and abstract into specific events that interviewees can recall, you can help interviewees answer more conceptual questions.

When both you and your interviewee feel comfortable with each other (something that might not occur for several interviews), you then ask more provocative questions. In interviewing about sexual harassment, you might now inquire what efforts were taken, if any, to curb the inappropriate actions of the boss. Or in interviewing about the culture of police departments, you might say something like this: "You told me that police officers have a deep sense of good guys and bad guys, and get off on being society's protection from the bad guys, and yet we continue to see corruption in drug units. Is this a real contradiction? Is it factually correct? How would you explain it?"

You can get away with asking provocative questions at this stage, because the interviewees already know which side you are on, and have learned that you will pay attention to their answers and really try to understand. When you have reached this degree of closeness with your conversational partner, you can question in almost any way that makes sense, short of rudeness or excessive pressure. Interviewees, though, become exhausted answering difficult or draining questions, so it is best to ask only one or two of the more difficult questions in a single interview.

TONING DOWN THE EMOTIONAL LEVEL

After discussing these more difficult questions, your goal should be to bring the interviewee (and yourself) down from the intellectual or emotional high, without losing the openness of the discussion or precluding continuation later on.

One approach is to return to a few less-stressful questions. After talking about tense matters, such as racial antagonisms in the development field, Herb has found that asking community developers to describe their victories in getting money from a city or foundation relaxes them, and yet maintains an appropriate level of frank discourse. Irene asked her interviewees in the budget reform project to explain the organization of the budget office as a way of continuing an open conversation yet pulling back from more provocative topics such as the role of politicians in financial administration. Asking people for documents you know they have—copies of budgets, project proposals, congressional testimony—should net you some evidence while moving the discussion away from stressful matters. In cultural studies, you can ask about where you should take pictures, talk about artifacts, or ask for details on how a ritual is carried out. In general what you are doing is returning to the descriptive part of the interview, while requesting help from the interviewee in ways that allow the interviewee to feel good about providing assistance.

This is also the time in the interview to let the interviewee turn the discussion around and ask you questions that you can answer in depth. After the interviewee has been so open, he or she might feel it only fair that you expose yourself some too. Or you can ask, "Now that you know what the research is about, is there anything that I should have asked but didn't?" Herb will also ask those experienced in advocacy for advice on some of the campaigns Herb undertakes as a citizen activist, returning to the more personal chitchat with which the interview began.

CLOSING WHILE MAINTAINING CONTACT

As the interview ends, you indicate that you are grateful for the time and ideas that the interviewee has shared: "This has been great. You have given me a lot to think about." You might ask, if you have not done so before, if the person wishes to be identified by name or wants the name of the group used. This is a reminder that the material belongs to the interviewee and that you will use it with respect.

On occasion, while ending the interview, conversational partners will suggest further topics or questions that they think you have missed. Herb had finished up his questions, stood up, and was ready to leave when one interviewee backed Herb down into a chair by stepping in his direction and loudly stated the following:

> One of the comments I was going to make to you about this work was . . . the most common experience that I have is absolute either disregard or disrespect for [community development organizations]. . . . There is a very, there is palpable disrespect and animosity, you know, toward CDCs.

As her closing comment, the interviewee had added a major theme that she felt Herb had missed. Herb picked up the thread and continued the interview along the lines she suggested and later explored that theme with other interviewees.

You should try to keep the door open to continue the discussion or ask additional questions: "Would you like me to send you a copy of my notes when I type them up, so you can see if I got it straight or if there is anything you would like to add?" Or "I wanted to ask you about how the house arrest program was working, but we never got to that. Could we continue this at another time?" Or you can simply ask if you can come back (or call again) to see what is happening with the programs or projects now underway.

After you have finished with the formal closing, the interviewee may resume the more casual chatting that marked the opening. Sometimes what is involved is just friendly banter, but often what is happening is the interviewee is indirectly delivering additional information, so you should pay close attention to it, and write it down as soon as you leave, and look it over in conjunction with the interview.

The separate phases of an interview, as described here, are not meant as a rigid guide that must be followed. Rather, presenting the interview as a set of stages offers a warning not to jump right into the middle of a conversation, unless the interviewee pushes you there. The model reminds you that people will not stay at emotional or intellectual highs for long periods of time, that they are likely to feel exposed or uncomfortable after intimate revelations, and that it is your responsibility to make them feel more protected and secure before you end the interview. Overall, the model makes you ask how well you have meshed the questioning with the steps of building a conversational relationship.

Variations of the Stage Model

The stage model best describes an ongoing relationship between you, the interviewer, and a single conversational partner. In practice, other forms of depth interviewing occur in which different approaches are required. Your goal in each situation is still to form an open relationship, obtain information in depth, and handle sensitive topics with care, but the pragmatics of the interviewing require a different approach.

MULTIPLE-PERSON INTERVIEWS

On occasion, you end up interviewing two or more people at the same time. In this circumstance the relationship between the interviewees is often more important in influencing what is said than the questions posed by the researcher. This relationship may already be established before the interview, so the researcher has no role in facilitating it; they either do or do not trust each other. The result is a kind of hybrid between an ordinary conversation and an interview.

In the following example, Irene had set up an interview with a city manager, but the assistant to the mayor joined in. Irene was asking the city manager (the top professional staff member) for a narrative description of how budgeting changed in the city, but the presence of the assistant to the mayor totally changed the discussion to one focusing on the relationship between the elected officials and the professional staff.

Irene:　　　　What about the comprehensive budget review? Where did that come from?

City Manager:　From the mayor and the council . . . Council members hear about services they did not know we offered. They go through the work of the departments and prioritize, shift funding to higher priorities. They take an intensive look at all the departments. Show every service, and relate it to resources. Let the council go through and make those decisions. Maybe they will make budget cuts, but more likely, it will be an educational process. Barry, maybe you have a better perspective on that.

Irene had intended to rephrase the question, to get a better answer to where the current budget process came from, whose idea it was, and what stimulated it, but at this point the assistant to the mayor interjected. He answered part of Irene's original question, what the system was intended to accomplish from his perspective, but he also changed the focus to the relationship between the elected officials and the staff.

Mayor's Assistant: I spent eight years as a council member. Now I am the mayor's assistant. It's an odd route, but then, I am an odd person. I see it from a different perspective. It has both strengths and weaknesses. From the mayor and council's perspective, they like the way it works here. There is a trust relationship with the manager. It's predicated on trust. The council cannot go into detail. Without trust, you get a series of managers and move toward a strong mayor model. That was happening. We avoided that with district elections. It's in the council's interest to trust the manager; it relieves them of responsibility. Council members can become knowledgeable in one or two areas. City of Phoenix—maybe we are brainwashed—but its fiscal house is in good order. It has come through distress well. Federal funds dried up. The manager was out ahead of the curve; the predecessor manager was good at that. It's an open system, trust. They do fight sometimes, but on balance, there is good trust between the mayor, the council, and the staff. It's a three-legged stool. Maybe it's four-legged; the fourth leg is the business community—and the press. Frank [current city manager, one of the interviewees] is of the same mold as Marvin [the previous manager].

Rather than continue answering Irene's question, the manager started responding to the assistant to the mayor.

City Manager: I am trying to keep up the philosophy.

Mayor's Assistant: Now its tough times. It's possible that the state will cut the shared revenue. There is trust; we are prepared to do that and come through, because we have done it before.

City Manager: Every year we cut back something. Even in the good years. You will see that on the list of changes over the past decade.

Mayor's Assistant: There is tremendous preparation on the part of staff; they bring the last inch to the council to decide. Cut down on council decisions, the staff does most of it. On the bond stretch out, the increase from five to eight years, the staff did 90% of the work and gave the council the last 10%. The council went and had a war.

City Manager: It wasn't too bad.

Mayor's Assistant: No it wasn't, because we were handed a managerial package. Otherwise, it would have been an all-out fight.

In this excerpt, several things are happening. First, the two men are mostly attuned to each other. They are in a relationship already, which means that they do not have to establish one during the interview and are able to go right into a controversial issue tying together council politics, managerial relationships, and budget outcome. Very little of the ensuing discussion is about Irene's question on how the budget process came about. Irene had little choice but to remain silent. The mayor's assistant had an opportunity to tell the manager what he thought about council-manager relations, and even if the question the researcher asked was not on this subject, he was going to answer it anyway. The rest of the interview went on like this, with the two men discussing issues with each other, after the interviewer asked a quick and seemingly simple question.

The relationship between Irene and either of the interviewees was more or less irrelevant. What shaped the course of the interview was the already established connection between the two interviewees. Fortunately, the interviewees were discussing matters concerning budgetary politics, so Irene did learn from what she heard.

TELEPHONE INTERVIEWS

Using the telephone is not a preferred way to conduct depth interviews, but if the research involves people all over the country and you lack the resources to travel long distances, telephone interviews may make more sense. Also, telephone interviews can be useful for follow-up questions after you have read an interview with a person with whom you talked face to face. In his current research on advocacy for community renewal, during one brief period Herb had to check out descriptive material on lobbying over a bill with interviewees in Washington, DC; St. Louis; and New York City and then follow up for details with activists in organizations located in Washington, DC. Only phone interviews were possible.

Telephone interviewing requires modifications to be made to the stage model. It is more difficult to engage in casual small talk on a telephone during the business day and interviewees may want you to get to the point quickly. The result may be less time to build trust before asking questions.

Herb attempts to compensate by building in multiple contacts before the actual phone interview. Herb attends conferences where he tries to meet face to face the people he anticipates he might eventually call. At conferences most people are too busy for an interview, but usually there is sufficient time to briefly explain what the project is about. Later, Herb follows up with an explanatory letter describing the project and asking for a telephone appointment. He then calls up to make the appointment, trying to use this initial brief call as the informal, rapport-building stage of the interview. He answers questions the conversational partner might have, chats about common experiences, and suggests what topics will be covered in the subsequent call. The actual interview is then a second call, by which time at least some relationship has been established.

At times, though, you have to conduct telephone interviews with someone you have not met face to face. In that case, it is important to be sure to include material in your letter requesting an interview that indicates that you are safe to talk to, that you know some of the same people, have been active in the same organizations, or are part of the same ethnic group, social club, or fraternity or sorority—anything that makes you seem more familiar and reliable. Herb sends along some of his writing with this letter so potential interviewees can see what the result of the interview is likely to be. In his call to make an appointment, he spends time not only outlining the project but also discussing these mutual ties. Sometimes interviewees ask about these connections to make sure that the interviewer really does know these people or really is a part of the group.

A second problem with telephone interviews is that it is difficult to sense when your questions are sensitive, when you should back off, and when the interviewee is sufficiently relaxed and confident that you can try those questions again. You cannot see visual expressions of stress or anxiety on the phone. You may have to put into words communications that are normally done nonverbally: "Are you okay with this topic? If this is stressful, we don't have to talk about it." Or maybe, "please let me know if I inadvertently ask you something that you feel uncomfortable talking about and we will go on to something else." Some techniques for lowering the intensity level do not work at all on the phone, for example, asking for documents such as organization charts or budgets, but equivalent techniques can involve asking where information is stored on Web sites.

Follow-up phone interviews (after either a face-to-face discussion or a previous call) can also be scheduled to talk about very limited and specific issues. To set up such calls, Herb will often e-mail a conversational partner, asking if a brief call to discuss a specific topic is okay. They nearly always agree and on several occasions the question Herb posed was specific enough that the interviewee answered electronically right then and there.

Evaluating Your Interview

Although interviews are like ordinary conversations in some key ways, they are also different enough to warrant practice and reflection on how they can be improved. You should not expect yourself to be terrific at it the first few times you try to interview, though interviewees are often helpful and will give good answers even to clumsily worded questions. What is important is that you read over your interviews with a critical eye and look for places and ways to improve. Even people who have been interviewing for years sometimes get forgetful, try to take shortcuts, lose their focus, or need to review their interviews to figure out what they need to change.

Look at your introduction. Was your description of the topic too broad, too narrow, or too abstract, giving the interviewee incorrect signals about what you wanted to know? You may need to approach the subject in a different way. Did you go overboard on describing your credentials and intimidate the interviewee? Were you negligent in not reinforcing the interviewee's sense of competence?

Closely examine the transcript to see how the interviewee responded to the overall topic. Did the person have an easy time matching his or her experiences to your questions? Did he or she narrow your topic down or alter it? You need this information to help you tailor the topic to what your interviewees know and are willing to share. Pay particular attention to those moments when the interviewee appears to be answering a different question from the one you asked.

Sometimes you will discover that though you began with one idea of what the study is about, you learn that the interviewees think a different aspect of the problem is important. For instance, Irene had structured an interview with a budget director around the topic of how and why the city had changed its budgeting. When she read over the interview later, she discovered that the question the budget director was actually answering was one that she had not thought of asking: How does the role of the budget office change when the form of government changes? Because the city she was studying had recently shifted from a council manager to a strong mayor form, the difference in role of the budget office between these two governmental forms was highly salient to the budget director on a day-to-day basis. In answering a different question from the one posed, the interviewee was expressing his opinions on what the questioning should be about. In general, answers that seem not to relate to the questions asked often mean that your research questions need to be reworked.

Sometimes, you will notice that your questions did not get the hoped-for depth. Try to determine why. Did you miss some key places where you should have asked a second or third question? Did you fail to ask for examples? Did you discourage the interviewee from responding at length by interrupting a long reply? Did you skip opportunities to follow up incomplete answers? Did you accept a generalization when you should have questioned it? Did you phrase too many questions to invite a yes or no reply? If the interviewee answered briefly and cautiously, did you then encourage the interviewee to speak his or her mind? Did you express your own opinions in too a strong way? If the interviewees contradicted you, did you get defensive rather than curious and supportive? If your interviewee seemed tense, look over the interview to see if you asked difficult and stressful questions too quickly. Also check to see if you backed away quickly enough and gently enough when your questions provoked stress.

In the final step of this self-evaluation, ask yourself if your interview also worked as a conversation. Did your questions flow naturally from the answers you heard while staying on topic? Were you carefully listening to what was being said and responding appropriately rather than trying to steer the discussion down some predetermined path?

Conclusion

You choose conversational partners who are knowledgeable about what is important in their world. When they understand correctly what it is that you want to learn, these interviewees can teach you with minimum guidance on your part. On occasion, interviewees have told us to be quiet, to listen and let them talk, and then proceeded to teach us what we wanted to learn. Still, you cannot count on your interviewee taking the topic and running with it, and so you have to carefully plan out questions in advance, a topic we discuss beginning in the next chapter.

But interviewing is more than learning how to word and ask questions. As this chapter has argued, an interview is part of a developing relationship in which issues of mutual interest are explored in depth. Its success comes about when you have chosen knowledgeable interviewees, built a good relationship, and asked the appropriate questions.

In the end, how do you know you have done a good interview? It is a sign that things are going well when your interviewees anticipate your questions and answer them before you ask them. When you are getting depth and detail, you are doing things right. It is great when the conversational partners so want you to get it right that they point out subtleties that you would otherwise miss. It is even better when the interviewees suggest lines of questioning for you or raise questions that you did not think about but are relevant to the topic. When conversational partners reach out, touch your shoulder, say "It was fun," and invite you back, you know the interview worked.

Finally, you know that the interviews are working when you feel yourself absorbed and excited as you reread your transcripts and find yourself eager to share what you have learned with others. The interviews are working when you find answers to the questions that you originally posed. In addition, the project is successful if you discover many questions and answers that you did not realize were important when you began the research.

7

Structuring the Interview

Interviews are structured conversations. You organize an interview by combining *main questions, follow-up questions*, and *probes*. Main questions are worked out in advance to make sure you cover all the major parts of your research problem, whereas the follow-up questions ask for explanation of themes, concepts, or events that the interviewee has introduced. Probes help manage the conversation by keeping it on topic, signaling the desired level of depth, and asking for examples or clarification. The main questions help you make sure you are answering your research puzzle; the follow-up questions and probes ensure that you get depth, detail, vividness, richness, and nuance.

Good Answers

In the responsive interviewing model, you are looking for depth and detail, vivid and nuanced answers, rich with thematic material. If you are not getting answers with those characteristics, you may need to alter your wording or spend more time building trust.

DEPTH AND DETAIL

Depth and detail overlap but the ideas are conceptually distinct. Detail means going after the parts, the items in a list, the particulars. If a young man tells you he went out with a beautiful woman, you might want to know in detail what *beautiful* means to him. You might say, "Beautiful, in what way was she beautiful?" or "What about her did you find beautiful?" You are looking for a list of characteristics. In questioning about a process, event, or ceremony, you might ask about a sequence:

What happened first, what next? You could ask who was at a meeting, how long it lasted, who sat where, who spoke, what was said, what action preceded and which followed. To ascertain a list of steps you often present a series of how and what questions: "How did you learn to cook nonfat meals after the heart attack?" "What cookbooks did you use?"

By asking for detail, you encourage the interviewee to provide the specifics that enable you to understand the unexpected or learn that what at first appears to be a minor concern is in fact important. In asking hospital employees the details of their jobs, you discover that working mandatory overtime and doing back-to-back shifts, though common, lead to mistakes and increased anxiety. By asking community developers how they finance their projects, you may learn that some needed projects do not get funded because of changing fashions among foundations or the lack of understanding of government officials about what poor neighborhoods lack. When you look for details, you can ask about how something happened, how a particular word is used, or focus on a specific event or object, a photograph, picture, or award: "Can you tell me something about those photographs on the wall? How did you come by them?" "Your organization won a prize for that project; how did that come about?" Details provide the precise evidence on which you later base your conclusions.

Depth involves asking about distinct points of view while learning enough of the history or context to be able to put together separate pieces of what you have heard in a meaningful way. Depth implies searching for an answer that goes beyond the superficial, beyond the first response to a second and third level, and maybe more.

In eliciting depth, you do more than ask the interviewee to continue on the topic in the way he or she had been doing. You can also communicate in your questions that you feel there might be other alternative explanations and other perspectives. If you were studying interpersonal attractiveness and your interviewee told you how handsome or beautiful his or her new friend is, you might ask if he or she has ever been attracted to someone who is not beautiful or handsome, or whether it matters whether the person has a good sense of humor. If your questioning can get the conversational partners to describe elements of attraction other than good looks, you might learn that they are attracted to people who have self-confidence, who think about others, or who are passionate about something, be it golf or reading or politics or choir practice. Once you have elicited these components of attractiveness you can look for refinements, limits, or exceptions. "You said you found people with humor attractive, but what about someone who joked all the time? Would you still find that attractive?" The result is a deeper understanding of what attractiveness means.

When you are looking for depth, you also seek explanations from conversational partners who have had diverse experiences or hold different opinions. For example, an African American community leader might charge that racism caused the government to turn down his redevelopment group's applications for funding. To get more depth, you explore with him what racism means, as well as what alternative explanations he might have considered and rejected for why the applications were turned down. In the same study, you would also explore reasons for the rejection with government officials, perhaps asking whether they were concerned about the ability of the redevelopment group to complete its work or if the funding agency had run out of money. In seeking depth, you explore alternatives.

Depth and detail differ but complement each other. To illustrate the difference between going after depth and going after detail, suppose you are doing a life history with a middle-age woman and she tells you that she recently invited her mother to move to her town. Going for depth, you ask questions that require a thoughtful response, such as "Was encouraging your mother's move a difficult decision for you?" To suggest your concern with details, you can ask, "What was happening in your mother's life when she decided to move?"

Much of the time you want both depth and detail. Suppose your interviewee tells you that her mother expects her to take her to the dentist and to her doctor's appointments. You then ask for more details: "What happens when you take her to an appointment?" She answers, "You know, I pick her up and bring her to the clinic and sit with her while she waits for the doctor, and then I take her home." You are getting detail, exactly what took place, but still lacking depth, because you do not know what any of this means. You continue looking for depth, asking, "Wouldn't it be easier on you if you dropped her off and came back for her an hour later?" She answers, "I can't go anywhere else and come back for her, because she gets too nervous." From this answer, you begin to understand what dependence means and how it is felt. You have the depth of the interviewee's reasoning and the details to back it up. Detail adds solidity, clarity, evidence, and example; depth adds layers of meaning, different angles on the subject, and understanding.

VIVIDNESS

In addition to depth and detail, the interviewer should design questions to evoke vivid descriptions. Vivid anecdotes or examples allow the reader to picture what is being talked about and to respond not just intellectually but also emotionally. To obtain vivid reports you ask for narratives or request step-by-step descriptions of what happened. The freshness and clarity of the answers create a vivid narrative.

Consider this example that Jim Thomas shared with us from his prison research: "[This guard would] mess with guys, and then he'd say, 'Go ahead and beat me.' And one day, somebody came up to him and hit him with a pipe. He's got a plate in his head now, [laughs] and he was lying on the floor, and blood was gushing, [laughs] and he was crying like a baby: 'Please don't kill me, please don't kill me.' He thought he was going to die right there." This description is vivid and when used in conjunction with others similar to it provides a convincing description of prison violence. Talking about violence in the abstract does not reach the reader the same way that episodes like this do.

Vividness also comes from asking background questions and learning enough about the overall context to personalize your report so that you can present your interviewees as real people rather than abstractions. Ask follow-up questions to pull out details from the interviewees' quotations that reveal their style, humor, or particular insights. Learn enough about the situations your interviewees confronted or experienced to properly interpret what they say: "A normally easygoing and diplomatic person, the mayor sputtered with anger when a citizen questioned the city council's judgment. . . ."

Vividness also comes from asking for descriptions of iconic moments or images, and following up on highly charged summary explanations. Maybe a husband made a belittling remark about his wife in front of guests, or maybe a politician broke a rule to gain some short-term advantage. Tiny episodes like these may contain the seed of a much larger story. They are concrete instances, small enough to understand, familiar enough to recognize, and laden with meaning. You ask for incidents like these in your questions: "When did you first think that your marriage might be disintegrating?" Or maybe in a study of a major conflict you ask something like this: "You have described the meeting where the fight occurred, but did any of you see it coming? Were there any prior hints about the tensions?"

NUANCE

Nuance is about showing that things are not always true or not true, that they may be true in part, or true in some circumstances or at some times. Rather than black or white, nuance implies that there are multiple shades of gray. Nuance requires obtaining precise descriptions, not blue, but cornflower blue, not just love, but love with energy and joy. Nuance highlights subtlety of meaning. What exactly does it mean to say you love someone? Is there a little fear mixed in with the love, or a little dominance? How is the idea shaded or toned? Questions should be designed to elicit nuance. When you get an unshaded answer, you ask for more refinement.

You can encourage interviewees to provide nuanced answers by wording questions, especially main questions, to avoid yes or no, black or white responses. Rather than ask, "Are you in favor of abortion?" inviting a yes or no answer, your main question asks, "What do you think about abortion?" inviting a more complex, shaded reply. You do not inquire whether the student culture accepts cheating as okay, inviting a yes or no answer; instead you ask under what circumstances cooperation between students is considered okay and under what circumstances such cooperation would be considered problematic.

You continue to seek out nuance with your follow-up questions. Suppose you asked your interviewee what his or her experiences have been with love and the interviewee replies, "Well, my parents loved both us kids." To get some nuance, you might then follow up by asking how they showed their love. Suppose the answer was "My mom used to tell us all the time that she loved us." Your follow-up question might be "What about your dad?" Maybe the interviewee's answer would indicate a difference in the way his or her parents showed their love: "He used to take us to ball games, and to work with him. He would show us all around and introduce us and say, 'These are my boys.' He was proud of us." With this answer you are beginning to hear the nuance, the difference between talking about love and demonstrating it by giving time to your kids, and you are also learning about the relationship between pride and love.

When you are looking for nuance, you question broad statements that seem one-sided or overstated. "My life has been one great failure." Surely there have been some good times as well. Asking about them is likely to introduce nuance into the discussion. The bolder the generalization, the more it invites further questioning. "We always get our work in on time." Always? You mean every single time? If the answer is "Well, not every single time," you then ask about the exception. If the interviewee persists in defending the "always" reply, you can pursue the reply a number of ways: by asking what *on time* means, whether they ever get work done before deadlines, whether they have any role in setting the deadlines or the ability to move deadlines if they prove unrealistic. Or you question how they adapt if the task changes midcourse, or if someone on the team gets sick or switched to another assignment. Each of these questions is likely to obtain a more nuanced understanding.

RICHNESS

Richness means that your interviews contain many ideas and different themes, often including those that you did not anticipate when you began the study. Richness allows depth interviewers to unravel the complexity of other peoples' worlds.

Richness comes through hearing extended descriptions and long narratives on what occurred. Suppose you are asking about a controversial issue that came before the city council and have encouraged the interviewee to describe at length the meeting at which a decision was made. The interviewee discusses the vote on the issue of concern but also mentions that there was an acrimonious exchange between the council members, that information was abruptly demanded of the professional city staff, and that though citizens made strong comments, the council appeared to ignore what they said. You have obtained depth and detail on the decision that was your initial concern, but have also discovered several new and important themes. You have learned about how council members relate to one another in a meeting, you learned about the subordinate role of the professional staff, and you found out how citizens' comments are handled. These multiple themes constitute a rich answer.

Richness is evoked by encouraging the interviewee to elaborate. You listen quietly and intently when an interviewee is giving detailed answers or is presenting narratives or stories. You encourage the interviewee to continue talking through continuation probes: You appear intent or suggest that the interviewee is doing wonderfully and you want to hear more to elicit more elaborated and refined material. Even when a story or narrative seems complete, you ask for more examples, because each example will be a little different, adding themes or concepts or putting a new slant on them.

Main Questions, Follow-Up Questions, and Probes

To structure interviews that are on target, that elicit depth, detail, vividness, nuance, and richness, you create a mix of three kinds of questions: main, follow-up, and probes.

MAIN QUESTIONS

Main questions are the scaffolding of the interview, the skeleton of it. Main questions encourage the conversational partner to talk about the research puzzles that motivate the study. Main questions ensure that the research problem will be thoroughly examined and that each part of a broad topic will be explored.

A main question translates the research topic into terms that the conversational partner can relate to and discuss. Your initial research question itself is usually too broad and abstract for an interviewee to answer. Herb is very interested in theories of resource dependency. He wants to know how their dependence on banks and foundations for funding affects the direction activist organizations take. His research question (in a grant proposal) might be as follows: "Resource dependency theory indicates that economically powerful organizations set the activist agenda. If so, how can activist organizations implement a community agenda?" As phrased, such a research question would sound abstract to most conversational partners who would not know how to begin in answering it. So Herb creates main questions that are more concrete and easier to talk about: "I've learned from your Web page that your organization is partnering with [big bank] to teach the poor about financial matters. Could you tell me how this program came about?" (This question asks the particulars of the relationship of a small group with an organization that provides funds.) If this interview question does not elicit a full-enough answer, Herb will follow up, asking whose idea the project was in the first place, and if it was a project that the community came up with, he might ask how the organization won support for it.

The researcher normally prepares main questions prior to the interview. In determining what to include, the researcher may obtain ideas from books or articles, documents, Web publications, prior interviews, or observations. Main questions have to be carefully thought through and expressed so as not to restrict or predetermine the responses but at the same time cover the research concerns. The goal is to encourage people to talk about their experiences, perceptions, and understandings rather than to give a normative response, company line, or textbook-type answer.

You should work out a limited number of main questions for any one interview. Though there are no fixed rules, experienced researchers rarely prepare more than half a dozen, and of those, expect to actually ask only three or four. If you have too few, and one question happens to be inappropriate, the interview may peter out, but if you prepare too many, you may be tempted to try to ask all the questions rather than encouraging the conversational partner to provide extended answers to the questions you have asked. If you rush through a dozen questions, you will not get sufficient depth on any of them.

FOLLOW-UP QUESTIONS

Follow-up questions are specific to the comments that conversational partners have made. In working out follow-up questions, the researcher *listens hard to hear the meaning of what the conversational partner has said* and then asks additional questions to explore the particular themes, concepts, and ideas introduced by the conversational partner. Follow-up questions are crucial for obtaining depth and detail, and can help in obtaining more nuanced answers.

If you have initially posed sufficiently broad main questions and encouraged your interviewees to reply at length, the resulting answer is likely to be rich and present many choices about what to follow up. You cannot possibly follow up on every interesting matter; the interview would lose its focus and you would run out of time. You normally follow up on those matters that seem most important to the interviewee and that speak to your research question. You are likely to follow-up on matters that are puzzling or unclear and that suggest concepts, themes, or ideas that you did not anticipate, that take you in new directions in understanding your research topic.

Follow-up questions can be presented during the same interview in which the concept, theme, intriguing idea, or unexpected thought was introduced, or they can be asked in subsequent interviews with the same conversational partner or even with different individuals. In answering your main question about an advocacy campaign, an interviewee might describe the coalition involved. You might decide to follow up during the interview asking about how this coalition came about or what role different organizations played in the campaign. Or you might try to get an interview with the head of the coalition and ask her or him what roles the different members play.

Novice interviewers initially have difficulty working out follow-up questions while doing an interview, but with practice following up on your feet gets easier. Do not get anxious if you look over your notes and notice many places where you could have or should have followed up and failed to. You can usually conduct a second interview with the same person and then ask the missing questions, or find other interviewees to whom you can ask these questions.

Being able to follow up during an interview seems impressive, but it is normally a function of being prepared rather than being extremely quick at thinking on your feet. Follow-up questions that appear to come about on the spur of the moment are usually in actuality a result of previous analysis. Before you talk with Ms. Smith, you will have already interviewed Mr. Jones and Ms. Earl, analyzed what they said, and from that analysis worked out that you want to follow up on certain matters. When these matters are raised by Ms. Smith, you recognize them immediately and ask the follow-up questions that you had worked out from your prior interviews.

PROBES

Probes are techniques to keep a discussion going while providing clarification. Probes ask the interviewee to keep talking on the matter at hand, to complete an idea, fill in a missing piece, or request clarification of what was said. Other probes ask for examples or evidence for particular points. Probes elicit more details without changing the focus of the questioning. In ordinary conversations, people feel they should not babble on lest they bore the listener. Probes are ways of combating the tendency people have to not go into detail, instead encouraging people to offer a variety of answers and do so in detail.

The wording of probes is almost formulaic, with identical questions used in a wide variety of interviews depending on which are most appropriate at the moment. However, the wording of the probe must make sense in context. If someone says to you, "We went to the mall," you would not ask, "Can you give me an example of that?" But you might ask, "What happened next?" Overall, the wording of probes is not problematic. They are simple, short, routine, and just have to be appropriate to what the interviewee has said.

When to Use Main Questions, Follow-Ups, and Probes

After your introduction, you normally start your interview with your first main question. You may have prepared a handful of main questions, but only after you feel that the first question is fully answered, at least as far as the interviewee can remember, and you have asked needed follow-up questions, do you pose the second main question. In asking subsequent main questions, you want to show how each links to what you have just been discussing, so the conversation does not sound choppy. You might say, "We have been talking about how this previous budget reform got started, but I would also like to know what you are doing now, whether there have been any recent changes in budgeting." If you have planned your main questions to cover your whole topic in a logical way, they should fit together naturally and not sound abrupt or unrelated to each other.

Generally, you follow up when something new or interesting is said that seems to speak to your research problem. An interviewee may come up with an intriguing generalization that warrants exploration, may suggest a more nuanced view of the subject than you anticipated, or present some new word or phrase that addresses your research question. You listen hard for these moments in your interview and then ask about them.

You may also want to follow up on inconsistencies but without sounding as if you are trying to catch people in contradictions. Try to explore an apparent inconsistency in a gentle way: "You told me before that the hats were green, but just now you referred to them as blue. Are they sometimes green and sometimes blue, or do they just look blue to you sometimes?" You do not follow up on every apparent inconsistency, lest you sound like an inquisitor, but do so just enough to figure out how much weight to put on given answers. Blatantly inconsistent descriptions provide weak evidence.

Follow-up questions can occur at nearly any time in an interview, once the first main question has been posed. However, you will find that you are asking more follow-up questions toward the end of an interview and toward the end of a project, after you have had time to figure out what the themes are that you want to explore in greater detail and depth.

There are no rules about how much follow up to do, but err on the low side so you can hear all that the interviewee wants to tell you without many interruptions. If you leave some issues unexplored, you can usually follow up during a second interview. Leave the interview site, transcribe and reread your interview, do a preliminary analysis of it to see what the important themes are, and then determine which issues were raised that you did not ask about but would prove useful in answering your research puzzle. Select from this list the most important ones to follow up. Then try to make a second interview with the same person. If you ended the first interview with a polite request—such as "May I get back to you if I have questions when I go over the interview?"—it should be relatively easy to call and say, "I was going over my notes from our conversation and there were some things I didn't understand; I was wondering if we could set up some time for me to ask you about those points?"

A second piece of advice is that there are some occasions when you should not follow up, even if something seems puzzling or wrong to you. Sometimes when you are interviewing you run into a front or an account. Putting on a front means that someone is taking on a somewhat exaggerated role and sticking to it to create an intended image (Goffman 1959). Headwaiters in restaurants may put on a front of extreme courtesy and formality to create a tone for the restaurant; police in tough neighborhoods create a front of fearlessness and brutality, because they believe that any sign of gentleness or flexibility will be perceived as weakness and make them a target of violence and mockery. Accounts are self-justifying explanations, socially acceptable reasons why people have done things that would normally be considered wrong (Lyman and Scott 1968). If you perceive that you are encountering a front, or that the interviewee is avoiding blame, asking questions that would break down these self-presentations is normally not a good strategy. Listen, observe, get down the details, and then at some other time interview the same person on the identical topic but this time try to word the questions in ways that are less likely to evoke a front or accounts—for instance, by asking about specific examples, cases, or experiences.

Interviewers sometimes evoke accounts without meaning to. You may be inadvertently giving an accusatory or judgmental edge to your questions that encourages people to try to justify themselves. If so, tone down that part of your questioning and watch for any secondary messages of blame you may be conveying.

You can ask a follow-up question either during the interview itself or in a subsequent interview. In contrast, you have to make the decision to probe on the spot, as probes request the interviewee to elaborate on what they have just said or to explain it further. You may find that you are doing more probes at the beginning of an interview than you do later. Probes are used to signal the level of depth you are looking for in an answer, and once the interviewee has understood that providing depth and detail are okay, you have accomplished that goal. Similarly, if you are asking about key terms that you do not understand, interviewees will get the idea that they need to explain technical terms, acronyms, or even procedures that are routine to them but that outsiders such as yourself will not know.

In general, try to keep your probes limited in number and unobtrusive. If possible, stay silent for a few seconds (that's hard to do) and wait for the interviewee to continue, or nod or gesture in ways that communicate "more, please." You should probe for missing information or ask for clarification of garbled sentences only if you are pretty sure the information is likely to be important. If you probe too often or too intrusively, you might stop the flow of the conversation. An interviewer who says, "Yes, I understand" once or twice during an interview may convey support, but someone who does it 20 times comes across as mechanical and shallow. An interviewer who asks, "How do you know that?" once may get an answer about how the interviewee learned something, but if you ask it several times, you create the image of not trusting the opinions or conclusions of the interviewee. If overused, probes can backfire.

Structuring Interviews by Combining
Main Questions, Follow-Up Questions, and Probes

All responsive interviews are built up by combining main questions, follow-up questions, and probes. Metaphorically, putting together the main questions, probes, and follow-up questions is a little like playing golf. You have a series of holes, each of which you approach with a main question, a big long drive that you have planned out in advance. Depending on where your drive lands, you follow up with other shots, choosing clubs with different shapes that are the most likely to get you close to the green from where you are. If you hit the ball into the rough—that is, get an answer that is vague or incomprehensible—you choose a specialized club, the probe, that helps you get past the difficulty. You continue the probing and following up until you get the ball into the hole. You repeat the process again on the next hole with another preplanned main question, follow-up questions, and probes, as needed. The holes are connected in a logical order and give structure to the whole game. Just as the choice of club depends on where your ball lands, your choice of follow-ups and probes depends on what you hear in answer to your main questions.

In a golf game, the course is laid out for you; the number of holes is fixed. That would be the equivalent of having a fixed number of main questions to cover your topic, but in responsive interviewing, you do not have that level of structure. You may have one main question, with lots of follow-up questions and some probes, or you may have several main questions, with fewer follow-up questions and probes. The balance between types of questions may shift from one interview to the next. The effect is like playing golf on a new course with a different number of holes every time you play.

Example: Balancing Main Questions,
Follow-Ups, and Probes

Let's examine an excerpt from an interview from one of Irene's projects to see how she balanced a main question with follow-ups and probes. Irene's research question was as follows: "Has the federal government learned how to control deficits, and if so, where and how has this learning taken place?" She interviewed a number of experts who had been close to the federal budget process. One of those she interviewed was Tom Cuny, a retired budgeter with strong feelings about how budget concepts, such as balance, were manipulated and evaded. Irene's first main question was "Was there any learning between Gramm-Rudman-Hollings [budget balancing legislation passed in 1985] and the Budget Enforcement Act [passed initially in 1990, and later renewed]?"

Tom: Gramm-Rudman-Hollings wanted truly dramatic reductions in spending. The first year we will just nibble [at programs] and then [spending will] fall off a cliff. By the time we reached the cliff, no one wanted to fall, we changed the law. By contrast, with the Budget Enforcement Act, we can control through the appropriations process the nonmandatories, set targets, the sum of which will be budget targets for that period. The idea was that if we squeeze the nonmandatory items to stay within the totals, we should come out at Valhalla. But we misestimated revenues, overestimated them, and underestimated mandatory spending, and had no mechanisms to fix it. The deficit kept rising, it was out of our hands. Both GRH and BEA were fatally flawed.

I am not advocating or disadvocating a balanced budget, but from a balanced budget perspective, both were fatally flawed.

. . . Three years ago when the Balanced Budget Amendment [to the constitution] started to look like it might go through, Hartman wanted to redefine the budget before the amendment got enacted. Hartman never met a capital investment he didn't like. He wanted to define budget to exclude new investment on capital and only include depreciation, which is uncontrollable by definition. [Cost is] controllable only when you invest. If the budget excludes the point of control, you lose it as a budget.

Irene: That was the intent presumably. [*A probe to encourage Tom to continue to talk.*]

Tom: Yes, put it out [of the budget] when you could control it. Put it in [the budget] when you couldn't control it, when it is just record keeping.

Irene: He did not succeed at that? [*This was a follow-up question, intended to get more depth. It suggests a modification of the*

(Continued)

(Continued)

> *main developing theme. Interviewee argues that people evade budget controls; interviewer suggests they try but are not always successful.*]
>
> Tom: Yes, but there has been lots of effort to take capital out. People invent gimmicks to have their cake and eat it too. In my 25 1/2 years at OMB [Office of Management and Budget] and CBO [Congressional Budget Office], I constantly ran across people who try to have their cake and eat it too.
>
> Irene: Have we had any directional movement on these issues? [*Follow-up refers to the interviewee's theme—evasion is pervasive—and looks for modification, softening, or nuance.*]
>
> Tom: There has been no directional movement. The basic [budget] concepts have been there all along. What we have learned is a multitude of ways to evade the rules we set up, to pretend we are doing what we aren't doing. Supply-side economics is snake oil. Balance. If Clinton hadn't used snake oil to attack the Republicans on cutting entitlements, backed Dole into a corner, Dole wouldn't have had to push the snake oil of tax cuts.
>
> The main question referred to specific legislation by name, signaling the interviewee that the researcher knew at least the core elements of the topic and that a detailed answer would be appropriate. The interviewee answered the main question by saying that both the earlier and the later legislation were flawed as tools of balancing the budget and briefly explained why and how. Then he took a slight detour, telling a story, the final paragraph of which is quoted above. The point of the story was that some advocates of capital spending were trying to protect items they thought might be cut by the proposed constitutional amendment to require a balanced budget by taking those items out of the budget. His argument was that people who wanted to continue to spend would find ways to get around spending limits.
>
> To keep him talking Irene tried a probe that did not elicit very much, so she then asked a specific follow-up exploring the difference between trying to evade a control and successfully evading that control. The follow-up did elicit a reply, but not as Irene had expected.

Instead of discussing the success or failure of the efforts to evade the rules, Tom returned to his theme that the effort to evade the rules was continuous. In doing so he introduced another example of what to him represented evasion of the balanced budget principle, tax breaks as a stimulus to the economy to balance the budget. He argued that offering tax breaks in the name of budget balance was snake oil, that you do not balance a budget by reducing revenue.

In this last answer, the interviewee introduced a new theme, that partisan attacks produce partisan short-term gain strategies on the other side that erode the clear concepts on which good budgetary management is based. Irene failed to follow up here, because she failed to see the theme in the density of the whole interview. Instead, having gotten a clear answer to her main question—the government had learned nothing about how to eliminate deficits, in his opinion—and being unable to elicit any nuance on this question, Irene went on to her next main question. (The excerpt above is only a small part of the interview.)

The overall balance between main questions and follow-up questions differs depending on the purpose of the interview.

Several interview patterns are dominated by the initial main questions. An evaluation interview is about determining the effect of a policy or program change on some population, such as the effect of a new welfare policy on clients, administrative agencies, and costs. In such cases, an interview would contain main three main questions—one asking how clients were affected, one about the agencies, and a third about costs—and then each of the specific issues would be followed up for detail. Life histories trace common cultural patterns, such as what grade school was like, what the rules of dating and sexual exploration were when the interviewees were young, how they found their first job, or what happened when a parent got ill. These interviews are structured through a small number of main questions, one for each stage of a person's life. Oral histories explore how individuals experienced a historical event, such as a war, coup, or epidemic. The goal of oral history is to present the interviewees' perspectives with the minimum possible amount of interpretation or selection by the researcher. Because many others will be using the transcripts of these interviews for different purposes, achieving clarity, thoroughness, and evidence are the most important goals. Oral history interviews typically are structured around a small number of main questions, with few, if any, follow-up questions, but with numerous probes, some for clarity, others for getting examples or evidence, some just to keep the interviewee talking to provide added detail.

Other interview types depend more on the follow-up questions. If the goal of the interview is concept clarification, there should be only one or two main questions with a number of follow-up questions, each tapping some nuance of the concept. Probing is less important and done primarily to keep the conversation going rather than to search for detailed evidence. If you are undertaking a case study to find out what happened and what it means, you prepare a handful of main questions tapping what each interviewee should know. The rest of the interview, however, should be based on both follow-up questions and probes.

As the foregoing discussion suggests, the structure of responsive interviews can vary greatly. Still these variations can be loosely grouped into three patterns that we have named *opening the locks*, *tree and branch*, and *river and channel*. Some interviews actually do fit precisely within these types, but more often an interview is a combination of several. Keeping these structures in mind can help when you are deciding how many main questions to ask and how extensively to follow up or probe.

OPENING THE LOCKS

The opening-the-locks pattern is most common early in a study when the researcher is somewhat naïve about the matter at hand but is pretty sure the conversational partner is well informed. The goal in using this pattern of interviewing is to obtain a broad portrait of what is going on to suggest what specifically needs to be explored in depth later.

Opening-the-locks interviews are structured around one or two main questions designed to encourage the conversational partner to talk at length and in depth on the matter at hand. For instance, you might ask a lobbyist to describe the politics surrounding a legislative bill or ask the chief financial officer of an organization how a budget was determined. You could ask a teenage aficionado of computer games what the games are about or the director of a social-service agency how it survives during hard times. If the researcher and conversational partner are both aware of an event that appears to illustrate an important theme, asking what the event signifies can be a way to design the main question. "What was really going on at that meeting do you think?" or "Was that some kind of turning point?" The hope is that a single main question when asked a knowledgeable conversational partner will be like opening the locks on a river, allowing the waters (information) to rush forth.

Many of Herb's initial interviews are of the open-the-locks variety. For example, as part of his project on advocates for housing for the poor, Herb began with one opening-the-locks question by asking political activists how their organizations framed—that is, how they gave public definition to—issues. He heard numerous examples as well as illustrations of tactics that were used, few of which he knew about before. In subsequent interviews he asked follow-up questions on the examples and the tactics that several of his interviewees had raised and that Herb now understood were important.

TREE AND BRANCH

In the tree-and-branch structure, the researcher divides the research problem into more or less equal parts, and each part is covered with a main question. In an evaluation interview, a researcher might want to know how a job training program increased the participants' skills and confidence while also wanting to learn what impact the training program had on the trainees' income, family stability, and choice of place to live. Main questions would be prepared on each. In an exit interview, the researcher might want to know what made the person quit and what the attractions of the other job might be, so again these topics would be broached in separate main questions. In this model, the interview is likened to a tree with the trunk as the research problem and the branches as the main questions, each dealing with a separate but more or less equal concern. In the interviews, the researcher would try to ask all the main questions and then follow up on each to obtain the same degree of depth, detail, vividness, richness, and nuance.

In preparing questions in the tree-and-branch model, you need to be sure that the main questions are logically related and in your wording ensure that the transitions between the main questions make sense to the interviewees. For instance, if you were trying to construct a history of an event, the main questions might follow a chronology. What happened first? What happened next? This is the normal way that people share narratives. Or suppose you were interviewing about living in a retirement home and have done sufficient participant observation to be able to prepare three main questions to cover what you feel are different yet equally important parts of life in the home. The first asks, "How good is the care from the staff?" The second asks, "What is the social life like at Golden Acres?" A third main question might be "Do you keep up contact with family and old friends?" Your conversational partners will recognize the importance of each question but might be unable to intuit a relationship between the questions. To make the relationship between the main questions clearer, after talking about care given at the home, you could continue the interview by asking, "Does the staff focus mainly on physical health, or do they also pay attention to recreation and social life?"

RIVER AND CHANNEL

Though you want to obtain depth in a tree-and-branch interview, you are also interested in breadth, making sure that most of your main questions are asked of each interviewee. In contrast, you choose the river-and-channel pattern when you want to explore an idea, a concept, or an issue in great depth, following it wherever it goes. You might never get to some of the main questions, because you followed up on one of them and then continued by following up on the follow-ups rather than asking other main questions. It is as if you picked a channel of a river and traced it wherever it went. The river-and-channel model is most helpful when you want to explore one theme in depth and detail, want to understand it well, and are willing to focus on that issue to the exclusion of other themes. With this pattern each interview may end up examining different issues, but these issues usually speak to related themes.

Assume you are studying how government decisions get made when agencies disagree. You begin by asking as a main question about competition between agencies and learn that several disagree on how a job retraining program should be run. You decide this is an appropriate and illustrative case and follow up on that specific disagreement asking what happened, how it happened, whose interests were at stake, and how it was resolved. You have pursued that channel to its conclusion. In another interview you are told about a conflict over which agency should manage a housing program and once again follow up that issue in detail asking what happened, how it happened, whose interests were at stake, and how it was resolved. You might repeat this pattern several times, in each case pursuing one topic in detail while ignoring others. At the end of a series of interviews, you have collected a set of rich, albeit separate, examples that when seen together suggest broader reasons why agencies disagree. You may end up learning about domain conflicts (each agency thinks the work is their responsibility) or how funding conflicts are or are not resolved.

Preparing Conversational Guides

Responsive interviewing can be nerve-racking. During an interview you have to figure out not only what people are saying, but also what they mean, and then work out appropriate, thought-provoking follow-up questions. To handle the fear that you will not be able to think fast enough on your feet to do good interviews or that you might lose track of what you intended to ask, some qualitative researchers prepare *conversational guides*—protocols, jottings, question matrices/checklists, or outlines—that give guidance on what main questions to ask and of whom.

Once you are in an interview, having a conversational guide in hand does not necessarily mean that you should rely on it. On numerous occasions, we have shown up to the offices of people we were to interview with written questions in hand, only to find that after the initial greetings, the conversational partner dominated the conversation by discussing what was on his or her mind that he or she thought would be of interest to us (and the matters usually are). On a recent occasion, after a brief chat with Herb, his interviewee started talking about his thoughts on how and why the goals of his organization had to change. He went on for an hour and a half and only then asked Herb what Herb wanted to talk about. In these cases, prepared questions are tossed out the window or saved for use at a later time.

However, in many projects the initial interviews are intended to cover a set of reasonably standard topics and can be planned in advance—attempts to scope out what is going on in a subculture or how an organization works, or to find out what happened at different stages of a person's life, or how people were affected by the same historic events. In these circumstances, it is possible and wise to prepare an *interview protocol,* which is a written version of the main questions. A protocol is the most formal of the conversational guides and is written out in full in advance and as such can be shared with the conversational partners before the interview and, when necessary, submitted to institutional review boards.

Even with a formal interview protocol in hand, you can ignore it if the interview follows a different path. If the interviewee anticipates later questions in their earlier answers, you simply skip the later questions. Further, the questions you put on your protocol are not cast in concrete and are often changed as you learn of new, important matters about which you now want to ask all your other interviewees. For instance, in your initial protocol you may have one question about budgets of nonprofit organizations and in your first interview learn that there are major differences among operating budgets (paying basic salaries, lights, heat, rent), service budgets (helping clients with their problems or whatever it is the organization does), and policy or advocacy budgets (paying for work to change laws and regulations). These distinctions are probably important enough that you should revamp your protocol to make sure you include questions on each type of budget in later interviews.

How many of the questions on a research protocol need to be covered in an interview? Ideally, you would like to cover them all, but that rarely happens, especially if the interviewee is forthcoming. Failing to get through all your questions is not usually a cause for worry because it usually means you are receiving rich descriptions. If you have some important left-over questions, you either reschedule to continue the interview, or obtain the missing information from different conversational partners. In his study on community-based housing and economic development projects, Herb had three main questions on his protocol: one on how the project was chosen, one on community response to the project, and one on technical problems in implementation. When a conversational partner spent all the allotted interview time answering only one of these questions, Herb was not concerned, because he planned to talk with several dozen other people and could cover the other topics with them.

Though formal protocols have their advantages, there are times when you require a less formal guide. The simplest is a set of what we term *jottings*, because they are items that are just jotted down while observing a meeting or watching an event. These rough notes then suggest the questions that are later asked of the conversational partners.

Jottings are also kept during an interview to guide follow-up questions. It is bad form (perhaps bad manners) to interrupt a conversational partner, especially one who is on a roll, to ask a follow-up question. Instead, as the interviewee talks, jot down the follow-up question and then, when he or she is finished, ask it. Even though Herb usually records his interviews, he also takes notes, doing so in a steno book that has a line down the middle of the page. On the left side he writes down abbreviated versions of what the conversational partner has said (in case the recording device fails) and, more important, on the right side he jots down key words suggesting the follow-up questions that can be asked during that particular interview.

Written questions, whether formal or informal, are useful, but they can be distracting to a new interviewer. If you rely on them to suggest the next question rather than listening to what the conversational partner has just said and then adjusting the question to those comments, you may sound like you are repeating a rehearsed list rather than engaging in a conversation. To provide overall organization yet allow for spontaneous conversation, some researchers just make themselves a list of issues that they want to discuss with the interviewee but do not write out the wording of the questions. Herb used to tape these lists to the walls of his study and then copy the relevant parts before each interview; nowadays he keeps his checklist in a computer file.

Checklists change rapidly, especially during the earlier stages of a study. For example, Herb started his study of community development with a checklist that looked something like the following:

1. Descriptions of the community projects
2. Organizational history
3. Relationships with government

After a few interviews, Herb learned that the organizations he was studying received help from other community groups and joined with them to form coalitions to lobby. He also learned that the directors of these community groups had strong ideological beliefs about what should be done to improve communities. He modified his checklist by adding these three items:

4. Relationship with other community organizations
5. Coalitions
6. Philosophy (ideologies) of community development

Especially when you are not asking all your interviewees the same question—if, for example, they know different things or have seen different parts of a process—it can be very useful to write yourself a master checklist of what you need to find out and who is likely to know it. This list can then guide you in drawing up each particular interview. There may be several people who know one piece of information you are looking for but only one person who knows another piece you need. When you are interviewing the only person who knows something you need to find out, be sure and ask that question; if you do not get to some of the other questions, you know that there are other people you can ask. As you obtain particular pieces of information, you can check those items off your list. The matrix also provides a guide to what you need to learn and from whom.

In recent projects, rather than keep a huge matrix, Herb keeps a master list in his computer on which he writes down the topics and ideas to explore, logs whether or not he has done so, and notes with whom, among his various conversational partners, a particular issue should be raised. He updates this list regularly, checking off the pieces of information he has collected in sufficient depth, and adding any new items that he now feels should be discussed. Irene is a little less systematic and simply maintains an overall topic outline with major and minor points she wants to raise. She prepares a new outline for each interview after looking over prior interviews and background documents to find out what else she has to learn.

Using outlines to prepare for each interview, rather than a list of specific questions or a topic list, helps you distinguish between the main questions you plan to ask and possible examples that can be raised when needed to help stimulate discussion. You can use a main heading in the outline for each of your main questions and subheads for examples you could raise. Having this kind of backup is not only relaxing for the interviewer but also allows you to prepare both for interviewees who are more comfortable talking about broader issues first and those who prefer to begin by discussing specific matters.

The following excerpt from one of Herb's working outlines illustrates how they work. The roman numerals represent topics to be covered in main questions (but without proposed wording), the lowercase letters suggest either more focused questions or anticipated follow-up questions, and the arabic numerals offer specific examples to be used if the broader questions prove too abstract to stimulate conversation:

   I. Organizational problems
      A. Maintaining qualified staff with low salaries
         1. Ms. Jones, who just quit to work at a bank
      B. Working with a community board
         1. Scandal of board member getting priority on apartment
         2. Last fund-raising campaign
      C. Obtaining funds for basic organizational expenses

  II. Exemplary projects
      A. The facade improvement project (mentioned in report)
      B. The cooperative furniture factory

Before the interview, Herb prepared main questions for each of the roman numeral topics. For roman numeral II, for example, he prepared the following question: "Could you describe the most interesting (successful, least successful, controversial) project your organization has done?" From his prior interviews and documentary research, he knew that if the conversation floundered, he could prompt his interviewee to continue by mentioning specific examples such as the facade improvement project or furniture manufacturing cooperative that he had included in the outline.

Whether you use protocols, outlines, or checklists, the guide is a free-hand map to the conversation, pointing out the general direction but not specifying which nooks and crannies will be explored. Guides enable the researcher to balance the need for predictability with the freedom to explore unanticipated topics. Guides can help prevent getting lost in cascades of follow-up questions. Early in the project, the guide should be simple and reasonably short, lest you build in too many assumptions about what you want to learn.

Besides helping you structure the questions, the physical guide also acts as an interviewing prop. Holding a guide makes you look prepared, and you know what you want to learn. Giving a copy of the guide to the interviewees may reduce their anxiety, because they know they will not be asked questions they do not know how to answer. The downside of giving interviewees a guide beforehand is that they may race through the questions without giving the interviewer much chance to follow up.

Summary

This is the second of four chapters on conducting an interview. In the first, we argued that an interview is part of an evolving relationship. In this chapter, we discussed the three types of questions—main questions, follow-up questions, and probes—from which interviews are built and then suggested different ways that these questions could be combined in a formal interview. In the next two chapters we describe how to determine what to ask as main questions and as follow-up questions, indicate how to word these questions, and present illustrations of a wide variety of probes.

8

Designing Main
Questions and Probes

I nterviews are designed around a balance of main questions, follow-up questions, and probes. In this chapter we first describe ways to determine what the researcher should ask in the main questions to cover the overall research problem. We then suggest how to word these main questions so that the interviewee can answer them by drawing on his or her own experience. Next, we describe how to ask probes that encourage the conversational partner to provide needed detail to flesh out narratives and stories.

Main questions elicit the overall experiences and understandings of the conversational partner but might not provide the requisite depth to answer the research problem. Follow-up questions build on what the interviewee has said to get a better and deeper understanding of the interviewee's answers. In the next chapter we indicate how to determine when to ask follow-up questions and how to word them.

How to Formulate Main Questions

Usually, you cannot just pose your research problem to your conversational partners, because it is too abstract to elicit a meaningful answer. Only academic social scientists would understand what you mean if you asked whether resource dependence explained organizational decisions. Interviewees would have trouble answering a question about what makes their marriage work, because they may never have thought about it and do not really know the answer. Instead, you need to translate your research puzzle into one or several main questions that your interviewees can answer more easily based on their experiences. To explore resource dependence, you can ask organization leaders how they decide what the organization will do and listen to see if they are influenced by those providing the organization's funding. To find out what makes marriages work, you can question married couples about the activities they do as a couple, how they deal with conflicts, what they ask of each other and how reliably they get what they ask for, what expectations they had when they got married, and whether those expectations have been fulfilled. This handful of main questions that the interviewees can answer based on their own experiences provides the scaffolding for your interview.

You can move from your research problem to a specific set of main questions in two ways. With the first approach, you know enough about the topic to be sure that if you obtain certain specific information, you will be able to answer your research question. In this situation, to design the main questions, you note what information you need and then work out a main question to elicit each piece of this needed information. With the second approach, you have a research puzzle in mind, but you are not yet sure what specific information will help you resolve it. You do know, in general, what goes on in your research setting and can divide up what happens into specific activities or components. In this second approach you devise main questions to encourage the interviewee to discuss each of the separate activities or components. You listen for information in the answers that addresses your research question and then work out follow-up questions on those specific answers to provide the information needed to solve your research puzzle.

ASKING MAIN QUESTIONS TO OBTAIN THE INFORMATION YOU KNOW YOU NEED

When you know what information you need to answer your research puzzle, working out the main questions is straightforward. You create separate main questions that ask about each of the pieces of missing information. The pieces of information you are looking for might be as simple as who met with the mayor when the zoning map was prepared or as complex as outlining a whole series of activities or steps in a process that explains the research puzzle.

Suppose your research problem is "How can a local government knowingly run deficits when it is illegal to do so?" When Irene began to research this problem, she anticipated from her knowledge about local government that three pieces would be required to address this puzzle. The first relates to the word *knowingly*. To answer the research problem, she needed to know who knew about the deficits, and what they did when they discovered them. The second part of the puzzle concerns the question of illegality and the possible consequences for the participants. Did the participants know it was against the law to run deficits? Did they imagine that they could keep the deficits secret, or did they think that even if the deficits were made public that there would be no consequences? As the third part of the puzzle, she had to know how the participants viewed the fiscal problems they confronted, what alternatives they saw, and why they picked this option. These three issues were turned into a handful of main questions. When she put the answers together, she was able to figure out how a city could knowingly run deficits that are against the law (I. S. Rubin 1982).

But how do you figure out what pieces of information you need? To do so, you build on your background knowledge of the topic, as well as your understanding of the logic of the situation being examined. Recently Irene wondered, as her research puzzle, "Could government learn?" and to explore this broader topic decided to examine whether previous experience with budget deficits taught government officials how to handle them when they reoccurred. The logic of the research problem and her own knowledge of government suggested that the puzzle had two parts, each of which would lead to a main question. In the first, she explored whether current decision makers have access to prior organizational experience and learning, that is, is it even possible to learn from the past? Is information stored in the organization in some way that officials can get at? Second, she tried to learn how decisions are actually made and whether this information based on prior organizational experience is referred to and used. She argued that it is possible to learn from the past but wondered if officials actually did so. To answer the first part of the research puzzle, she worked out main questions to learn if elected officials and career bureaucrats remember what happened in the past, had access to documentation of past events, or knew someone who remembered the events. In wording the main questions that called up the conversational partners' experiences, she began by asking whether the interviewee recalled the budget cuts of the Reagan administration 20 years ago, if the interviewees kept up contacts with old-timers or retirees, or if there was a place in the organization where they could look up past reports or memos on the subject. To answer the second part of the research puzzle, she prepared main questions to track the ways in which decisions are currently being made, and as the interviewee answered these main questions, listened for steps in the process that sounded like reliance on past experience. When sufficient detail was not provided in the answers or puzzles still remained, she then hunted for these pieces of the research puzzle through follow-up questions (I. S. Rubin 2003).

ASKING ABOUT THE COMPONENTS OF THE BROADER SETTING

Sometimes you do not know the specific information required to answer your research question. If you worked out the initial main questions based only on your guesses, rather than on actual knowledge, you might unduly restrict what experiences the interviewees rely on in providing the answer. Rather than learning from the interviewees' experiences, you would be simply testing your own ideas and losing the opportunity to get outside your own preconceptions. How do you guide the interview but not limit the questions to those based only on your initial guesses?

While you might not know in detail what happens, based on your observations, reading, and preliminary interviews, you should have an idea of the overall types of activities that go on in the research setting and be able to work out a list of these activities and component parts. You might not know enough to ask about a cricket match, but you do know in sports that there are *teams* and *competition* and ways of *scoring*, and you can ask questions about each. In wording these kinds of main questions, you ask for descriptions of each of the component parts. You phrase these main questions so that they cover each of the separate components or activities in ways that slant the answers toward what you want to learn about your research puzzle. You listen carefully to the interviewee's response and extract any information suggestive of possible answers to your research puzzle. With this new information in hand, you then work out follow-up questions that focus in on those parts of the interviewee's answers that might shed light on your research puzzle.

For instance, suppose you are curious to learn how women's roles have changed over the last several generations. To ask for specific information based on your own ideas of how women's roles have changed would be to prejudge what those changes have been; at best, you would be posing questions about the past based on your present knowledge. You do not yet know enough to determine whether your ideas about what occurred are correct. However, you do know that people's lives occur in stages—childhood, school, marriage, raising families, working, retirement, and illness and death. You word the initial main questions around these important components of the life cycle. You start your interview with a statement mentioning that you are curious about how women's roles have changed and then ask a series of main questions about what happened during each stage of their lives. When your interviewees describe something that illustrates changing women's roles, you follow up to get more detail.

Or suppose your research question is how an organization that is now part of a multinational conglomerate has changed since being bought out.

If you were to work out main questions asking about ways you thought it had changed, you probably would hit on some important topics and receive meaningful answers, but you still might miss the perspectives of those involved. Alternatively, you can work out main questions on what you know in general that organizations do—recruitment of personnel, training, resource acquisition, budgeting, controlling production, marketing, and distribution. For each of these tasks, you can ask the interviewees to compare what they now do with what was done before being acquired. When you hear differences between the past and the present, you then can follow up to get more detail. In this way, you can explore your research question based on the conversational partners' understanding of the matter rather than your own preconceptions.

MAIN QUESTIONS BOTH EXPAND AND EVOLVE

Main questions are not determined once and for all at the beginning of your research. As you learn more about what is important to your interviewees, you add main questions regarding issues they have raised that you now know more specifically address your research concerns. On occasion, you discover that your initial main questions are so far off base that they need to be completely changed and then you need to reinterview individuals to ask these newer questions.

In his current project on how national support organizations help local groups improve the housing and economy in poor neighborhoods, Herb initially thought they did so through technical assistance and training and worked out main questions on these topics. He discovered from his preliminary interviews that the national organizations were now emphasizing their advocacy work to encourage government to provide more funds rather than their technical assistance to the individual neighborhoods. Herb changed focus, dropped main questions on training and technical assistance, and added some that focused on how these organizations carried out their advocacy activities. His overall research question of how the support organizations helped local groups remained in place, but his main questions changed to reflect what the organizations were actually doing.

Wording Main Questions

In responsive interviewing, the exact wording of a main question is not crucial so long as what you ask elicits the understandings and experiences of the interviewees in ways that speak to the research problem. At times, in asking main questions, especially when we were nervous, we fumbled for words rather than working out a clearly expressed question only to find that the mere mention of a topic—the Citibank Merger, the 2001 rescission—was sufficient to evoke a long, detailed, and thoughtful response from our interviewee.

Though fumbling happens, it is not the recommended procedure. With more precise wording you allow the interviewees the scope neces-sary to present their own experiences yet ensure that those experiences speak to your research topic.

SOME GENERAL PRINCIPLES FOR DEVELOPING MAIN QUESTIONS

First, make sure you give your interviewees the opportunity to answer as they see fit. Interviews normally begin with broad questions that are relatively easy to answer from the interviewees' experience and that do not box the interviewee into particular responses.

Be cautious about imposing your own understandings or examples in presenting a main question. Doing so is tempting, especially if the inter-viewee is not responding quickly and you want to provide examples to get the conversation going, but this approach limits the interviewee's freedom to respond. Suppose you are studying what families teach the young about dating and begin by asking a question that is framed in your own experiences: "When I was a kid, my grandmother always warned me how serious a mistake it would be to get pregnant before marriage. Did your relatives ever say things like that to you?" There are so many assumptions built into your wording that the interviewee would have a hard time fit-ting her own experiences into the answer. A better approach would be to ask if the interviewee had conversations with relatives about dating, and if the answer was yes, ask about what was said.

Second, most of the time, you should not pose your research problem directly to your interviewees. Instead, translate it into questions that are easier for interviewees to answer from their own experience. Rather than asking her research question, whether agencies responding to budget pressures cut away the basic resources necessary to carry out their work rather than eliminate waste (I. S. Rubin 2003), Irene worked out a set of main questions eliciting interviewees' descriptions of what happened when the budget was slashed. After she heard their first-hand descriptions and then asked some follow-up questions, Irene judged for herself whether what was cut was essential to the agency's work.

Another major principle is to avoid questions that encourage or allow a yes-or-no answer. For instance, if you ask, "Was your supervisor generally fair to you?" you might get a quick yes or no and then silence. A better wording might be "Could you describe your relationship with your supervisor over the time while you worked here?" There is no way to answer a question worded this way with a yes or no, and the interviewee is likely to look at the relationship from a number of angles, maybe including changes over time, giving you a richer reply.

A related principle is to avoid using the word *why* in main questions, even if you are interested in learning why something happened. People are comfortable talking about their experiences but often do not know how to respond to the more abstract question of why. Instead ask about their experiences and responses and from what you have heard work out the reasons why.

Try to avoid main questions that elicit opinions, at least until later in the interview. Early on, if you ask an opinion question, people will answer and then throughout the interview will try to be consistent with their response, even if they later think of contradictory instances or subtleties. Rather than ask, "In your opinion, has the organization improved since you began to work here?" you might ask, "What changes in the organization, if any, have you seen while you worked here?" If you feel you have to ask an evaluative question, try to hold off until near the end of the interview, after the interviewee has given you a range of examples and a variety of ideas. Or if you need to ask such a question early, word it in a balanced way that elicits both the good and bad. "What do you like most and least about your job?" is a better main question than "Tell me what you like best about your job."

FORMULATING THE MAIN
QUESTIONS SO INTERVIEWEES CAN RESPOND

You rarely present your research problem as a main question, because research problems tend to be phrased formally and often in academic jargon. You need to rework your research concern into a series of main questions that are answerable by your interviewees. Doing so requires using vocabulary, terms, and concepts that your interviewees recognize and phrasing matters in ways that encourage interviewees to answer based on their own experiences and perceptions. You learn the vocabulary through participant observation and reading newsletters or other documents and then ask general informants about details of the research setting with which you are not familiar. Before your formal interviews, you try out the questions on general informants and encourage them to tell you how they react to the way you have worded your questions.

Main questions should be answerable by interviewees in terms of their experiences and knowledge. How people grow old in America is a broad and difficult question, but asking individuals what changes aging has brought about in their lives may be a practical approach to eliciting answers to your research question. Main questions normally avoid asking about how other people think or feel. Querying a daughter on how she copes with her mother's aging is fine, but asking her how her mother feels is not.

Avoid using academic jargon in your questions, because it will seem mysterious to most interviewees. Suppose you are a sociologist studying teenagers' behavior and have worked out a research question on how *differential association* affects teenagers' choices of entertainment. Differential association is a sociological theory that argues that whatever groups people interact with most intensively influence their values. In exploring this research question, however, you would not go up to a 15-year-old and ask, "Could you explain how differential association affects your behavior?" Most 15-year-olds would not have any idea what you mean. Instead, you would ask your interviewee who he or she hangs out with, what he or she does with the group, and what group members think is a cool thing to do. If some of the teenagers report that they hang out with members of their church, they spend a lot of time in choir practice, and going on tour to sing would be cool, and others report that they hang out with older kids in the neighborhood, they spend a lot of time learning to hustle for cash, and think it would be cool to drive before they are of legal age, you would have a start to answering your initial research question without introducing the academic jargon.

WORDING BROAD-SCOPE MAIN QUESTIONS

A central principle in wording main questions is to start out broadly to help you learn more about the topic and then rework the questions as you learn more to come up with narrower and more specific inquiries. When you begin a project, you may need to discover what occurs in the research setting, learn about the overall background of a problem, or even find out the conceptual lenses through which your interviewees interpret their worlds. In such cases, you begin with a very broad initial main question to obtain the needed overview.

A major type of initiating main question is termed a *tour*, in which you suggest to your interviewees to act more or less as guides, walking you through their turf while pointing out what they think is important on the way. Tour questions are worded quite generally: "Could you *tell me* about what you *do here*?" or "Could you *step me* through this process?" (modified greatly from Spradley 1979). In beginning a study on how professors get grants for academic research, the tour question might be worded as follows: "Suppose I wanted to prepare a grant proposal, could you *step me through* how you do that?" Or if you wanted to know about teaching, you could ask, "Could you *tell me* how you prepare for class?"

Tour questions can also be a bit more focused. For example, you can use tour-type questions to make comparisons across time. A tour question in a study to compare how a university is cutting back now with what it had to do twenty years ago might begin with "Can you tell me what happened during the budget cutbacks in 1987?" followed by a parallel question for the present day. A broad tour question in a study of student life could be worded as "I'm interested in what students do at this university; could you tell me about a *typical day*?" A slightly narrower wording would be "Could you tell me what you did *yesterday*?" Such questions are intended to obtain an overview of what occurs within a given cultural arena.

After you have some general familiarity with the cultural arena, you might then ask more targeted tour questions to learn about specific events that you now feel are important for understanding the culture. These narrower tour questions are called *minitours*. In the student life example, you might ask, "Could you tell me what happens at a typical football game?" or "What is a typical frat party like?" A slightly different wording simply asks, "What happens?" "Could you describe *what happens* during a marriage ceremony [or a cricket match or a burial or a Thanksgiving meal]?" To medical people in a hospital, a tour question might be worded as "*What happens* once someone arrives in the emergency room?" Another phrase used in minitour questions is "How do you go about . . . ?" For instance, "How do you *go about* implementing a new law?" These minitours still allow the interviewee full discretion on what to describe, but they are focused on specific areas that the researcher feels are culturally important: sporting events for understanding student life or actions in the emergency room for learning about the culture of a hospital.

Tours are the most general way of wording an initiating main question, but many other broad opening questions can be used. For example, in early interviews in evaluation work, you might ask a broad question, such as "Overall, what has *been your experience* with this project or program?" Irene starts out her interviews on government contracting with the private sector by asking managers what their experiences have been with contracts. Doing so allows the interviewee sufficient scope to offer more or less positive examples. Or you can ask the interviewee what is important about a particular set of events. For example, in interviewing female principals, Chase asked about the highlights of the interviewee's work history and what the interviewee *saw as important* or *turning points* in her career (Chase 1995). With this approach, you ask the interviewees to point out what they consider crucial. These events or occurrences then suggest the follow-up questions for subsequent interviews. In addition, you might later ask what criteria the interviewees used to determine what was and was not important.

These broad initiating questions encourage the conversational partners to provide in an unfiltered way their own take on an issue and as such often evoke unexpected themes. When Herb asked his interviewees to provide a step-by-step description (i.e., a tour) of how their organization lobbied, he heard much that he already knew but also heard an unexpected theme, that organizations that all supported the same legislative proposals competed for who would get the credit for getting them passed. Because a broad tour question does not limit what the conversational partners can talk about, Herb's interviewees discussed their battles with their allies, an important part of their world. To Herb it was a new idea and suggested many questions he needed to ask other interviewees.

Another way of asking initial broad questions is to ask about *hypothetical examples*. Fine and Weis used a hypothetical example to begin a discussion about the difficulties faced by the poor in Buffalo: "If President Clinton were to come to Buffalo, what kinds of things should be dealt with here, and what specifically would you like him to do about it?" (Fine and Weis 1998, p. 29).

You can also try *comparison* or *contrast questions* by asking the interviewees to sort their experiences into opposites, such as the best and worst or the most favorite and least liked, and then immediately follow up by asking what made these experiences fall into one or the other extreme. Or you can ask the interviewee to compare two things, such as two pieces of legislation, two events, or two administrators or leaders, or ask for comparisons over time: "Can you tell me about the neighborhood that you live in now? How is it the same or different from the neighborhood that you grew up in?" (Fine and Weis 1998, p. 163).

MORE FOCUSED MAIN QUESTIONS

Many interviews begin with very broad questions and proceed to more focused ones. If the interviewer is already familiar with the setting or process being studied, he or she may begin with moderately focused questions. At this point you are working out the questions that are intended to get the particular information you need to answer the research question. Your wording has to be specific enough to get that information but still broad enough to allow the interviewee to describe what it is that he or she knows. As you learn what events or concepts describe the interviewee's world, you incorporate these into the wording of your questions. When you use words such as *tax-credit, affordable housing, rescission, reconciliation bill, tax expenditure,* or *plat* in your questions, community developers, budgeters, or planners quickly figure out that you are attuned to their world. When the researcher is clearly informed about an issue, the interviewee is more likely to provide the requisite detail.

You can ask *chronology questions* about what happened at a specific date, time, or season or when specific events took place. In oral histories, you ask what people *were doing* or how they *reacted to* (depending on your focus) well-known events. If you are trying to trace through a particular conflict, and you already have the chronology, you might want to find out about each step in detail. "*What happened* after the letter with the supposedly secret information was published?" "What happened when the mayor raised the issue at the city council meeting?" "What happened when you met privately with the mayor?"

Having discovered the stages of the process from either background reading or preliminary interviews, you then can ask more focused main questions on each stage. Such *stage questions* are often worded as "Could you tell me about what happened when . . .?" Life stages include childhood, education, dating and marriage, work, raising children, illness, and death. Careers may be divided into stages, finding and working with a mentor to learn the ropes, working up the ladder, dealing with competitors or rivals, becoming a supervisor, and easing toward retirement. With a stage question, you focus in on a time and then ask the interviewees what happened then.

Stage questions are versatile and are used in many studies. For example, scholars who examine public policy recognize that legislative bills go through an initial formulation, preliminary hearings, and markup sessions, and then are voted on by subcommittee, full committee and each house separately, and finally, there may be a conference to resolve differences between the bills passed in each house. In working out a series of focused main questions, you ask about each of these stages for the legislative proposal you are interested in. For instance, "I noticed that the conference committee dropped a key portion of the house bill. Can you tell me what happened?" You could work out similar questions for each stage, showing in the question that you saw (or learned about) the outcome and now want your interviewee to explain how it happened or what it meant to them.

When you have divided your research problem into separate parts, you need to make sure you have separate main questions for each part. In cultural studies, you learn from your initial broad questions, often tour questions, about important events, ceremonies, and icons that typify or illustrate cultural values. You now structure a series of more focused main questions to ask about each one. What happens at a wedding? What occurs during Lent?

As you go further into your project and have asked main questions that are intended to get the specific information you determined you need, you are building toward a tentative answer to your research problem. At this point, and not before, you might want to work out some fairly narrow and explicit *confirmatory* questions to find out how your interviewees react to your emerging interpretation or explanation.

In one project, Irene was trying to figure out why a city was running deficits even though doing so was illegal. She had done a lot of background reading and had conducted a number of exploratory interviews (with tour-type questions) to put together a sequence of events that preceded the deficit, including a tax reduction that restricted revenues and a labor strike that increased costs, each suggesting a tentative explanation. She then worked out a series of *confirmatory* main questions, each asking about one of these possible explanations for the deficit. In one question, she asked interviewees to provide narrative descriptions of how the tax reduction came about. In another she explored the labor settlement. Once she had obtained the narrative details, she then asked her interviewees what they thought the contribution of these two events was to creating the deficit. Note that her opinion question was asked late in the interviewing, after she had elicited the descriptions of each of the key events.

QUESTION WORDING CHANGES
IN RESPONSE TO THE INTERVIEWEE

When answering your questions, interviewees sometimes change the wording and answer their modified version rather than what you asked. Do not get frustrated if this happens. Most likely the interviewee is merely putting your question in his or her own language, something that you would have done if you had known how. At times, though, your conversational partner is intentionally rewording the main question to help you in a gentle, courteous way. Your interviewee might be telling you that you have misunderstood something or might be trying to answer a related but more meaningful question than you actually asked. A whole path of inquiry was opened for Herb when his conversational partner changed a question asking about how his organization "worked with" another group and started explaining how his organization "competed with" this other group.

Purpose and Wording of Probes

Main questions structure an interview by focusing on the substance of the research problem. Probes help you manage the conversation by regulating the length of answers and degree of detail, clarifying unclear sentences or phrases, filling in missing steps, and keeping the conversation on topic. They also help the researcher put together a narrative by placing what is said in order by date or time and by sorting out which answers are more dependable, less biased, and based on more credible evidence.

You create a warehouse of possible probes and then pick whichever ones you need at the moment. Probes can be verbal or nonverbal. Verbal probes are usually short and simple, such as "Could you tell me a little more about that?" and "Go on—this is great." Nonverbal probes include waiting a bit for the interviewee to continue talking, leaning forward to express interest, and busily taking notes in ways that signal the interviewee to keep talking.

MANAGING THE CONVERSATION

Probes help manage how interviewees answer questions. Some probes signal to the interviewees that they should expand on a point by providing richer, more detailed answers. Other probes gently steer conversational partners back to the topic when they veer too far off the subject.

Continuation Probes

A *continuation* probe encourages the interviewees to keep talking on the present subject. A continuation probe might involve little more than saying, "Mmm hmm. So . . ." or it might entail repeating part of what has just been said but with a questioning intonation. "You bought the ducks at an auction?" Or you can say, "Then what?" or "and . . . ?" and pause until the interviewee continues.

If the interviewee interrupts him- or herself, resulting in an incomplete thought, you can ask for a *completion* of that line of thought by summarizing or repeating part of the last sentence. "Before we talked about the strike, you were saying that the union was all absorbing. . . ." That invites either an explanation of "all absorbing" or a completion of the original thought. In the following example, MacCleod repeats the last phrase, but prefaces it with "what do you mean?"

Interviewee: At first, they [his parents] wanted me to be a lawyer. Ever since I went to Barnes. But there's no way I could do that. I need a job that has action. I need to be active. I couldn't sit behind a desk all week to make a living; that wouldn't be right.

Interviewer: What do you mean, it wouldn't be right? (MacLeod 1995, p. 77)

If you repeat the wrong part of the answer—maybe because you were startled or puzzled—you can steer the interview off course. For instance, a conversational partner had been detailing her problems with the welfare system by describing how welfare officials ignore bad parents.

Interviewee: And Division of Youth and Family Service don't even do nothing to them. And those are the ones they should investigate. But they don't do that. They always bother the ones who just made one mistake. And, you can't get rid of them. They follow you everywhere you go.

Interviewer: They follow them? (Fine and Weis 1998, p. 202)

The probe encouraged the interviewee to keep talking but redirected the conversation to the wrong part of the answer. The important part of the answer was the focus of the agency on the wrong parents, not the agency following people around. A better probe here would be "Just one mistake?"

If someone has answered by presenting a list and commented only on the first item, you probe for completion by asking, "How about the second item on your list?" Or if one has been omitted, you can ask, "We skipped the one about the bike ride; can we talk about that now?"

Elaboration Probes

Elaboration probes and continuation probes are a little different. Continuation probes ask the interviewee to keep going and you don't know where they will lead; by contrast, elaboration probes ask for more detail or explanation of a particular concept or theme that you selected from what the interviewee has said.

If someone makes a broad comment, such as "There is a lot of conflict around here," at that point you do not have enough information to formulate a focused follow-up question on a specific conflict or, for that matter, even know if you want to do so. Instead, you can use a continuation probe, maybe a bit of silence and a hand gesture, to say you would like to hear more. Another approach might be to ask for an elaboration: "Such as?" "Could you give me an example?" or "Can you tell me more about that?" You could say, "That sounds interesting, what can you tell me about those conflicts?" Elaboration probes elicit factual detail. Note the formulaic wording: "Such as . . . ?" "Could you give me an example?" "Can you tell me more about that?" and "What can you tell me about . . . ?" You can use these wordings almost anywhere, regardless of the content of the interview.

In the following example, the interviewer asks the interviewee to elaborate on one point in her answer. This specificity changes a continuation probe into an elaboration probe. In studying the childhood of poor people, Lois Fine was talking with Virginia:

Virginia: I grew up on Dodge and Rollers . . . in that neighborhood. There was always a gang around, but the difference that I noticed, in the same neighborhood today is the gangs—when we were growing up—had a tendency to take care of their turf, or their neighborhood and now the gangs don't. They have a tendency to just milk it for what it's worth.

Lois: Can you say more about that? What do you mean that the gangs took care of their neighborhood? (Fine and Weis 1998, p. 166)

"Can you say more about that?" is a standard continuation probe, but then the interviewer adds an elaboration probe, asking the interviewee to explain a particular point.

Another common way of getting people to elaborate is to ask for a story. "Hmm," you might say, "sounds like there is a story there." Or you could ask, "Maybe something else was going on . . . ?" Either encourages the interviewee to provide more explanatory detail.

Attention Probes

An *attention probe* is meant to let the interviewee know that you are listening carefully, which often encourages people to elaborate. As an attention probe, you can just look interested or say, "Okay, I understand" or "That is interesting." Another approach is to ask, "Can I quote you on that?" Whether or not you need permission, you are telling the interviewee, "I am listening intently, you phrased that point extremely well, and I would like to get it down and use it just the way you said it."

Clarification Probes

A clarification probe asks the interviewee to explain something that you simply did not follow, for example, to help clear up garbled grammar or ambiguous pronouns: "You said she did not want to go to a nursing home. Was that the social worker who said that or your mother?" A clarification probe might involve little more than looking puzzled and asking, "What?" or might involve saying, "Can you run that by me again—I am afraid I didn't follow it."

Clarification probes might involve checking up on specific important points. For instance, when an interviewee in a poor community had been complaining about the behavior of the police, given the racial sensitivities in poor neighborhoods, the interviewer asked a clarification probe: "White cop, black cop, both?" (Fine and Weis 1998, p. 34).

At times, a sequence of probes is required to be really sure of what is being said, as shown in this example of questioning about why poor people are not involved in neighborhood block clubs:

Interviewer: Do you belong to a block club?

Interviewee: The block club I won't join. I totally hate their views, I mean, they're like, "Get them out, kick their ass," just—

Interviewer: Who is saying "Get them out, kick their ass"?

Interviewee: Oh, people who live a few doors from me. And, they're very prejudiced.

Interviewer: So, they're white?

Interviewee: Yeah.

Interviewer: Whites want to kick out the blacks?

Interviewee: Exactly. It doesn't matter to them if they're good or bad. You know if they're renters or owners. They just want them out. (Fine and Weis 1998, p. 47)

Sometimes the technical vocabulary is unfamiliar, or the steps in a process may not be clearly outlined. When our colleague Jim asked a computer hacker how he got into a university computer, he got the following answer:

> They don't know their own system's security procedures, and we just got the book. We read it, and I ran it, and we got it. He saw us, I guess. We were using an ID of some guy whose account was canceled, and they asked who we were, but we were lucky and social-engineered it and he told me to get out, so I did. So we didn't do anything other than get in, ya know? But, that's what all we wanted.

Jim then used a clarification probe: "Could you run that one by me again? I am afraid I still don't understand how you did that."

Try to avoid asking too many clarification probes on technical issues, lest you sound hopelessly ignorant. When you do ask them, try to keep them unobtrusive, asking them almost in passing:

Interviewee: There were several RIFs [reductions in force], lots of continuing budget pressures. The I bureau . . .

Irene: I bureau? [*overspeaking*]

Interviewee: . . . Information Bureau was reinvented. But as they were doing it, they were hit with another budget cut. It is hard to plan. There are disincentives for public managers to doing long-range planning.

Steering Probes

Sometimes a conversation goes off track and you need a *steering probe* to lead back to the intended path. A simple steering probe is to say, "sorry, I distracted you with that question; you were talking about . . ." and fill in the blank with the topic just before you both got distracted. Once, Herb had engaged an interviewee in a conversation about a political battle in the Whittier community in Minneapolis. The interviewee got distracted when Herb mentioned a similar fight in an adjacent neighborhood, Farview. After listening for a bit, Herb interjected, "Sorry, I distracted you by asking about the tensions in the Farview neighborhood. Circle back a bit and let's explore what the tensions were in the fight over the park in Whittier." The steering probe both stopped the discussion on the Farview neighborhood and acted as a continuation probe on the problem in Whittier.

PROBES ASKED IN ANTICIPATION OF THE ANALYSIS

In addition to helping handle the mechanics of a conversation, probes are also used to obtain specific information that will help you later when you analyze what you have heard. *Sequence probes* are asked to put together events in proper order; *evidence probes* seek information to assist you in determining which version of an argument or whose answers to a question should be weighted more heavily; and *slant probes* provide clues about whose side your interviewee is on and how to interpret his or her answers.

Sequence Probe

With a *sequence probe,* such as "Could you tell me what happened step by step?" you learn the order of events, what came first and what came next. You ask sequence probes to help unravel causation, especially when interviewees seem to have blurred the ordering of events. For instance, in Irene's study of a city in financial trouble, managers blamed the unions, claiming the union's obstinacy created a costly contract settlement that contributed to the fiscal stress. To examine management's interpretation, Irene used a series of sequence probes, first asking when the budget initially showed a deficit, then when the union contracts were negotiated, and when additional salary and benefits came on line (I. S. Rubin 1982). When she added this material to information about management's strategy in the negotiations, she concluded that managers, responding to fiscal stress, tried to break the back of the unions, which then caused the unions to become more militant and demand larger salary increases rather than the union militancy causing the fiscal stress. Finding out the sequence suggested the cause.

Sometimes as a sequence probe you ask directly, "When did that happen?" but people's memories can fail on details, so don't push for a specific date if the interviewee hesitates. Instead, probe for other events that occurred around the same time, events that the interviewees or you can more readily date. Irene had heard three different dates as to when a budget innovation began. Using a sequence probe, Irene got one interviewee to remember that the innovation occurred just after he was hired, and of course, he remembered that date.

Evidence Probes

Because you may ask several people about the same issues and get different answers, when possible, you need to figure out whose answers you should lean on more heavily. Evidence probes ask about how a person knows and how they came to their conclusions.

Generally researchers give more weight to first-hand accounts and to answers that emerge from experience than to answers that come from general knowledge, newspaper stories, or narratives read or heard. Thus, one evidence probe is to ask how much first-hand experience interviewees have had on the subject. In an interview on cutbacks in government, you could ask something like this: "I know your office was involved in designing the layoffs. Did you personally have anything to do with it?" You can also ask questions, such as "Were you there at the meeting when he said that?" In the following example from Fine and Weis, the probe puts a screen on future answers so that the interviewer is hearing only about first-hand experiences:

Interviewer: You told me about the violence that you experienced when you were a child with your stepfather and your mother. Is there any other violence that you ever experienced personally?

Interviewee: Oh yeah, on the streets. Yeah; I've seen people shot. I've seen people pull the trigger, I mean that's as violent as you can get.

Interviewer: What are your reactions to these things? (Fine and Weis 1998, p. 63)

When we ask experience probes, we sometimes emphasize words such as *personally* or *you* to convey that we are interested in hearing about things the interviewees know first-hand.

To find out if your interviewees have evidence behind their generalizations, you politely ask for an example: "You said many of your clients come from multiproblem families. Could you give me an example?" Or you can delicately ask for evidence in other ways as well, such as "How did you find that out?"

Asking for an example is usually fairly straightforward. But if you are going to probe further, you have to do it delicately, because it is offensive to ask people to prove what they say. After hearing a generalization, you can ask, "What occurred that made you think that?" For instance, if a professor says, "Students are less well prepared than they used to be when they come to college," you probe by asking, "Do you have some specific instances in mind or are you speaking in general?" If someone tells you something that sounds incredible, you can laugh and say, "You must be joking; that is too wild to be true." That politely invites further evidence or a denial: "No, it's true; I saw it with my own eyes" or "Well, I exaggerated a little for effect." Another approach for obtaining evidence is to ask the interviewee to relay step-by-step what happened or what was said, almost as if he or she had recorded it. If a conversational partner tells you, "She told me to start looking for another job," you could ask, "What were her words, do you remember?" or "What did she say, exactly?"

Slant Probes

Slant probes help you determine the lenses through which people see and interpret their worlds. A labor organizer is likely to have a biased view toward management, whereas many in management can see no good whatsoever in labor. If interviewees present strong opinions without grounding them in experience, you should be suspicious that the answer may be biased. If you are getting a one-sided presentation, in which only weaknesses or only good points are mentioned, you have evidence of slant. Sometimes, however, slant is not that obvious and you need to explicitly check for it. In doing so, you do not want to sound as if you were charging the interviewees with something immoral or with being narrow-minded, so slant probes should be phrased gently. You might ask, "How did you feel about [the topic]?" or "Did [the event/person] make you angry?"

Sometimes the interviewee will make a strong statement indicative of an underlying slant or bias—"They hope that black folk will fail"—and pause for your response. A quizzical look or a quick "Really?" or "Is that so?" usually will encourage the person to continue and explain or justify his or her slant. A more explicit slant probe in this case could be "Are you saying that downtown really wants black folk to fail?" If the answer is still yes, then the interviewee's attitude toward downtown should probably be considered slanted, not necessarily wrong, just marked by a strong opinion that might shape other answers.

Our general advice on probes is that even though they are not difficult to word or to ask, you should not probe on everything, lest you focus too much on details and not enough on the main points. Too much probing interrupts the flow of answers, annoys interviewees, and may sound patronizing. You probably would not want to say, "Real good" after every answer, for example. Remember that good interviews usually consist of a balance between main questions, follow-ups, and probes. Even experienced interviewers sometimes use probes when a follow-up question would be better because probes are so easy. If you catch yourself doing this, try to cut back on your probes and listen harder to pick up the places you might want to follow up instead.

Conclusion

With main questions and probes, you should be able to get answers that together address the overall concerns of your research problem. The answers should be reasonably complete, clear, and on topic; you should also have a good idea of how much weight you should give each answer. What you have heard, however, may not be self-explanatory. It may raise new issues that you do not yet understand, or the answers may not provide enough context to figure out which concepts and themes are most important or how they go together. Getting this depth and understanding on the issues and ideas raised by interviewees is what you accomplish through follow-up questions. We describe how to follow up in the next chapter.

9

Preparing Follow-Up Questions

Y ou ask follow-up questions to get more depth and understanding about an idea, a concept, a theme, an event, or an issue suggested by the interviewees that you feel speaks to your research concerns. In addition, you follow up to make sure that your information is balanced and thorough. Follow-up questions also enable you to explore unanticipated responses and obtain nuanced answers when the initial response is too general, simplistic, or dogmatic. Some follow-up questions are worked out and asked during the same interview in which the topic of interest is mentioned. In addition, after an interview is finished, you carefully examine the transcript, figure out where else you could have followed up, and then pose these questions in subsequent interviews.

What to Follow Up During an Interview

You listen hard during an interview and when you hear oversimplifications, new ideas, or relevant stories, or if you notice that information has been omitted, you try to follow up on the spot. The key is recognizing these points in the interview as they happen.

OVERSIMPLIFICATIONS

You would follow up after hearing a superficial response to a main question or a summary statement that sounds too strong, too simple, or too broad. If you hear a conclusion, such as "Most of the time we can provide services more cheaply in-house than if we have to contract out with the private sector," you might feel that the comment is too broad and follow up by asking, "How can you do it more cheaply?" or "When might it be cheaper to contract with the private sector?" Or to obtain

173

more details, you would query, "Can you give me an example of when you had to contract with the private sector even though it was cheaper to perform the service in house?"

NEW IDEAS

If the interviewee introduces new ideas, unanticipated themes, or perspectives that contradict what you have concluded from other interviews, a follow-up is usually in order. In Irene's study on contracting, one interviewee answered a question about whether there were some functions that were inappropriate to contract out for by saying that it was wrong to contract for attorneys' services because of the possibility of conflict of interest; previous interviewees indicated that there was nothing for which it was appropriate to contract out. You might follow up this contradiction by pursuing the idea of a conflict of interest. You could ask, "Are there possible conflicts of interest with any other professional services, besides attorneys?" Or you could ask for examples: "Is that a hypothetical possibility, or have you actually heard of instances in which attorneys had conflicts of interest? If you know of some cases where this occurred, what can you tell me about them?"

MISSING INFORMATION

If a fact, event, or explanation appears to be intentionally omitted, or is only hinted at without being developed, you might want to follow up on the spot. Recognizing these missing pieces requires that you have already done background work on the topic. For example, in one of Irene's interviews, she asked a longtime city manager for reasons the budget process changed. He gave her a list of reasons, but omitted financial stress, an item often cited in the literature. Irene immediately followed up, saying, "I noticed you didn't mention fiscal stress as a reason." The manager responded that he omitted fiscal stress because city staff were always managing resource scarcity, so its presence did not change anything. His omission was intentional, and his explanation added a new theme to Irene's developing model, distinguishing between ongoing problems and episodic ones.

STORIES

Another cue to immediately follow up is when you hear a story that seems relevant to your research problem. You want to be sure that you fully understand the underlying theme and its implications. Stories are usually told to communicate a message but do so in an indirect way (see Boje 1991; Boje 1995). Stories may also provide particularly vivid arguments.

Before doing the follow-up, you have to recognize that a story has been told and then wait until it is completed before asking the question. Sometimes you know a story is coming if the interviewee either introduces it by saying, "Let me tell you a story about that" or begins by setting a scene as you would in a play. At other times, stories may be brief and told without preamble, so they are harder to pick out during the interview. In either case, to recognize a story, look or listen for the following:

1. Stories are told smoothly, with little fumbling or backtracking. The interviewees may have told them many times before, so they are familiar with their main lines.

2. Stories are often told as adventures, such as how my grandparents came from the old country without any money and started a business, or how when in Thailand Herb and Irene got, and got rid of, Teddy the Himalayan Black Bear.

3. Longer stories are carefully structured. They may begin with a time or place setting, introduce characters, describe some event or complexity, and then offer a resolution. Not every story has all these parts, but it would not be much of a story if it did not contain some buildup and a dramatic event.

4. Stories are often marked by haunting symbols or condensed, summary images that convey a great deal of emotion and multiple meanings.

5. Stories might be marked by a change in speaking tone. Short incomplete sentences are replaced by fully elaborated ideas, or the interviewee sits back, takes center stage, and begins a long description.

6. Sometimes the researcher asks a question and gets an extended response that seems not to speak to the question. The disjunction between question and response can be a clue that the interviewee is telling a story.

In one of Irene's interviews on how an agency was run, an informant started off with a story about his dissertation instead of responding to what Irene had just asked. The disjunction was so great, Irene felt that he had to be telling a story and that if she listened carefully enough, she would catch a theme. His story was about his failure to get a dissertation research award from the General Accounting Office (GAO) after being told that all applicants would receive one. But a couple of weeks later he was told he did not get it and when he asked around to find out why, he discovered that the topic of his dissertation was considered too risky for the agency.

He concluded the story by saying that the GAO was a cautious agency. The story enabled the interviewee to simultaneously make a criticism and provide evidence for it, while introducing a new concept and gently directing the researcher's attention to it. Irene followed up by exploring what was meant by *cautious agency* in more detail, to figure out the ways in which cautiousness was shown, and learn why some agencies were more cautious than others.

Preparing Follow-Up Questions for Later Interviews

Whether or not you ask follow-up questions during the interview, after the interview, you examine the transcripts to see what needs to be explored further. You look for where concepts need to be clarified and where the implications of themes need to be examined. In addition, you look for places where you lack sufficient information on ideas introduced by your interviewee and then follow up for thoroughness.

FOLLOWING UP ON CONCEPTS

By exploring in depth terms that interviewees routinely use to describe their world, you learn the central features, rules, goals, and values of the interviewees' lives and worlds. You begin by rereading interviews to see what terms are used and ideas implied that need further clarification. You note the technical words that were used or ordinary words that are used in a special way, ask yourself if knowing what they mean to your interviewees is important in answering your research question, and whether the word is used beyond what it ordinarily means, and if so, then work out a follow-up question. You can look up the literal meaning of a word such as *rescission* in a dictionary (or perhaps a text on public budgeting), but when you read the term in an interview transcript, the interviewee may use it in a way that implies more than the dictionary definition. You might then follow up to explore this additional meaning.

Sometimes your interviewee uses a phrase that sounds so common and ordinary that you do not immediately recognize that it might be an important concept. While interviewing about municipal budgets Irene heard the common phrase *the bottom line* but thought nothing of it at that time. When she reread her interview, however, it occurred to her that the phrase *the bottom line* is a business term, and as an accounting concept does not apply to government budgets. What is this private-sector term doing in the vocabulary, in the worldview, of public officials? This insight suggests working out two different series of follow-up questions. One approach would be to explore what the concept of the bottom line means in a public-sector organization. A second approach would be to look for other private-sector concepts that have been brought over into the public sector, and if you find them, examine how their meaning has changed.

As you look over the interviews you will also note concepts that the conversational partners did not explicitly label but that you now feel should be followed up. Often these ideas are mentioned in separate pieces scattered throughout the interview. For example, at different points in an interview, a wife might accuse her husband of not understanding her needs, failing to listen to her and later being careless with family money, and staying out late too often. On rereading the entire interview, you note that these separate ideas are related and label them *marital tensions*. You might then want to follow up to learn how serious these stressors are, or whether they are offset by sweet and attentive behavior.

Distinguishing Minor and Major Concepts

Though you might want to learn the meaning of each term your inter-viewees use, you do not have the time and they will become impatient. Before working out a follow-up, you have to determine whether the concept is a minor technical term (which you can look up on the Web or in a book) or an important clue to explaining a piece of the culture or providing a missing piece to the research puzzle.

Some technical concepts at first do not seem important, but when you inquire you discover that they are suggestive of broader ideas. If someone were to interview Irene about her cooking, they would be treated to terms such as *tortilladora* (a press for making tortillas) and entertained with the details of different food dehydrators. By themselves, these terms do not need clarification because they are simply descriptions of machines. But if you were to ask a follow-up question to Irene, for example, about when she got a dehydrator, or why she got such a big and expensive one, you would learn that this purchase was part of a response to a heart attack and a determination (Herb calls it an obsession) to eat healthy, tasty foods. Now you would know something important about Irene and the meaning of cooking in her life. Similarly, for firefighters, the term *looped main* is a technical matter meaning that water can get to places through two distinct paths. If you followed up on what this concept means, you would find that this term carries with it the idea of extra capacity in time of need, a kind of security blanket that responds to the anxiety of dealing continually with life and death issues.

How can you tell the difference between minor technical terms and ones that might help you unravel your research puzzle? One way is to look for patterns in your interviews. A second is to pay close attention to items that seem important to the interviewees, either by their cost (the food dehydrator, looping the water mains), by the efforts conversational partners take to get them or avoid them, or by the emotion evoked when they are mentioned.

Irene was interviewing a fellow cardiac patient about how the patient's husband was responding to her illness. One day her interviewee talked about getting her nails done weekly and said that her husband did not mind, despite the cost. Getting her nails done was not necessarily significant, but in context, it suggested to Irene that this woman's husband was indulging her, not watching the pennies, that he knew and accepted how sick she was and wanted to please her in any way he could. There were two concepts here that should be followed up: One was the acceptance of the severity of illness, and the second was indulgence. The indulgence concept was apparent because it was part of a pattern that occurred in the other interviews with the same person.

Though sorting out important concepts can be difficult, sometimes they leap out at you. For instance, when our colleague Jim was interviewing in a prison, in response to a main question about prison life, a prisoner explained that boredom was his worst problem. Jim followed up:

Jim: What kinds of things do you do in prison that keep you from becoming bored?

Prisoner: You can join gangs, play chess with your cellie, go to the [exercise] yard, drink, join the JayCees, get into the education program, or just lay around your cell watching TV, if you don't have a [job] assignment.

Startled, Jim probed for clarification.

Jim: Uh, "drink?" Did you say "drink?"

Prisoner: Yeah [*laughs*]. Drink. You know, drink.

Jim: As in "drink, drink?" Like . . .

Prisoner: As in drink, booze, hooch, firewater, joy-juice, alcohol, ya know?

Jim: [*laughs*]

Prisoner: Got news for ya. Anything you can get on the outside, we can get in here.

The concept of drinking alcohol inside a prison stood out not only because it was startling, but because of the effort needed to get that alcohol in a prison.

FOLLOWING UP ON THEMES

As you go over your initial interviews you see what themes have been presented but not explained in any detail. These call for follow-up questions. A theme may indicate how people feel, such as people are tense about the wedding ceremony or the new legislative proposals have made housing activists wary. Other themes offer explanations for why something occurs: Because of White House pressure, budget agencies are distorting their performance reports. Themes show how two or more concepts are related: Holding a wedding ceremony increases tension. Pressure from the White House (pressure is the concept), *causes* agencies to distort their performance reports (distortion is the concept).

Sometimes you can pick up on themes during the interview, but just as with concepts, they are easier to see as you examine your interviews afterward. In the following case, Irene followed up immediately on a theme (and even though asking "why?" is usually not a good approach, in this case no harm resulted).

Irene: Why did these [budgeting] changes take place?

Pat: A budget crunch hit in the late 1960s, and private sector people on the council said they handle problems like that with industrial engineering. As we got into it, it became clear that we also needed to look at effectiveness, not just efficiency. PPB [program planning budgeting system] was the rage in the late 1960s, we picked it up.

Irene: You were not one of the five-five-five cities, were you?

Pat: No [*he lists one or two that he can remember, and Irene adds one*]. A lot of this comes out of national trends. We picked up ZBB [zero-based budgeting] when the federal government did. Council members asked us if we did it.

Labor relations contributed to the adoption of the MBO [management by objectives] portion. Also, it was a national trend. We had had unions, but it was the mid-1970s before we recognized them and bargained collectively. We passed a meet and confer. With that, executive salaries were becoming tied to the union negotiations, putting caps on increases. "Why aren't you controlling the executives' salaries?" they asked. The answer was pay for performance. Managers will get from 0 to 10% increase based on performance, to justify the executives salaries.

In this exchange, the themes are expressed directly in answers to the main question with some repeated in several contexts: The city picked up planning programming budgeting systems because it was the rage in the 1960s, adopted zero-based budgeting when the federal government did, and adopted management by objectives because it was a national trend. The interviewee goes so far as to say, "A lot of this was based on national trends," offering his own summary of multiple examples. The analyst would have to be asleep while reading the interview to miss this statement of the theme of following trends. There are also unexpected subthemes, such as that management salaries increased because of the union pressure to increase the salaries of rank-and-file members, and that increased managerial salaries in turn created pressures to cap the managerial increases or justify them in terms of performance. In later interviews each of these themes was explored further to obtain needed depth.

Sometimes you recognize a theme because the interviewee virtually shouts it out. During one interview Irene was asking about how collusion occurs in contracting but instead of an answer on collusion she got the following: "There is a significant amount of corruption that simply lacks exposure. Worker compensation scams/corruption in police (including correctional offices at the state level) and firefighters are examples." Analysis of this passage suggests the idea that there is a lot of corruption in everyday events where no one is looking for it, suggesting to Irene what she should explore in more detail.

When you are exploring a particular theme, you first try to clarify what it means, perhaps by asking for examples: "Can you think of any other everyday corruption besides worker compensation scams?" You continue by making sure you understand the terms within the theme and then how the concepts mentioned relate to one another. In the example, the key terms are corruption and exposure. After you are sure you understand what was meant by each term, you might want to explore how they are related and follow up even further: Do some forms of corruption get a lot of exposure and others only a little or none? What is it about corruption that gets attention? If there were more exposure, would there be less corruption? Is it the commonness of the corruption that makes it relatively invisible? Exactly how does this relationship work, as the interviewee sees it?

Once you understand what the theme implies, you explore how solid the evidence is for it: "Did you run across these scams when you were a court administrator (in other words, is what you are telling me based on first-hand experience)?" Sometimes you can ask directly, "What led you to that conclusion?" or "What makes you say that?" If the interviewee can deal with a mildly confrontational question, you can ask, "How could anyone know how much of this type of corruption there is, if it truly lacks exposure?"

Finally, you can work out questions to examine the limits of the generalizability of the theme: "What conditions do you see that decrease or increase the amount of everyday corruption? Have you ever worked in a place where the level of everyday corruption was low?" If the answer is yes, then follow up again with "What were the circumstances that limited the amount of corruption in that case?" Note that it would be inappropriate to ask the interviewee whether his or her model applies everywhere, because he or she could not possibly know the answer from first-hand experience, but if the interviewee has worked in more than one place, you can ask him or her to compare the level of corruption in both places. If you are going to ask these follow-up questions of different people than those whose interviews suggested the theme initially, you need to find out first if they agree that there is everyday corruption. Sometimes one interviewee sees something that others do not or that others are unwilling to talk about.

Example: Following Up on Themes

Suppose you were interviewing doctors about compliance, that is, whether and when patients follow their doctors' recommendations. You have already asked your interviewees for reasons they think that some patients do not take their medications regularly. Some of the doctors tell you that the medicines have side effects that vary from annoying to serious, and that patients stop taking the medicine to avoid these side effects. To explore how this theme of side effects causing cessation of taking medicine is understood by doctors, you could ask what they mean by serious side effects and what types of side effects cause patients to stop taking medicines.

If you wanted more evidence in support of this theme, you would ask questions about how doctors discover that patients have stopped taking their medicine, or whether there are ways for patients

(Continued)

(Continued)

to report on side effects. If it turns out that there is no systematic way for doctors to know about minor side effects or failure to take medicines, you would have to question the evidentiary base for their generalizations.

To check out how generally the theme extended, you might question about overcompliance, patients who do what the doctors say, regardless of whether it makes sense, for example, if the medicines are making them dizzy or nauseated or not making them feel better. Or you could ask about other reasons that patients do not comply with physicians' recommendations. You could talk to a variety of doctors who have poorer or richer patients, or sicker or healthier ones, and see if they give the same explanations for lack of compliance.

Following up themes often requires a sequence of questions, where what you ask next depends on what you just heard. You can prepare the initial follow-up question, but where the interview goes after that is not predictable. Suppose in an evaluation project you were interviewing people in a poor community about what changes in primary health care occurred after a new clinic opened (that is, you begin with a comparison main question). The interviewees tell you they now go to the clinic rather than visiting the emergency room at the hospital, suggesting the theme that the new clinic causes a decrease in emergency room use. You would want to explore this answer since reducing emergency use was the hoped-for effect of the new clinic.

Because you know what the key terms mean, your first follow-up might be to explore mechanism: "*How* did the new clinic reduce emergency room use?" You can ask a general question comparing the service they used to get at the emergency room with the service they get at the clinic, and maybe follow up that answer with specific inquiries on whether the clinic's long hours or free medicines have been helpful. Or you could ask for more detailed comparisons, such as "Was the service quicker at the clinic than at the hospital?" or "Are the nurses friendlier at the clinic than in the hospital emergency room?" Keep in mind that you can work out these follow-up questions only if you have background knowledge of the clinic's operations, including the free medicine and the long hours of operation.

Following up on themes that speak to your research questions is vital, but you need not follow up on every theme you hear and do not fully understand. Suppose you are interviewing students about life in the dorms, and find out that loud music on the floor is a particular problem. In their answers, interviewees may mention particular vocalists or musical groups. You probably would not follow up and ask about the music students listen to, lest you lose the thread of the interview that is focusing on problems in the dorm. Instead, you could ask how people accommodate to loud music by inquiring if students have a place to go to study when the dorms get noisy, or if there are rules against loud music. You can ask if the rules are enforced, or what happens if a student reports the loud music to a dorm employee. Follow-up questions must lead you closer to answering your research problem.

FOLLOWING UP FOR THOROUGHNESS

Thoroughness does not require asking about everything; it means you do not leave major threads hanging, ideas incomplete, or key terms undefined or unexplained, or fail to figure out the mechanism that explains the themes. Thoroughness requires exploring alternative explanations and material that challenges your preconceptions. It means filling in key blanks, missing information, missing steps in an argument, or missing events in a sequence. What seems missing will differ from study to study, but following are some suggestions on what you might hear that would indicate that a follow-up question is required.

Partial Narratives and Stories Referred to Only Briefly

You follow up when a narrative is incomplete, for instance, when you have heard only one side of a fight or if important steps seem to be missing. If in an interview a city official brags about how he or she lured a mall to the town, you might want to ask whose idea it was initially, whether subsidies were provided, and what negotiations occurred with the mall developers, and then find out if there was any opposition.

Sometimes interviewees refer to a story, perhaps giving it a label, but do not actually tell you the story. If the story seems to speak to an emerging theme, you almost certainly have to follow up for the missing story. Maybe you have been interviewing about how the mayor deals with developers and in passing your conversational partner mentions "the envelope under the table." What envelope under the table? What is the story here to which the interviewee is referring? Was there a payoff? Is the mayor on the take?

Ambivalence

When interviewees express marked ambivalence, there is often a not-yet-tapped explanation underlying the ambivalence. In Herb's early interviews, community developers sometimes said that protest actions were terrific and sometimes said that they were highly problematic. Herb followed up by asking when protests were appropriate and when they caused more harm than good and by doing so learned how carefully advocacy strategies were worked out.

Terms Mentioned but Not Defined

Sometimes interviewees use unusual or suggestive terms, or change the terms you have used, but then do not explain any further. In one interview, Irene asked the interviewee if he felt there was collusion among possible bidders for contracts to provide services for cities. The interviewee said no, but that there was *enhanced standing*, leaving the term undefined and requiring Irene to follow up to learn what it meant. She found that *enhanced standing* was short hand for saying that local firms with a good track record had a marked advantage in the bidding process.

Terms Defined but Without Examples or Explanation

Frequently terms that appear to be significant are used without details or examples, strongly suggesting a follow-up. In one of Irene's interviews in Washington, the interviewee offered the following term and definition: "We created the deficit *lock box* at this table! The deficit reduction trust fund. It was an accounting gimmick." The interviewee defined the term *lock box* as a deficit reduction trust fund, but without examples Irene could not understand what it meant. The interviewee claimed—with apparent pride—the deficit lock box was created right here at this table, but then suggested that it was an accounting gimmick, which made it sound like something that you would not want to brag about. To make any sense out of this, she had to follow up to ask for more details on what *lock box* meant. She found out that some budget reforms are more symbolic than real, an important theme in her work.

Concepts Implied but Not Stated

Sometimes an interviewee implies a concept without stating it, inviting a follow-up question. In the following example, the researcher had been diszcussing how earmarked funds, money targeted for a given purpose, affected the workload of a government agency: "They [the fees] are *earmarked* at INS [Immigration and Naturalization Service]. If the relationship between the fees and workload is reliable, it's okay, but it is not always. What is the advantage of doing it *this way or that way*? It is unknown territory. We need to move into it." The phrase *this way or that way* suggests that there are other as yet unnamed ways of handling the problem of linking fees to workload but does not specify what these might be. You would follow up to find out about these unnamed techniques by asking, "How could the relationship between workload and fees be improved?" or "What are some of the other ways of doing it besides the way it is being done right now?"

The Missing Middle

It seems easier for most interviewees to describe continua by pointing out what is on each end rather than talking about the murk in the middle. People often contrast free enterprise and government control, ignoring that many, perhaps most, cases are in between. To explore this murky middle you ask about in-between cases, such as a regulated industry or a private firm that has received special tax advantages.

Questions Not Answered or Answered Evasively

As you review the interviews, you will note places where you received only partial answers to what you felt were important questions, especially on controversial matters. You usually want to follow up but have to figure out a way of doing so that is not offensive.

From previous interviews Herb learned that some of the housing organizations he was studying wanted programs only for the extremely poor, whereas other organizations lobbied for programs that helped the lower-income working class. One interviewee mentioned without providing any explanation that these rival organizations had joined together in a coalition to lobby for a major bill. Herb wondered how the ideological gaps were bridged:

Herb: How, how do I put this? There's no nice way of putting it. You have people in that coalition who have, are targeting at very different income levels.

Interviewee: Yeah. It was actually a lengthy structured debate about that and a compromise of which the, the final position was one that came out of a process of compromise. Um, but there were certainly people, uh, organizations that

> were more interested in the more moderate income, and people more on the low-income side.

Herb: Um, hmm.

Interviewee: And there were also divisions on the issue, uh, which was also, uh, resolved about what extent is this new production, to what extent is it preservation.

Herb: Um, hmm.

Interviewee: Or is it a mix, and what's the mix? And, uh, those were two sort of major things which got thrashed out I think satisfactorily.

The interviewee acknowledges the differences between the groups and indicates that there were some compromises but still does not give a clue to what those compromises were. This lack of detail (from a usually forthcoming conversational partner) made Herb suspicious that there was an interesting story, so Herb followed up by asking people from the different organizations to describe the negotiations and learned from each why certain concessions had been made.

Wording Follow-Up Questions

Wording follow-up questions takes some practice, because the phrasing depends on exactly what the interviewee said. In this section we provide some guidance and illustrative patterns on how to begin until you work out your own approach.

SOME PRINCIPLES IN WORDING FOLLOW-UP QUESTIONS

The wording of follow-up questions should directly reflect the content of what the interviewees have said. When you follow up during an interview, you summarize what has just been said and then ask your specific question. When you follow up in a later interview, you include in that question a précis of that part of the previous conversation that stimulated the follow-up. To inquire about information missing from a previous interview, Irene worded her follow-up question like this: "You said last time that you prepared some material to help fight back against the cuts. What did you prepare?"

Wording of follow-up questions should indicate that you not only heard the words said by your conversational partner but were also aware of their emotional content. As the following example shows, it is easy to follow up on the words that were expressed but harder to follow up on the feelings:

Interviewer: How did you feel when your father died?

Interviewee: I was really torn up. Really bad. I couldn't sleep for a few days, missed a few weeks of classes, and I cried constantly.

Interviewer: Has anybody else in your family died in the past few years?

The follow-up question sounds logical, but it ignores the pain in the previous reply, so it comes across as almost callous. At the same time, the interviewer fails to explore the evolving theme of the consequences and management of grieving. Better follow-up questions would stay closer to the material. The question "Did you have anyone to talk to about what you were feeling?" shows empathy while encouraging the person to elaborate on the concept of grieving.

In follow-up questions, try to avoid using the word *why* in your query when you are trying to figure out a cause. *Why* is the proper English word, but it is so abstract that interviewees may have trouble answering. Indirect questions may work better. For example, you could ask, "Did you ever figure out what led up to the fight?" (meaning: why did the fight occur?) or "What contributed to the increase in the deficit?" (meaning: why was there an increase in the size of the deficit?). Asking "When you quit your job, what pushed you over the edge?" is equivalent to asking why you left your job, but avoids the word *why*. Possible phrases to substitute for the word *why* include (but are not limited to) *what influenced, what caused, what contributed to,* and *what shaped* something you are interested in.

Example: Suggesting a Reason Instead of Asking "Why?"

One way of avoiding asking people why directly is to suggest a reason yourself and invite interviewees to discuss your suggestion. The following excerpt from one of Irene's interviews shows how this can be done. The subject is a proposal to turn the Patent and Trademark Office (PTO) into a performance-based organization (PBO), that is, transform it from a tax-funded government agency into a more independent organization that operates like a business, charging fees for

(Continued)

(Continued)

> services. The interviewee explained that the Patent and Trademark Office, which is located in the Department of Commerce, was trying to become more independent of the department when the opportunity to be designated a performance-based organization came along.
>
> *Interviewee:* The Patent Office already had a proposal to encourage a government corporation. When the PBO idea came along, we took PTO organization into it and folded it in. It was the furthest along. They had done a NAPA [National Academy of Public Administration] study, etc. It was easy to fold in, draft in, add a CFO [chief financial officer], and performance standards and bonuses.
>
> *Irene:* And, incidentally, that would keep PTO in the [Commerce] department.
>
> *Interviewee:* Even as a corporation, it would stay in the department.
>
> The follow-up question (which was worded as an incomplete declarative sentence) *suggested a reason why* the Department of Commerce supported the idea of a performance-based organization, namely, that the department would still have some control over a performance-based organization but would have very little if any over a corporation, if that were the outcome. The interviewee was invited to agree or disagree with this reason; at this point in the interview, he disagreed, but later he agreed that keeping the Patent and Trademark Office in the Department of Commerce was part of the department's PBO strategy.

Another approach to asking why without doing so directly is to search for causal statements in the interviewee's comments—for example, "He hit her because he was so insecure" or "They cut our budget because they thought we were playing partisan games"—and then follow up by proposing alternative reasons and asking the interviewee to react to them, for example, by suggesting, "Maybe she goaded him sometimes about the fact that he wasn't bringing in any money" or "Maybe another reason was that your agency represented a big chunk of the budget and they could not get enough money unless they cut your agency."

You choose the level of directness and challenge that matches the stage of the interview relationship, the depth of answers you are already getting, and the sensitivity of the subject. You want to make sure that you do not stress the interviewee with your question. At the extreme you can leave the option of answering to the interviewee. For instance, on learning that an organization was in financial trouble, Herb followed up with this question: "If this is too stressful, don't answer, but what happened when you did not have the money to meet the payroll?"

In general, the more trust that has been built up in the interview relationship, the easier it is to word a follow-up question in a direct way. Herb had heard that Chestnut, an advocacy organization, was bad-mouthing another organization that Herb was studying, and yet the two were coordinating efforts. With a conversational partner with whom Herb felt particularly comfortable, Herb asked this follow-up question directly: "Chestnut has a reputation of being hard to work with, yet I've noticed you are working with Chestnut on this issue. How is that working out?"

A relatively gentle way of following up on sensitive material is to *throw out the rabbit*. The phrase describes a form of sermon in African American churches. Throwing out the rabbit involves a series of non-threatening follow-up questions that allude to sensitive subject matter without directly asking about it. By doing this, you indicate that you are interested in the matter but are not pressing for an answer. As an example, one of Herb's conversational partners who is usually forthright was skirting the issue of his organization's relationship with his community's city council member. Herb, suspecting that he had accidentally touched on something sensitive, changed his questioning pattern and began to throw out the rabbit. Each time the conversational partner mentioned city participation in any neighborhood project—tree planting, a stop sign, a shopping center, and so on—Herb followed up with a question on what the city council person did. Each time, Herb got a short, direct answer with little detail. Herb was patient and continued to ask about the city council person's role on different projects, without pushing for the detail that the interviewee seemed reluctant to provide. Later the conversation turned to how this community group dealt with zoning cases. This time, without Herb having to ask, the conversational partner explained that the council member was infuriated with the community group because by contesting controversial zoning cases, the community organization made it more difficult for the official to collect bribes for fixing the outcomes. The reason for the interviewee's stress and the brief answers became apparent without Herb having to push or ask why. The rabbit was caught.

Asking follow-up questions about inconsistencies you have heard requires a gentle, nonthreatening approach. One way is to include in the wording an option that reconciles the apparently inconsistent statements: "You mentioned that Mr. B retired, but I had heard that he was fired. Do you think he retired in anticipation of being fired?" Alternatively, you can suggest that the two themes sound contradictory, and ask the interviewee to explain if in practice they were as contradictory as they sounded in the interview.

A different approach is required when following up a story. First, patience is required not to ask a question too soon, as interviewees usually have invested a fair amount of emotion in the stories they tell, and so it is important to them to get the story out completely. Follow-up occurs, if at all, only after a story is finished and then only cautiously. You rarely want to follow up on the factual content of a story by asking, "Is it true?" or "Did it happen that way?" Instead, you focus on what the story means to the interviewee, what he or she is trying to say in this indirect, but vivid way. At the same time, though, you cannot ask directly what the story is about, because that sounds as if you were not listening. Instead, you word the follow-up question in a way that shows that you accept the premises of the story and then ask about the implications of what was said for the interviewee. For example, after a story about a heart attack, you can ask, "How did that heart attack change your life?"

If you suspect that your interviewee is being overly formalistic or offering a too simplistic gloss on the matter, being a *little* confrontational in your wording might work. If an interviewee offers a theme or explanation that seems too broad, you present situations in which the explanation does not hold and ask for comments. Sometimes you can explore a controversial point in more detail, disagree with what the interviewee has said, or offer alternative explanations. If it seems appropriate, you can even question the evidence they have used. When using these more confrontational approaches, you must be confident that your interviewee is comfortable with this kind of give-and-take and enjoys arguing with you.

PATTERNS IN WORDING FOLLOW-UP QUESTIONS

Novice interviewers are often anxious about whether they can come up with a decently worded follow-up question in a timely fashion. With experience, doing so becomes second nature, but it helps to have some patterns in mind for wording questions quickly.

Comparison

Asking interviewees to compare two things they have talked about is a common approach in wording follow-up questions: "How would you compare your old job with your current one?" You question about similarities and differences, or ask for a description of what something was like at some point in the past compared to right now. You may want to know if a later event is similar to an earlier one or if a problem (like loud music in the dorms) seems to be getting worse or better.

Making the Question More Specific

Follow-up questions obtain more detail by pointing out what seems to be missing. Suppose you asked, "How did the federal deficit get so big in such a short time?" The interviewee might respond, "Well, the short answer is we increased spending and taxes didn't keep up." The answer is too general to be useful because there are too many ways this result could have occurred. Possible follow-up questions include asking about both sides of the budget equation, the expenditures and the tax revenues, to find out why expenditures increased and why revenue failed to keep pace. You might ask first about which programs experienced faster spending growth, and then continue to follow up to see what factors contributed to the growth of these programs. You can ask about how closely revenue follows the growth and slowdown of the economy, or whether there were changes in tax policy that reduced revenues. These narrower follow-up questions encourage the interviewee to provide more detail yet do not excessively curtail the answers that can be given.

Another way of focusing a follow-up question is to ask about each of the stages described in the answer to your main question. For instance, in Herb's work, developers describe leveraging, that is, taking a small amount of initial money for a project and using these funds to encourage business, government, and foundations to ante up more money. He needed to follow up to clarify what this important process entailed and from several interviews figured out that leveraging took place in four stages: (1) coming up with the initial project, (2) selling the idea to a supportive funder, (3) getting the public sector to be willing to absorb a gap, and (4) going to conventional funders, such as banks, with a project when the rest of the funding was in place. Each stage suggested at least one follow-up question. For example, for the first phase Herb asked, "How did you come up with the idea for the project?" for the second phase, "What about the idea attracted the funder?" and so on.

Making the Question More General

Sometimes the initial answer is so specific that it ignores a broader implication, so in your follow-up you address this broader issue. For example, as his conversational partner narrated his work experiences MacLeod heard a specific incident:

Frankie: I went in like a dockperson y'know, just unloading trucks and I ended up doin' pretty well. It was a friend of a friend that helped me out. I ended up going from a dockworker to a shipper to a material control specialist. I was sittin' on a computer all fucking day.

MacLeod's major research concern in this study of working-class inner-city people was the possibility of career mobility. Rather than asking about the specific job Frankie held, MacLeod proposed a broader follow-up—"Tell me about how you were able to move up"—which better focused in on his research interests (MacLeod 1995, p. 164).

Asking About Implied or Actual Contradictions

In a discussion about the rapidly growing deficit, an interviewee said, "We increased spending" in the active voice, but "Revenues didn't keep up," which is passive, implying no one did it—it just happened. If you think your interviewee can handle a bit of confrontation, you would ask, "Wasn't there a tax reduction about this time?" The follow-up question gently calls attention to a possible contradiction, suggesting that the deficit may have been a matter of policy rather than something that just happened, as the interviewee implied.

Irene was interviewing an official in an agency whose budget had been deeply cut. He spent 15 minutes describing all the impacts of these cuts, and then he said, "We [his office] haven't been touched; we are scheduled for an increase in staff." Irene, recognizing that this felt like a contradiction because she knew there was a hiring freeze, as her follow-up asked, "If you can't hire new staff, how can you expand?" He answered, "We try to lure people from other parts of the agency to transfer into our office." That answer opened up a new line of inquiry, about how an agency adapts to a changing mission when its total number of staff is fixed and about what incentives are available to lure able members from one unit or program to another.

Keep in mind that you need background knowledge to word follow-up questions well. The contradiction between the active and passive voice became apparent only because the interviewer knew that there was a tax cut at the time when the deficit was growing so rapidly. In the second example, Irene had known from reading documents that there was a hiring freeze, so that the expansion of one unit sounded difficult if not impossible to carry off.

Exceptions to the Rule

When you hear an interviewee draw a conclusion or make a generalization (state a theme), you want to follow up to find out the conditions under which this generalization holds. A simple wording might be "As far as you know, does it always happen like that?" Another approach involves asking for exceptions and asking more about them. Suppose you were interviewing about marital relations and the interviewee concluded, "I just think women are less likely to throw the machine against the wall when they can't get it started." You could follow up by asking for the exception: "Is there anything, in your experience, that makes women really mad, mad enough maybe to throw something?" Once you heard an exception to the rule, you could follow up to find out what makes the exception different.

Following Up Hints

The easiest follow-up questions to word are those that respond to hints presented by the interviewees. When interviewees allude to a matter but do not spell it out, they are often inviting you to follow up. When Wilson was conducting a study to find out why employers reject hires from a particular housing project, one employer told him, "If somebody gave me their address, uh, Cabrini Green, I might unavoidably have some concerns." That wording just about begs the interviewer to ask about those concerns. Wilson jumped to the bait, asking, "What would your concerns be?" (Wilson 1996, p. 114).

More generally, if an interviewee presents a theme or conclusion in a negative fashion, such as "Goya was not the painter of those pictures," the natural follow-up would be "Then who was?" The interviewee may not know, but has undoubtedly given the matter some thought, and will usually volunteer his or her ideas on the subject. Normally when someone says something did not happen or did not happen in a particular way, they are leaving an opening to ask, "Well then, how did it happen?"

Devil's Advocate and Challenge Questions

A somewhat more provocative way of exploring a theme or conclusion offered by the interviewee is to challenge it. You can challenge it in a variety of ways: by offering alternative and somewhat contradictory conclusions or mechanisms and asking for comment, by questioning the evidence underlying the theme or its generalizability, or by suggesting conflicts with other things the interviewee said.

A reasonably gentle way of challenging is to ask permission to play the devil's advocate. In doing so you are explicitly requesting the interviewee's permission to argue against the evidence, yet implying that the interviewee's case is strong enough to withstand the challenge: "You've said that banks are not loaning enough money because they are antiblack. Well, let me play the devil's advocate: Perhaps the banks are discriminating because they don't want to do business with the poor and blacks tend to be poorer?" This wording allows you to argue against the interviewee's claim of racism without sounding hostile by asking him or her to refute arguments others could make. Devil's-advocate follow-up questions often encourage the conversational partner to detail the reasoning behind the original statement: "It is race rather than class because the banks do loan money in poor white neighborhoods."

You can, of course, present challenging questions without mentioning the words *devil's advocate*. For example, you could ask, "How would you respond if someone suggested that banks don't make loans in black neighborhoods because there is a higher incidence of fires?" Or by putting the question in someone else's mouth, you can ask the question without sounding hostile. For example, on the bank loan matter you might follow up by stating something like this: "The *Chicago Tribune* argued in an editorial that the crime rates were higher in the black neighborhoods so investment is lower. How would you respond to that kind of argument?"

Missing Items

Wording questions to help you find missing material is usually easy. If you were interviewing about how a coup took place in a democratic country and the interviewee told you that a military unit attacked the presidential palace unexpectedly one night, killed the president, and then declared their general the new leader of the country, you might ask, "What about the media—did the military take control of the newspapers, radio, and television?"

Getting Past a Party Line

Follow-up questions are essential but difficult to word when you are getting a party line or a formally approved answer without any depth or spontaneity. One way to express these follow-up questions is to indicate what you already know, to make it appear useless to stonewall you any further. For example, when Irene was interviewing in a government personnel agency, she was getting only an official version from upper-level administrators. She then mentioned that she had been interviewing leaders of the union who had presented their picture, one that belied the official line, and that she would like the administrator's response. Her wording was "Look, I have one side of this argument already; I can go ahead with that, but I really would prefer to hear your side as well, and go forward with a more balanced view." The result was a much more informed explanation that got past the official version.

Asking What It Means

Sometimes you are following up to learn what a term or a concept means. Asking "What do you mean by [the term]?" may get you a brief definition when you want a longer and more thoughtful explanation. Our colleague Jim Thomas, when confronted with a slew of technical terms, focused on the one concept that seemed the most promising and asked the interviewee, a young hacker, to explain it so that those in the broader public would understand:

Jim:	You said earlier that you were "hacking" last night. What did you do?
Interviewee:	I was running numbers, you know, wardialing 288s, and got a couple of hits. So I cracked into a local dialup, found a PBX and hacked into one of 'em and tried one of 'em. I got in, and ran one and hit. A Unix system. After a few tries, I got root, set myself up, logged out, then hacked out a coupla more. . . .
Jim:	Now, if you were talking to a reporter, say somebody from the *New York Times* like John Markoff [co-author of *The Hacker Crackdown*], how would you explain to him, so he could explain to the public, what running numbers means?

To get the broader explanation, Jim asked the interviewee to imagine an audience that was interested but not at all knowledgeable. Similarly, David Hummon asked a hypothetical question about the concept of the small town: "Suppose you had a relative who never lived in a small town and who was about to move to a small town. If he or she wrote you and asked what small towns are like in general, what would you respond?" (Hummon 1990, p. 189). Another possibility is to ask what thoughts the term evokes in the interviewee's mind. Balshem used this type of follow-up to excellent effect to learn what cancer meant:

Balshem: When I say cancer, what does it make you think of?

Answer: Oh, God, I have this terrible thought of cancer—it's like this great big thing that's eating up the whole insides. This big black thing. I just think of it as black. This big black thing that just goes along like a Pac-man gobbling up your insides . . . The movie *The Blob*, remember the blob would eat up stuff and kept getting bigger and bigger? Well, that's kind of how I think of cancer. The great big blob of stuff that keeps increasing. (Balshem 1991, p. 158)

About 25 years ago, in a very influential book called *The Ethnographic Interview,* James Spradley introduced specific questioning patterns to explore cultural concepts. One of the patterns he suggests is termed a *coverage question,* meant to help distinguish closely related concepts from each other. For instance, when Herb was trying to figure out what the term *intermediary* meant, he asked, "Is the MacArthur Foundation an intermediary?" The answer was no. Then he asked, "Is the Local Initiatives Support Foundation an intermediary?" The answer was yes. Then Herb asked whether the City Housing Partnership was an intermediary. Some responded yes, some no. Then by asking further follow-up questions that compared characteristics of the organizations that were, were not, and were maybe intermediaries, Herb figured out what intermediary meant to his interviewees. Another way of clarifying the meaning of a term is to ask an interviewee to compare two overlapping terms. For instance, Stephen Groce studied copy and original performance musicians and asked them to describe the differences between musical artists and entertainers (Groce 1989, p. 397).

Example: How Does a House Differ From a Stop Sign?

Herb knew from previous research that protest activists used the concept of empowerment to describe any victory over government. For instance, getting the city to install a needed stop sign created empowerment. In a later study of development activists, he felt that the term was being used quite differently. Rather than ask, "What do you mean by empowerment?" which might elicit an abstract, text-book-type answer, Herb asked the interviewee, who previously had been a protest activist, to compare empowerment in the older way the term had been used with the newer way that those building homes seemed to be using the term.

Herb: How does a house really differ from a stop sign in the empowerment sense?

Interviewee: It is bigger, for one thing. And, it impacts people, I think, in a different way. I think quite honestly, [if] people have a decent place to live, to go home [to] every day, their ability to deal with every other issue that's out there is greatly increased. I don't have to worry about where I am going to live, what I am going to pay for rent—I can move onto that next step and worry about a whole lot of other things. If they got the stop sign and they are still worried about where to live, that stop sign doesn't take them to the next step. You know, it is a self-actualization thing. You take care of your most basic needs and then you can move on to the secondary level, up the ladder.

To hear how a term is used, you can request the interviewee to describe when else he or she would use the word. For example, the researcher might say, "You've described partnering on the school project—which of your other projects involve partnering?" Then the researcher could explore what partnering meant in each of these other examples.

To get the richness required, you may want to follow up with questions on each component of a theme or term. Suppose you were conducting a cultural study of academics and picked up the term *professional success.*

You probe for examples and hear different concepts such as recognition, changing a paradigm, promotion, citation in major journals, invitations to attend foreign conferences, and other measures of professional success. To work out the full meaning of the overall concept of professional success you follow up with questions about each of the component ideas, asking, for instance, "What do you have to do to get a promotion?" or "How do you know if someone has changed a paradigm?" Then in your analysis you bring these ideas together.

Another strategy for clarifying a concept is to question about the opposite of the idea you are following up. If interviewees frequently refer to a positive concept, a good teacher, a pious person, or quality housing, you might want to check what a bad teacher, an impious person, or poor-quality housing is. A good teacher might differ from a bad teacher in that the former shows concern about the students. That response suggests an additional follow-up question to learn what concern means and how teachers show they are concerned.

Asking for Minitours

If you conclude from your first set of interviews that you might find evidence about a theme from learning more about what happened at an event, you can follow up with a request for a minitour of that event. For instance, in the preliminary analysis of his current project, Herb worked out a tentative theme indicating that activists are torn between wanting to attack government regulators for not punishing banks that discriminate and desiring to work with the same regulators to force the banks to cease discriminating. Herb noticed that regulators with whom this hate-love relationship was occurring showed up at the meetings of activist organizations to discuss government programs. To find out more about this cross-pressure, he asked his conversational partners to describe (provide a minitour of) what happened at the meetings at which the regulators were present.

Is My Idea Right?

A further way to check out your emerging themes is to present them directly to your interviewees and ask how they respond. You only do this after you have completed many interviews, have several tentative themes in mind, and are confident that your relationship with the interviewee is solid enough that he or she will feel free to tell you if you are off base. For example, in the following excerpt, a police officer has just described how he became a municipal police officer. The interviewer was stunned that her tentative conclusion that family history encourages people to make a career out of policing was not mentioned, so she asked the interviewee about her idea directly.

Interviewer: Any family members or role models that encouraged you?

Interviewee: Absolutely not. I'm the first one in law enforcement in my family.

Interviewer: That's amazing. Usually there's someone out there.

Interviewee: No uncles, no friends. In fact I was on my way to some-place else and I got stuck along the way. (Moody and Musheno 1997)

Sequence

In trying to determine why something has happened, you work out questions that unravel matters backwards in time. Your follow-up questions ask step by step what happened before the event—the fight, the attack, the meeting—that you assume might have led to the events or feelings that the interviewees are now describing. When Irene was studying the effect of President Reagan's budget cuts on federal agencies, she noticed that her interviewees seemed almost paranoid about the way the cuts would be administered and wondered about this anticipatory dread. She suspected some past event had taught professional staff to fear the politicians and so asked follow-up questions about the interviewees' prior experiences with cutback. She learned that President Reagan's attacks on the bureaucracy reminded many of the agency staffers of times when President Nixon made partisan, personal, and anti-Semitic attacks on the bureaucracy a decade earlier. Asking about the past elicited the depth that made the present fears understandable (I. S. Rubin 1985). You can word such questions in a number of ways: "Have you experienced anything like this before?" or "What happened that time?"

Conclusion

In the last two chapters, we presented a variety of ways of wording main questions, follow-up questions, and probes. These wordings are options, not rules that must be carried out to get a good interview. Improvisation often works as well as following established patterns.

Main questions encourage the conversational partner to expound on *your* research concerns, by providing *their* experiences and perspectives. Through the choice of main questions, you make sure that by the end of the project you have the data you need to answer your research problem. Main questions are prepared in advance of an interview, though they change as the project progresses.

Probes help manage the conversation to ensure you get the depth, detail, and evidence that you need without unduly interrupting the flow of what the interviewee is saying. Probes can help keep the conversation on topic and will elicit the information you need to put together the pieces of a puzzle from separate interviews.

Follow-up questions *pursue concepts and themes that are introduced by the conversational partners* and frequently take the interviewer off in new directions. Follow-up questions provide an element of unpredictability to qualitative interviews that can be unnerving but also exciting. Most important, the information obtained from the follow-up questions helps achieve the goals of responsive interviewing: to arrive at new interpretations, achieve a deep understanding and rich narrative, and present strong and vivid evidence for what you conclude.

Taken together, these three kinds of questions bring about the thoroughness that is one of the hallmarks of responsive interviewing. Main questions are worded to cover the whole research problem; probes ensure that unclear answers are explained and questions are fully answered; and follow-up questions ensure that missing or implied information is tracked down, that contradictions are addressed if not resolved, that alternative explanations are examined, and that you learn about all sides of an argument and different perspectives on an event.

10

The First Phase of Analysis

Preparing Transcripts and Coding Data

*D*ata analysis is the process of moving from raw interviews to evidence-based interpretations that are the foundation for published reports. Analysis entails classifying, comparing, weighing, and combining material from the interviews to extract the meaning and implications, to reveal patterns, or to stitch together descriptions of events into a coherent narrative. Researchers construct from this analysis informed, vivid, and nuanced reports that reflect what the interviewees have said and that answer the research question. Though the analysis is based on the descriptions presented by the interviewees, the interpretations in the final reports are those of the researcher.

Analysis in the responsive interviewing model proceeds in two phases. In the first, you prepare transcripts; find, refine, and elaborate concepts, themes, and events; and then code the interviews to be able to retrieve what the interviewees have said about the identified concepts, themes, and events. In the second phase several paths are followed. You can compare concepts and themes across the interviews or combine separate events to formulate a description of the setting. In doing so, you seek to answer your research question in ways that allow you to draw broader theoretical conclusions. In this chapter, we describe the first phase of analysis, focusing on data preparation. In the next, we discuss how you pull out the descriptive narratives and work toward theory.

Guiding Characteristics of Data Analysis in Responsive Interviewing

In the responsive interviewing model, data analysis has several guiding characteristics.

NALYSIS OCCURS THROUGHOUT THE RESEARCH

Analysis begins early on when you examine the first few interviews to make sure your project makes sense and concerns matters important to your conversational partners. As you complete each interview, you examine its content to see what you have now learned and what you still need to find out. Based on this ongoing analysis, you then modify main questions and prepare your follow-up questions to pursue emerging ideas. When you are done interviewing, you then examine all the interviews together to pull out coherent and consistent descriptions, themes, and theories that speak to your research question.

QUALITATIVE DATA ANALYSIS IS NOT ABOUT COUNTING

Qualitative analysis is not about mere counting or providing numeric summaries. Instead, the objective is to discover variation, portray shades of meaning, and examine complexity. The goals of the analysis are to reflect the complexity of human interaction by portraying it in the words of the interviewees and through actual events and to make that complexity understandable to others.

INTUITION AND MEMORY DO NOT
SUBSTITUTE FOR SYSTEMATIC EXAMINATION

In conducting depth interview research, you will immerse yourself in the data collection and ongoing analysis for months, sometimes years, before beginning the final analysis. With this intensive involvement you develop a sense of what the data are saying and that sense is important and represents a good starting point for the final analysis. However, memory can be flawed and selective and what you think was said months before is *not* a substitute for careful examination of the actual transcribed words of the conversational partners. Analysis involves systematic coding and extracting of information from the transcripts rather than looking for confirmation of your initial ideas.

THE DATA UNIT IN QUALITATIVE WORK
IS AN EXCHANGE ON A SINGLE SUBJECT

In analysis, the comments made during an interview are broken down into *data units*, blocks of information that are examined together. Part of the analysis is in determining the appropriate data units, as they differ depending on what precisely is being analyzed. Data units describing events might take up several pages, whereas a quick explication of a concept might be placed in a small, phrase-length data unit. Data units can consist of a chain of follow-up questions and their answers that inquire on the same matter.

You can break down the same interview text into several interlaced data units. You would treat in its entirety a long paragraph describing part of the battle with the mayor as a single data unit detailing that event. That same paragraph might include a sentence describing the arrogance of the mayor and then later the sense of frustration of the citizens. Each of these individual sentences within the larger data unit would itself be treated as a data unit, the former describing the concept of arrogance, the latter the concept of citizen frustration. This single paragraph would contain three separate data units.

DATA UNITS ARE COMBINED IN DISTINCT
WAYS DEPENDING ON THE RESEARCH PURPOSE

Part of analysis involves combining data units on the same topic, both within single interviews and across the entire set of interviews. To figure out what a specific concept means, you look at all the data units where that concept is discussed and then bring together in one file the separate definitions, examples, and refinements. In working out what caused an event to occur, you examine and weigh the data units from separate interviews in which the conversational partners talk about the occurrence.

Anticipating Final Analysis:
Transcripts, Memos, and Summaries

No one can remember the content of multiple interviews over months or years, so researchers make permanent records of their interviews through either notes or recordings. If you take notes, you must type them up immediately; if you record the interview, you need to *transcribe* the recording, that is, listen to it and type what was said. Some interviewers just take notes from their recordings, but most prepare a full written version of their interviews.

Depending on their intended use (and the skill and effort of the researcher), transcripts differ in their precision. The most precise get down on paper exactly what was said, including grammatical errors, digressions, abrupt changes of focus, profanity, exclamations, and other indications of mood such as laughter or tears. Precise transcriptions include stalling words such as *um* and *ah* and spell words the way they are pronounced, such as "ol' boy networks" instead of "old boy networks." Silences, pauses, and hesitations are indicated (often in brackets). For those analyzing the use of language or monitoring psychological responses, the length of pauses is indicated in the transcript (Psathas 1995). Transcriptions also include events that interrupt the interview, such as when an interviewee answers the phone (see Poland 2002).

For most projects, transcripts do not need to be this perfect. Herb includes a lot of "uhmms" and "ahhs" but Irene puts in only a few to indicate the flavor. Rather than marking the length of a pause, she is more likely to put a statement in brackets, such as "[interviewee took his time thinking about this one]." We put into the transcript only the level of detail we are likely to analyze and include any information that might influence the interpretation, such as laughter or gestures of emphasis or puzzlement. If you transcribe the interviews yourself shortly after you have done them, you may remember important physical gestures, for example, a shrug of the shoulders, and you should try to include that gesture on the transcript.

Whatever the level of precision of the transcript, you need to be clear on the distinction between what the interviewees said and what you interpreted or summarized. If you are taking notes rather than recording, you need to mark in the text when you are quoting the interviewee exactly and when you are summarizing what you heard.

Creating a typed transcript from a conversation is laborious and requires your full attention. Going from recording to typed version is easier if you use a transcribing device operated by a foot pedal so you can stop and start the recording while keeping both hands on the keyboard. The more often you hear the recording, the more likely you are to type an accurate version. If, after listening several times, you still cannot figure out what was said, you should note in the transcript that something was unclear.

Voice recognition software is not yet able to transcribe interviews for you. It works for notes that you have dictated yourself, because you can teach the software to recognize your pronunciation, but the software cannot yet recognize different voices and accents. For the time being, you have to transcribe the interviews yourself or hire someone else to type them for you.

Transcribing the interviews yourself forces you to pay attention to what interviewees said and helps you prepare for the next interview. If you do not have the time, you may be able to get someone else to do the transcription for you; you then read the transcript before designing the next interview. The downside of having someone else type the transcription is that the person listening to the recording of the interview was not there, does not know the names of people or places mentioned on the transcript, and cannot fill in from memory parts that are inaudible. You have to go over transcripts done by others carefully to make sure that they have not introduced major mistakes.

While doing transcriptions, or reading transcriptions done by others, you should write down thoughts that occur to you in a memo file. You can jot a memo on any possibly relevant thought that is triggered by particular interviews. For example, one passage in an interview may make you think about a book or article you read or suggest a future research question; another may remind you of what you heard a week before in a totally different setting. Early in a project, memos suggest reformulations of research questions; a little later, they deal with the concepts, themes, and events you will ask more about. You can also include in your memos comments on how well you felt the interview went, as well as whatever bias or slant you detected on reading the answers. Toward the end of the project, your memos increasingly contain ideas on what themes and concepts to include in the final analysis and write-up (see McCormack 2000a; McCormack 2000b).

If a single quote suggests a theme, you put that quote in your memo, perhaps in a separate *notable quote* file. In a study done years ago, Herb was interviewing to learn about the work of economic development practitioners, people who are paid to bring new businesses to a city or county. After chatting for over an hour with Herb, one practitioner leaned back in his chair and summarized his comments with the pithy phrase "What we do is *shoot anything that flies; claim anything that falls.*" Herb put that quote in a notable quote memo and translated it into a theme that he asked about later on in more detail—that economic development professionals claimed credit for any project that seemed to succeed because real victories were far and few between (H. J. Rubin 1988b).

Whenever a good quote catches your ear, you should include it in your memos, follow up to determine its meaning in later interviews, and then use it to help you look for relationships between themes during the final analysis of the data. Such notable quotes are easy to recognize because they are well phrased, sum up hours of conversation, or provide a moral to a story. Some notable quotes seem to provide a direct answer to the research question. For example, during his project on community renewal, one of Herb's interviewees told a story, with this conclusion: "Well, the funder said to me, 'Lois, that was a really bad business decision 'cause that house, you could have made money . . .' and I said, 'I know that. And if I were in this to do business . . . I could make a lot of money for the organization . . .' But, I said, 'That's not what we're here for.'" (H. J. Rubin 2000, p. 21).

This quote suggested to Herb the theme that it was important for community developers to help poor people rather than simply make money for their organizations. He put this quote into a notable quote memo, followed up on it, and then used it as a central theme in his write-up.

When you have finished typing your transcription, you then write a summary of the contents of the interview. The summary should contain the name (or the pseudonym) of the interviewee, the time and location of the interview, the reasons the interviewee was included in the study, and how long the interview lasted (see Miles and Huberman 1994, p. 53). It then includes the main points made during the interview that address the research question and whatever concepts or themes that you have identified. To write a good summary, ask yourself what the central points are of each answer and in particular which ones are new, which support what you have already learned, and which modify your ideas. For example, after noting the time and place, the position held by the interviewee, and the fact that conversation was held in a private office, Irene summarized the content of one of her interviews as follows: "Interviewee argues that contracts for attorney services are different from other contracts because of the possibility of conflicts of interest if the attorney is also working for other towns in the area. This is a lesser concern with other professional contracts."

These summaries help guide your later analysis when you are comparing what was said across the separate interviews.

Beginning of Analysis

The first thing to do after preparing a transcript and updating your memos and summaries is to make multiple copies. Keep the original interview on your personal computer and make a copy to mark up for analysis. Print a hard copy to store in a different location and make backups on floppies, Zip disks, or CDs. You may want to maintain the original physical recordings, at least until the analysis is complete, unless there are confidentiality issues that require you to erase them immediately. If you have promised interviewees confidentiality, you may need to keep hard copies and recordings in locked file cabinets and password protect material on your computer.

With transcriptions, summaries, and memos in hand, you begin the analysis. During the data collection, you read every interview carefully before preparing the next one. As a result, you have a working idea of what important concepts, themes, and events are present. As you do the analysis, you examine these concepts, themes, and events across different interviews to combine the material into a coherent whole that portrays a culture, suggests solutions to policy problems, or describes what happened and what it means.

Analysis proceeds in several stages that often overlap. The first stage is *recognition,* in which you find the concepts, themes, events, and topical markers in your interviews. A *concept* is a word or term that represents an idea important to your research problem; *themes* are summary statements and explanations of what is going on; *events* are occurrences that have taken place (a public meeting, a battle in the letters-to-the-editors column); and *topical markers* are names of places, people, organizations, pets, numbers—such as dates, addresses, or legislative bills—or public laws. Physical artifacts can also operate as topical markers. Topical markers are not important by themselves but instead provide hooks that tie separate parts of a narrative together. If you are studying how people lobby, you might follow a particular bill that would be mentioned in the interviews with a specific legislative number that becomes the topical marker.

Next, you systematically examine the different interviews to *clarify* what is meant by specific concepts and themes and *synthesize* different versions of events to put together your understanding of the overall narrative. As you refine the meaning of each concept or more precisely state a theme, you will almost always think of other parallel ideas; learning what your interviewees mean by an *honest politician* forces you to work out what is meant by a *crooked politician.* As you clarify and synthesize ideas that are present, you generate new concepts and themes by *elaboration.*

After you find, refine, elaborate, and integrate your concepts and themes, you begin to *code* them, that is, figure out a brief label to designate each and then mark in the interview text where the concepts, themes, events or topical markers are found. Coding involves systematically labeling concepts, themes, events, and topical markers so that you can readily retrieve and examine all of the data units that refer to the same subject across all your interviews. Coding for events and topical markers is easy: Every time an interviewee refers to the events of 9/11, you mark that passage with the numbers *9/11.* Concepts and themes may be more troublesome, because to code them you need a precise definition to be able to recognize when they are present, especially if they are not explicitly mentioned by an exact name.

The distinct label you use for each concept, theme, event, or topical marker is termed a *code.* The overall relationship between the codes is called a coding structure. Thought is required to match your codes and coding structure to the purpose of your study. If you were coding tales about animals, you might set up individual coding categories for each animal: dog, cat, sheep, cow, goat, and horse. But if the purpose of the study is to examine how people conceive of animals, you might want to group animals in coding categories that reflect how interviewees see them, for example, as pets or as commercial animals. If the purpose is to learn how they are treated for scientific purposes, you might group them and set up codes such as *more like humans* and *less like humans.* For this type of analysis, you might not need the labels *dog, cat, sheep, cow, goat,* and *horse* at all.

The decisions the researcher makes when coding largely shape what he or she will be able to conclude during the analysis. If a researcher does not have a label for stress, he or she will not be able to develop themes based on stress. If the researcher does not have a category for animals more like humans, he or she will not be able to explain the choice of laboratory animals for experiments.

After you physically code the interviews by marking each data unit with the chosen labels, you *sort* the data by grouping all of the data units with the same label into a single computer file. Within this file you then can look for how the concept was seen overall, and then examine for nuances, that is, for subtle differences in the way the concept was used, or you can explore what an event meant to different participants, or you can look for systematic similarities and differences between groups of interviewees on the same concept, theme, or event.

How you approach the final stage of analysis in a cultural study differs from the tack taken with topical research. In the analysis of cultural data, the *final synthesis* involves combining the concepts to suggest how the overall culture operates. You might first describe how secrecy and confidentiality in an organization are taught and enforced and then work out a theme showing that, in the culture of the organization, studied secrecy and confidentiality together make sharing information difficult. In topical studies, in the last stage of analysis, you put together an overall evaluation of a policy or program or construct a description of events that have occurred and then explain how and why. In studying a failed organization, you might conclude from information in several interviews that the organization died because of corruption at the top levels, and then from examining other interviews put together why this corruption was allowed to persist unchecked.

RECOGNIZING, REFINING, DEFINING, AND ELABORATING

Once all of your interviews are in computer files, you look for the individual concepts, themes, events, and topical markers that speak to your research question and place an appropriately chosen label next to each data unit to allow you to retrieve the coded item. You cannot code for everything that is in your data, nor would you want to. Instead you look for those items that are most important for understanding your research topic by looking for those that you have already noted in your memo file or those that are suggested by published literature and speak to your research concerns. As you code according to these preexisting categories, you remain alert to other ideas that you might have missed and as they appear add them to your coding structure.

LOOKING FOR CONCEPTS AND
THEMES SUGGESTED IN THE LITERATURE

You can get ideas for important themes and concepts by which to code by examining published literature in your field. Research on organizational behavior suggests looking for concepts such as decentralization of decision making, hierarchical control, interorganizational communications, coordination procedures, and many other matters that describe how organizations function. If you were studying nonprofit organizations, you would expect to find concepts similar to those in the literature mentioned by your interviewees. Reading through literature on how organizations deal with budgetary constraints suggests looking for concepts such as deficit, borrowing, fund-balances, and earmarking, among many other items. You would expect to find similar concepts in your interviews if you were studying how universities cope when states cut back their funding.

Suggestions for themes to code for can also be found in published literature. In the published literature on big business, one important theme is that overlapping board membership encourages interorganizational coordination. Being aware of this theme in the business world, Herb looked carefully in his interviews with nonprofit leaders to see if being on one another's boards facilitated coordinated efforts.

Using published literature to suggest concepts and themes by which to code is perfectly legitimate. In fact, doing so will help you later on if you are trying to relate your findings to what others have already written. However, coding on concepts and themes from published literature requires care. If you use an established theoretical lens as your sole source for coding categories, you might miss the original insights in your own data; you end up testing someone else's theory rather than building one of your own. In addition, concepts and themes worked out for other studies might not precisely fit your data and you can end up trying to fit your square pegs into their round holes.

LOOKING FOR CONCEPTS AND
THEMES IN YOUR OWN INTERVIEWS

More important than borrowing concepts and themes from the literature is finding those that emerge from the interviews. You look for the concepts and themes in several ways, ranging from using common sense to more complicated approaches.

Questions You Asked

You begin by using common sense and looking at the explicit terms you asked about in your questions and include these on your coding list. If you questioned about budget deficits because this concept is central to your research question, then you certainly want to make sure the concept *budget deficits* is one for which you code. If your main question directly asked about a theme relevant to your research problem, for instance, that there is no political gain for the pain of balancing the budget, then, of course, you code on answers to that question, as they will speak to the theme.

Concepts and Themes Interviewees Frequently Mention

You can look for the concepts, themes, events, and markers explicitly raised by the interviewees. If, in a study of the federal budget, interviewees keep mentioning legislation for balancing the budget such as Gramm-Rudman-Hollings, they think it is important, so you would include it as a coding category.

After you have picked out the obvious coding categories, you begin to look for the more subtle ones, this time working out more carefully and reflecting on the meanings of what the interviewees said.

Concepts and Themes Indirectly Revealed

You may discover themes by looking at the tension between what people say and the emotion they express. If someone tells you he or she has adjusted now 10 years after a divorce, but you hear pain in the interviewee's voice as he or she tells you this, you may deduce a theme of denial of pain. A shift from active to passive voice during the interview might represent a distancing of the interviewee from the events, a denial of responsibility, or even a shifting of blame. "All hell broke loose" is different from "My letter caused a lot of tumult" in terms of who is claiming responsibility. Such tonal shifts might reveal secondary themes, such as a desire to avoid blame or ambivalence about having caused so much tumult.

Concepts and Themes That Emerge From Comparing Interviews

You can come up with ideas for concepts and themes by thinking about what different interviewees said on the same issues and then using the comparison to suggest the code. For example, if one interviewee tells you that growing old has its compensations and another tells you it is downhill all the way, the implicit contradiction might catch your eye and argue for a new combined theme: Some people are better able than others to see the advantages of aging. You might then look for reasons why. Maybe better health enables people to see things more positively, maybe an intact family creates a kind of contentment, or maybe prior experiences of hardship give some people a better sense of proportion, suggesting further themes.

Concepts and Themes Suggest New Concepts and Themes

The concepts and themes you have already identified in turn often suggest new, related concepts and themes. Suppose you have interviewed museum docents to find out why people volunteer for such work, what interests them about it, and what their satisfactions or frustrations are with it. You look at the transcripts and see that one docent described two paintings as world-famous and another indicated that some of the paintings were the pride of the museum's collection. You now have two codable concepts— world-famous paintings and the museum's pride—and you think these ideas might be linked. What links them is the pride the docents feel about the museum, which you think might be one of the reasons they volunteer to show the paintings to the public. This suggests a new theme that you would then look for further in your data to see if it was supported elsewhere.

Another way of working out new concepts and themes from your transcripts is by grouping together concepts that you have already labeled and then reflecting on what they collectively imply. Suppose you have interviewed students, and when you asked them what they liked best and least about school, they gave you a long list of complaints, each a codable concept. A number of these were about teachers. One student says about a professor, "He's totally disorganized and no one can read his writing"; the second one says, "The assignments are unclear and impossibly long"; the third one complains, "He doesn't explain ideas very well in class discussion"; and the fourth argues, "He is not available, doesn't return calls, and skips office hours." Separately each complaint is a concept. Then if you put these concepts together, you might want to call the result a bad teacher, defining this new concept as a professor who is disorganized, makes unclear assignments, doesn't explain the course material, and cannot easily be found. In creating this definition of the concept of *bad teacher*, you have built directly on the concepts you coded on—how organized the professor is, the quality of assignments, the clarity of explanations, and availability.

Looking at the concepts and themes you have already worked out can also suggest ideas for coding if you notice what seems to be missing. If you were coding for college sports and you had coded for basketball and football, you would then make sure you also coded for golf, baseball, and tennis. If you were studying social science majors and were coding for sociology, economics, anthropology, history, and psychology, ask yourself if you are missing political science.

Checking for parallelism in ideas also suggests concepts and themes. Do the coded terms reflect the same degree of depth and nuance? If you were coding for pets and you had set up coding categories for cats that included American short hair, Russian blue, and Siamese, you probably would not want to code the barking pets simply as dogs but rather as bull terriers, French poodles, and Labrador retrievers.

Typologies Suggest Concepts and Themes

A *typology* is a set of related concepts. The way you construct a typology and then interpret what it says can help suggest new concepts. When you create a typology, you first think of a particular concept, and then work out its opposite and decide the dimensions along which this concept varies. Consider, for example, the opposite concepts of good research and bad research, which suggest that the dimension along which they vary is quality of research. Bad research is dull, noninnovative, poorly designed, and badly written, and good research sparkles and challenges, is new, well designed, and engagingly written. You have worked out two opposite ideas and have indicated the criteria that define how they differ. Next, you add a second concept, again by comparing opposites, this time, good and bad teaching, that define a dimension of quality of teaching. You define good teaching as fun, innovative, and concrete and bad teaching as boring, pedestrian, and abstract.

In working out the typology, you then examine both of these dimensions at the same time, suggesting four types of professors: some who are good at both teaching and research, some who are good at one but not the other, and some who are good at neither. You then label each of these separate types of professors and in doing so create a new idea, a new concept, for which you can code. The ones who are good at both might be model professors; those good at neither, we could call turkeys; the ones who are good at teaching but not research we could call pedagogues; and

the ones good at research and not teaching, researchers. (The labels for
the new concepts do not have to be difficult.)

What you have done is construct a typology that accomplishes
several things. First, it forces you to be clear about what each of the
dimensions means. Next, it enables you to generate a number of themes
you can analyze. For example, once you have worked out the concept of
turkeys you would look over your interviews to see how turkeys are
viewed in general, how they get their positions and keep them, how they
behave, and what impact they have on other professors or students, each
aspect suggesting a possibly important theme.

Figures of Speech, Slogans, and
Symbols Suggest Concepts and Themes

As part of searching for concepts and themes in your interviews, carefully check out figures of speech such as similes and metaphors, slogans, and
symbols. These literary markers often indicate central concepts and themes.

Do certain metaphors get repeated throughout the interviews? If so,
they might reflect important cultural themes. For example, in interviewing policy advocates, both Herb and Irene have heard interviewees
refer metaphorically to legislative proposals as trains, as in "There was
only one train about to leave the station." The interviewees were using the
train metaphor to explain a theme, that they sometimes compromised
their legislative agendas in order to get their proposals attached to a piece
of legislation that was likely to get passed, that, like the train, was going
somewhere, even if not directly where they wanted to go. Some progress
was considered better than none at all. The metaphor that was widely
shared in the research arena emphasized politics as the art of the possible,
not the achievement of the ideal.

Though similarities in figures of speech throughout your interviews
suggest pieces of the culture, patterns of differences can also be useful in
revealing themes. If some of your interviewees talk about "jumping ship,"
and others talk about "bridges to the future," you should pay attention
to the contrast as suggesting important differences. Clearly one group
thinks the situation is hopeless, whereas the other sees a more positive
future, which suggests that you look for thematic material to see who feels
hopeless and why.

Examining slogans and symbols can also be helpful in uncovering
themes. Slogans such as "running government like a business" that reoc-
cur throughout your study often are short-hand statements of themes, in
this case, that business provides a proper model for government. Similarly,

symbols, especially when they appear throughout the study, are likely to point to themes. "9/11," for example, has become symbolic of a turning point, a loss of naïveté, and an increased feeling of vulnerability. It has also come to symbolize heroism, duty, and sacrifice, as well as determination to rebuild and fight back. That is a lot of meaning for three numeric digits and a slash. When you hear symbols such as 9/11 mentioned frequently, you can be sure that they convey a set of themes that you need to tease out of your interviews and make explicit. What were your interviewees trying to convey to you by referring to the events of 9/11? The answer is a theme.

Stories Suggest Concepts and Themes

When stories occur in nearly the same form in different interviews, they are likely to provide cultural themes. In her research in Washington, Irene often heard a story about the Center for Tax Justice, a tiny left-wing think tank that discovered that a number of major corporations were paying little or no taxes in the early 1980s. The center used that information to shame Congress into making the tax system fairer. This story has a David-and-Goliath element in it—the little policy shop that defeated huge corporations looking for continued tax breaks—but it also includes a cultural lesson, that Congress responds to embarrassment. So if you want to bring about change, you may have to embarrass Congress, a theme that the interviewees shared (see Yarwood 2003).

Small differences in stories that are widely shared can also be revealing of themes. If two interviewees repeat the same story but pull out different lessons from them or emphasize different parts of the story, the contrast may suggest themes you want to develop. When you know the whole story and an interviewee tells you only a part of it, you may wonder why part was left out, and that might lead you to some new insights to check out.

If you have collected stories from a number of interviewees, for instance, about organizational heroes, when you analyze them, you might want to check if people in the organization behave in the same way that the heroes in the stories behave or if there is a tension between the idealized behavior in the stories and the way people are actually acting. If there is a difference, you may have discovered a useful theme about what is expected normatively and what is practiced.

Creating Concepts Through Your Own Labeling

Often we recognize concepts because the interviewees use a word or phrase in ways that emphasize the idea's importance. Maybe the interviewee says, "Finding the right husband depends on luck." You decide that luck is an important concept and, naturally enough, call the concept luck just as the interviewee did. At times, though, you hear an idea that the interviewee does not summarize with a single term. In a discussion about marriages that last for many years, your conversational partner says that success in keeping a marriage together "depends a lot on whether you grow together; I learned to like action movies and he comes to the opera with me, and we both bird watch." You might call this concept *learning to share each other's interests* or *growing together*.

Creating your own label for a concept takes some thought to ensure that you do not distort the idea introduced by the interviewee. If an elderly person tells you her son never calls, would you label that concept *a complaint* or *loneliness*? Early in your analysis, you might not know and would have to reread the interview in context to see whether the interviewee was giving you a list of complaints or was talking about isolation. It might be that both meanings are intended and then you code the same passage as both *complaint* and *loneliness*.

Our colleague Jim shared with us the following excerpt from a conversation between paramedics. We have put labels on the concepts, using some labels that the interviewees used and making up some of our own, to show you how you can generate new concepts and themes by labeling. "It was slow tonight [**slow night**]. Some drive-bys and a few carry-outs . . . a cold one, a coupla bleeders, and a blue-icer [*example of slow night*]" [*distancing from bodily trauma*].

In describing the evening's routine, the speaker was using the vernacular of his profession to explain that it was a slow night. The interviewee explained what a slow night meant by giving a detailed example. He and his partner made a few routine stops and also transported several people ("carry-outs") to a hospital. The concept *slow night* is defined by the small number of drive-bys and carry-outs. The other odd terms, *cold one*, *bleeders*, and *blue-icer*, do not seem to be important ideas in themselves, but taken together, suggest that the paramedics have distanced themselves from the depressing nature of their work by giving nicknames to types of serious injuries. We labeled this concept *distancing from bodily trauma*. Once you have the idea that paramedics distance themselves to protect themselves emotionally, you can look for other instances of distancing in your interviews. Do paramedics distance themselves only from bodily trauma, or do they build walls around their feelings regardless of the source? Do they have other coping mechanisms besides calling their cases by odd names? If so, what are they?

Just as you give labels to concepts that might not be named by the interviewees, you also frequently provide a label to a theme. You do so by reading and rereading each passage and asking yourself what it is about, and if it presents a theme that relates to your research question, you work out a label that summarizes what was said in a codable phrase. Consider the following excerpt from an interview with Irene: "Many times someone comes to me and is concerned about what someone said or something they did and they try to make it an ethics issue when in fact it is simply that they don't like what someone does or says." Irene thought about this passage and summarized the theme as "People charge others with ethics violations to achieve their own ends." Herb came across the following passage in the transcript of an old interview: "It is a tough row to hoe these days, especially since financing has just dried up, but . . . it is tough . . . that is why we are doing it. That is why not-for-profits do it, because it is tough, because the for-profits won't do it." He summarized the possible theme as "Not-for-profits step in where others despair."

Once you have found a concept, theme, event, or topical marker and worked out what you think it means, you look for these same ideas elsewhere in all the interviews. You compare instances of the same idea and progressively define, refine, and label these emerging concepts. You continue doing so until you are comfortable that you have worked out a consistent understanding of each concept and theme and have noted most. You put all the concepts, themes, events, and topical markers you are going to use in the analysis on a coding list, and then use that list to guide your coding, or marking, of the text.

CREATING CONSISTENT AND REFINED DEFINITIONS

Before you mark the text with the codes you are going to use, you need to be sure that you have clear and consistent definitions that can be used throughout all the interviews. Suppose in a study of community activism you conclude that empowerment is an important concept. Either in your mind or, better yet, in writing you would work out ways of recognizing and labeling the concept by answering a series of questions. The following is adapted from Boyatzis (1998, p. 31).

1. *What am I going to call it (label it)?* Empowerment.

2. *How am I defining it?* Empowerment is a feeling that individuals have when they believe they can accomplish chosen goals. It is also political or organizational strength that enables people to collectively carry out their will.

3. *How am I going to recognize it in the interviews?* When people explicitly say they feel empowered, when they accomplish something new and important, especially against opposition, or when they succeed in areas in which they have failed in the past.

4. *What do I want to exclude?* Empowerment must emerge out of an activity carried out by the individuals or the groups in which they are involved. If others (such as supportive politicians and charities, etc.) provide the benefit or do the activity for people, it is not empowerment.

5. *What is an example?* One example is a protest in which a neighborhood forces government to provide extra policing on Friday nights.

The problem of coming up with clear definitions is that your interviewees might see some of the concepts or themes you are using in a slightly different way, which may mean that you have to adjust your labels and definitions to accommodate. You may need a broader term that includes several different but related examples, or you may need two or more narrower terms to capture the differences.

To assure yourself that you have good working definitions that hold throughout your interviews, you then try out your new definitions on a sample of your interview transcripts chosen to reflect the variation in your study. If you are doing research that deals with gender, be sure to include males and females in your minisample. If you are studying an organization, make sure you test out your labeling with interviews with some from the bottom and some from the top of the hierarchy. If your study is about a religious group, you may want to include some who are deeply involved and some whose participation is spottier. If your definitions hold up well in the minisample, you can keep them as is; if there are major differences in how the interviewees understand a term or theme, you then have to make some changes in the definition before doing the coding.

For example, suppose the concept you are defining is motivation for running for public office and you initially defined it as the reason that politicians give for their decision to begin a political career. As you look through your minisample, you find that some politicians in the interviews described the reason they ran for office in terms of career enhancement or to help their own community, whereas others claimed they wanted to do good for others. With such differences in meaning, you probably would not want to keep a single concept that includes both careerism and public service as motivation for office seeking; instead you would introduce two concepts, labeling career enhancement and helping your own community as *self-oriented motivation* and doing good for others as *selfless* or *public-oriented motivation*. You would then go back to working out how to precisely define each concept and recognize each in the transcripts.

If you divide one concept into two related parts (motivation for office into self-interest and public service), you will then want to choose labels for the new terms that still show how they are related, such as *self-interest motivation for office* and *public-service motivation for office*. That way, later on it will be easier to retrieve all the passages that refer to motivation for office, whether you are referring to public-service motivation or self-interested motivation.

In the example of politicians and motivation, the differences in how the interviewees understood the concepts were clear because the interviewees explicitly stated them. At other times, the differences may not be so clearly stated and you have to work them out yourself. In a study on what makes marriages break up, you might wonder whether what initially appears to be an easily understood concept such as marriage means something different to men than it does to women. To see if this is the case, you would examine separately the interviews from the men and those from the women. Men might emphasize responsibilities and sexual intimacy; women might emphasize emotional support and communication. The concept of what marriage entails might be so different that to lump men's and women's understandings under one term would be more distorting than enlightening. You could divide the broader idea of marriage into two concepts—men's idea of marriage and women's idea of marriage—or you could focus on the four more specific components—responsibility, sexual intimacy, emotional support, and communication.

Another problem that makes it difficult to precisely define a concept is that even when most of the interviewees use the same term, its meaning can change depending on the context of its use. For example, *community* might refer to both ethnic affiliation and physical neighborhood, depending on when and where the term is used. Or terms might have ordinary meanings and also special, technical meanings that do not quite mesh with each other. In both cases, you should probably code each use with a different label.

As you refine your definitions, you need to double-check to make sure you *really* understand the concept the way the interviewees use it rather than the way you define it using your own cultural lens. Misunderstandings can easily occur, especially when interviewees use metaphors to illustrate ideas but the metaphors are not shared between cultural groups. Suppose your Japanese interviewee said, "Everything fell into place, Sartori!" How would you define and code that passage?

Sartori is a Buddhist religious term meaning enlightenment and is a mystical experience. If you were unaware of the religious origin of this term, you might impose your own understanding that things fall into place because of methodical hard work rather than a mystical experience of enlightenment. When a term sounds unusual, especially when used in a different cultural context, you may have to do some extra work to find out what it means to your interviewees.

PHYSICALLY CODING THE INTERVIEWS

The next step in analysis is to go through all the transcripts and then, using the definitions that you have worked out, place a label or code next to each data unit where the matching concept, theme, event, or topical marker appears. Coding allows you later on to quickly locate excerpts from all the interviews (as well as from observations and documents if you have coded them) that refer to the same concept, theme, event, or topical marker and then examine them together. You can retrieve all data units that refer to empowerment or each interviewee's rendition of what occurred at the secret meeting to discuss the incentives. Coding allows you to sort statements by content of the concept, theme, or event rather than by the people who told you the information.

When you are marking the text, you have to keep your mind engaged. You cannot code mechanically because you need to concentrate hard to make sure you find instances of concepts and themes that interviewees did not present in a single word or when you have to infer the concepts or themes from a broader statement. You must constantly judge whether the text provides an instance of the concept or theme for which you are looking. Attention is also required when coding interviews for several matters simultaneously, though you would probably not want to code for more than a couple at a time simply because it is too hard to concentrate on so much at once.

There are different ways of putting codes in the text, each mostly a matter of taste. Some people code in the text itself, darkening the key words they want to look at later. Legislative bill HR1120 becomes **HR1120** when the bold typeface is turned on. When the expression in the text is not the same as the label you are using, some people insert the label in brackets. The interviewee says "I think my boss is a son of a bitch, conceited ass." The coded manuscript looks like this: "I think my boss is a son of bitch, conceited ass [**hostility toward boss**]. Other coding systems involve placing the particular coding category in the margins of the transcript.

Text	Code
When I first met him I was thrilled. He was fun to be with, good-looking and had a lovely way of teasing me. After we talked for a while, I learned that we both liked birding and taking long walks	Attraction
On December 17th, my policy director and I talked with the representative's chief of staff about HR1214. He indicated that the representative would support the bill if we could get it out of committee	Lobbying for HR1214

When you have complex codes in which some concepts and themes are subsumed within others (called hierarchical coding) and you want to show this relationship in your codes, it is handy to create an outline, and then use the numbers from the outline as your codes to show how the separate coded items relate to each other. If the main topics are designated with roman numerals—I, II, III, etc.—subtopics below them are designated with capital roman letters—A, B, C, etc. All the items that come under roman numeral III are related to each other, and all the items under III A, III B, etc., are subparts of III.

Herb used this outline procedure in the coding for his book *Renewing Hope*. For example, his fourth main topic was projects, so it was called IV in roman numerals. Projects were broken up into the definition of success, types of projects, and stages of projects. The stages of projects were in turn broken up into six topics. The coding outline appeared as follows:

IV. Projects
    A. Defining success
    B. Projects by types
    C. Projects as stages
        1. Predevelopment dreaming
        2. Financial overviews—typical packaging
        3. Multiple partnering as financing
        4. Community linkages
        5. Clients
            a. Enabling the client
            b. The dysfunctional client
        6. The traumas of construction

If Herb read in a transcript a discussion about a dysfunctional client, he coded it IV-C-5-b. The outline was created after extensive reading and rereading of the interview transcripts. This kind of coding scheme allows you to see the relationships among your coding categories and to use the computer to call back for examination any level of the outline. Thus, you can look at all the data units that talk about dysfunctional clients, all the sections that say anything at all about clients, or all the information about the stages of a project. Using an outline such as this makes coding somewhat easier, because if an interviewee talks about projects without specifying the stage or the way of judging success, you can just label it IV: Projects.

Example of Coding With a Computer Program in Mind

Herb and Irene both rely on Nota Bene's (a word processor) embedded coding and retrieval system called Orbis. With Orbis, all words in the text are automatically coded (though we tell it not to code for ordinary words such as *the* or *is*). If we are looking for any word that occurs in the text, Orbis will find every instance of it and return all those instances to us, each with the amount of text we specify, such as the sentence or the paragraph in which it occurs. With programs that search and retrieve text, there is no need to specifically write in names or dates or any topical marker. However, Orbis cannot find words if they are not in the text, so we have to make up and then put in codes for concepts that might not be designated by any specific words in the transcript, and we also have to put in codes for themes. If a person said "I felt great after the council agreed to put in the stop sign" we would write in the text the code "$$empowerment" and the program would find it for us along with the text around it, and put it in a file we designate. We use the $$ signs to indicate that we have created the term rather than found it in the text.

CODING USING THE GROUNDED THEORY APPROACH

In our approach to coding, you examine your interviews and look at the literature to gain ideas on what themes and concepts for which to code, develop new concepts where appropriate, and then work out the definitions prior to doing the physical coding, but our approach is certainly not the only way. Many qualitative researchers prefer to use the *grounded theory model* (summary compiled from Boyatzis 1998; Charmaz 2000, 2001; and Strauss and Corbin 1990). This model argues that coding, recognizing concepts and themes, and theory development are parts of one integrated process. Further, the concepts and themes must emerge from the data without the use of the literature. Grounded theorists code each passage of every interview as they go along rather than develop a separate list of concepts and themes that are then applied to the interviews.

Through what is termed *open coding,* that is, coding as you go along, grounded theorists have worked out a systematic approach that often results in fresh and rich results. The downside to this approach is that it requires an enormous amount of coding, much of which you will never use. Analysis in grounded theory does not distinguish between themes and terms that are more central and those that are more peripheral to the research topic, because the topic and hence the main themes are evolving throughout the project. Concept recognition, coding, and theory development are part of a continuous and seamless package. By contrast, in the responsive interviewing approach, the phases of the work are more distinct, and the learning from the earlier phases is used more in the later phases.

Though analysis in the responsive interviewing model is more efficient than in grounded theory, there are times when the grounded theory approach to coding is preferable. If you are analyzing someone else's data—for example, if you are conducting some research using oral history archives or are sharing interviews in a group research project—you do not have the kind of experiential learning that went into the production of your own interviews and that initially suggests possible concepts and themes. In that case, grounded theory's line-by-line approach to coding is essential. Or if you have used your own interviews for one project but would now like to look at the data a different way to see what else is in there, a grounded theory approach can be useful. Similarly, if you are concerned that the literature and existing theory might be putting blinders on you so you cannot see what is in your data, the grounded theory approach to coding might provide an antidote. In looking for concepts and themes in the grounded theory approach, you examine each line or phrase, ask yourself what the interviewee meant or felt, and then summarize the answer in a word or phrase.

If you use an open coding process, in which you read your interviews and mark off and code each passage as it occurs, you may not have consistent meanings to your codes, and your idea of what the codes mean may change as you later see how particular interviewees expressed themselves. As a result, you may have to recode to accommodate what you are finding. That can get tedious, especially when you have thousands of pages of interviews and have to recode several times. Open coding works better in shorter projects and in projects in which you are very familiar with concepts you are looking for. You may have a kind of coding sheet in your head, if not written down.

You can use an open coding framework without all the assumptions of grounded theory, coding as you go, rather than preparing a list, refining the concepts, and then marking them in the text. In this hybrid model, part-way between the responsive interviewing formal coding schema and grounded theory models, you need not code every passage or term but select only those concepts and themes that are most closely related to your research question. The more focused your interviews, the more efficient this hybrid is.

Conclusion

The first stage of the final analysis involves more than just preparing the data; it entails finding concepts and themes, figuring out what label to give them, and determining whether you want to show the relationship between the codes in your coding schema. The decision of what to code, and how to define your key concepts and themes, is the part of the analysis in which you compare how ideas are expressed across interviews to refine the meanings, elaborate concepts and themes, and suggest what needs to be added. To complete the analysis, you still have to put these concepts and themes together, show how they answer your research question, and pull out broader implications.

11

Analyzing Coded Data

O nce you have systematically coded your interviews, you try to figure out what these coded data mean. You begin by clarifying and summarizing concepts and themes, grouping information around particular events or stories, or sorting information by groups of interviewees. You do so by using either your word processor or specially designed software for qualitative data analysis to retrieve all references to a particular concept, theme, event, or topical marker. With the items now grouped, you search for patterns and linkages between the concepts and themes or draw together different events and their alternative versions to form a rich descriptive narrative. Finally, you step back to figure out the broader implications of your findings and ask how widely and under what conditions they hold.

Building Toward Narratives and Description

You systematically examine concepts, themes, and topical markers, sorting them into appropriate groups, comparing them, and looking for patterns and connections. In cultural studies, you combine what different interviewees have said about the same concepts to refine your understanding of what each concept means. In topical studies, you compare and weigh contrasting descriptions of events to work out your own interpretation of what happened.

SORTING AND SUMMARIZING

To begin, you bring together all of the data units given the same code into a single computer file and then summarize the content of each file.

In summarizing the content of the file, you list main points in the text associated with the coded category with minimal judgment on your part. If in describing a good professor some individuals mentioned openness and responsiveness and others discussed the clarity of lectures or the fairness of examinations, your summary of the good professor would include these four traits: openness, responsiveness, clarity, and fairness. You do not omit any concepts that were indicated or emphasize some over others. By itself a summary can be useful, because not everyone knows what other people think about a topic, for example, how students view good professors or what the reasons are that someone runs for office the first time.

As a second step, you can examine the summary you have written and ask yourself what seems to be missing and try to figure out why. If none of your interviewees mentioned that a good professor is up-to-date on the literature, gives practical examples, or has a good sense of humor, maybe that means students do not need to be entertained, and maybe they take for granted that the professor is well informed because they so seldom encounter a professor whose information is wildly out of date. You think about both what is present and what is missing to help generate some initial themes.

SORTING AND RANKING

To help you generate additional ideas, you can sort and rank material within each file of coded data. Suppose you were conducting exit interviews and you initially pulled out data units that contained the coded concept *complaints*. When you summarized the file, you found complaints about parking, dissatisfaction with personnel evaluations, and concerns that computers are out of date. In your summary you also noted that people were mildly annoyed by parking problems but very irritated about the out-of-date computers because they made it to difficult for them to do their work. The fact that some complaints were considered minor and some major suggests that you rank-order the complaints from the most to the least serious. You can use ordered information in a variety of ways. You might ask whether the most serious problems were addressed or ignored, or whether the most serious problems affected all the employees or only some of them. You could question whether the problems that bothered people the most were those that hampered their ability to get their work done or simply those that occurred most frequently.

SORTING AND COMPARING

Once you have worked out preliminary ideas from examining the sorted files of coded data, you then sort your files a second time, this time to see if when you group your interviewees by their background characteristics, the coded data from their interviews highlight the concepts, themes, or events in distinct ways. Do managers see outdated computers as a minor problem, whereas employees see it as a major problem? Do younger politicians have different views toward questionable fund-raising techniques than more experienced ones? Do first-generation college students differ in what they want to get from their education from those whose parents went to college?

Most often your sorting will be based on obvious differences in background characteristics of the interviewees—men or women, black or white, labor or management. But you can sort in other ways; for instance, you might want to group interviews in terms of how a specific concept was used, irrespective of the background of the interviewee. For instance, in Herb's project interviewing community developers, many of them talked about the importance of respect. Herb gathered all of the passages in which he had coded the concept *respect* and sorted them into separate files in terms of who the interviewee said was providing the respect: bankers, municipal officials, or foundations. He then summarized each of the subfiles and compared the summaries. Herb found that community developers felt they were being treated with respect from banks and foundations when these funders listened to community ideas rather than trying to impose their own. They felt that city officials were treating them with respect when the officials removed administrative hurdles and simplified permit processes. When he compared these discussions, Herb first noted the differences, but then he also noticed what they had in common: Respect, to community developers, meant removing the obstacles that they faced in their work.

The comparisons you make suggest further questions to ask of the data that then help you better understand and theorize about what is going on. Once Herb had determined what respect meant to the community developers he was studying, he once again divided his data, this time into two groups, one of more respected and one of less respected activists. He compared the two groups to look for the differences and found that the community activists who concentrated more on bricks-and-mortar (construction) projects felt they were more respected than those who worked on social services, suggesting an important bias on the part of the funders. This finding suggested examining further to figure out how those community activists who provided social services funded themselves and if and how they avoided the lure of doing bricks-and-mortar projects.

Example: Using Sorting and Comparing to Build an Integrated Analysis

Irene used the simple analytical tools of sorting, ranking, and comparing to build a theory about how agencies respond when they are under serious budgetary attack. She first picked a bureaucratic agency whose budget was seriously threatened as her research site. In the analysis of her interviews, she looked to see what kind of criticism accompanied the budget threats and coded for the concept *criticisms*. She put all the text that included criticisms of the agency into a single file. Next, she prepared another file of coded data units on *agency responses*, and then compared the two, looking for matches or lack of matches between the criticisms and responses. She noted which criticisms evoked reactions and which did not. She rank-ordered the complaints according to how serious they appeared to the agency officials and examined the coded data to see why the agency considered some more urgent than others. She then compared how different agencies responded to similar criticisms, building toward theoretical conclusions about how agencies respond to criticisms when their budgets are threatened.

WEIGHING AND COMBINING

Weighing and combining help you synthesize different versions of the same event or separate explanations of the same concept or theme, allowing you to pull together different events into a single descriptive narrative. For example, in cultural studies, you may have heard a term in one interview used in a casual way, gotten a more formal definition of it in a second, and in a third, heard good examples of what the concept means in practice. In a fourth interview, you may have heard subtle distinctions that you missed. In the combining stage of analysis, you put these coded pieces together to fully explain the concept. In topical studies, you design the interviews so that each person is asked only about what he or she knows best. You now have to integrate these pieces to describe and explain what happened. For instance, to understand how local community groups design and implement development projects, Herb combined relevant portions of the interviews of those who knew most about the financing, those who were experts in physical construction, and those who knew how to negotiate political support.

Combining separate and overlapping parts of a narrative or complementary understandings of a concept is straightforward. If some people describe how a celebration was prepared and others what happened at the ceremony, you can put these two pieces together in a file of descriptions of the ceremony. Combining material is more complicated if you are trying to link several distinct concepts into a single theme. You have to first infer how the concepts are related from the way they are described by the interviewees, or perhaps you work out how they might be related and then go back to the coded interviews to look for evidence that either supports or modifies these logical guesses.

For example, in his study of economic development practitioners, Herb first summarized his interviewees' complaints about their work from the coded file on that topic. One set of complaints referred to the uncontrollability of the work environment, that is, how hard the interviewees worked seemed to have little impact on the outcome of creating new jobs. Another common complaint was that economic developers felt they spent excessive time on ineffective busywork, such as sending out brochures. Herb reasoned that these two ideas could be combined into a single theme, that the inability to control outcomes led economic development practitioners to increase the amount of busywork they did. With this theme in mind, he reexamined each of the separate coding categories, one on uncontrollability and the other on busywork, to see where and how they overlapped and in doing so found examples of the connection between uncontrollability and busywork.

Combining results is more difficult if your interviewees disagree with each other. In such circumstances you have to *weigh* the evidence from different interviewees to check out how credible each report appears to be. By weighing different versions as you combine the descriptions, you create your own interpretation of what happened and what it means.

In weighing different versions of the same events, you can take any of several approaches. One is to check to see if one interviewee's rendition is based on actual participation or first-hand observation, especially if done over a long period of time; if so, you rely more on the first-hand version. You also check for slant or bias and then rely less heavily on a strongly biased interpretation. You typically weigh more heavily a version of a narrative that is backed up by documents, copies of memos or consultant reports, newspaper clippings, budgets, studies, or annual reports.

You can weigh evidence through internal analysis. A statement such as "I knew she was drunk because she was walking down the hallway and kept bumping into the wall and saying, ''Scuse me'" seems to be strong enough evidence that the person was inebriated. On the other hand, if you hear waffle words, such as "around then" or "I don't remember exactly, but this is what I think happened," be cautious in accepting what was said. If a person contradicts him- or herself in ways that you cannot easily reconcile, you may not want to lean on such interviews very heavily. From comparisons with other interviews, and especially if you have done observations, you can usually judge what types of details a person seems best able to recall. Some people may have a good eye or ear for mood, recording the tone of an event or meeting, whereas others remember votes taken, promises made, or the content of discussions. You rely more heavily on the type of information you feel the interviewee remembers best.

INTEGRATING, CHECKING, AND MODIFYING

Now you integrate different parts of your findings by first checking them for accuracy and consistency and then modifying them if you conclude that your initial interpretations were not quite correct. Suppose in a study of university retention you worked out a summary theme saying, "The university is biased against adult students." When you look for evidence for this finding, you return to the coded data and this time compare the complaints made by the younger and older students. If these complaints match, you would then modify your initial finding and argue that the university is not responsive to student demands overall, but is not particularly biased against adult learners.

Next, you ask yourself if your version of what you have heard, analyzed, and integrated is complete and whether it seems credible. If your interpretation sides more with one group than another, double-check to see that you have sufficient evidence to justify the assessment you have made. Or, if you are claiming that one set of events caused another, make sure you have evidence documenting precisely how the cause brought about the effect. In Irene's study of severe fiscal stress, she concluded that poor management contributed to the fiscal stress, but she needed to show step by step how that happened to make her conclusion convincing. From examining step by step the chronology of events that her interviewees had presented and that she had put together in her coded data, she found that rather than reduce expenditures or try to raise revenues (the traditional responses to fiscal stress), the manager early on tried to bust the unions, with the expectation that weaker unions would receive lower wage increases. But, in response to that effort to bust the unions, union members were angered, struck back, and won much higher salary settlements, which only added to the fiscal stress. Irene was able to document every step of this process by piecing together complementary stories from both the managers and the union leaders.

The Second Stage of Your Data Analysis: Building Toward Theory

What you have accomplished so far provides a solid base to begin writing the narrative and descriptive part of your study. You can explain to your reader what concepts mean in the cultural group examined by bringing together explications of cultural concepts with examples that illustrate them in practice. You can present vivid descriptive material of the culture: what goes on at a wedding in a specific ethnic group or what is the acceptable way of handling dissent in an organization. At this stage of analysis in a topical study, you can put together events in chronological order or work out your own explanatory narratives: what happened in the political campaign or how the university changed under fiscal stress. You can describe the difficulties employees had when working for the company or why a social program worked or failed. You can now present a credible and accurate description.

Next, you want to extend your reach and look for the broader implications of what you have learned. You do so by asking how your findings can modify, extend, or perhaps even create social, political, or behavioral theories. Theories are sets of statements that bring together concepts and themes to explain how things happen or why they took place the way they did. A theory links concepts and themes into an overarching explanation that not only addresses the immediate research question but also creates broader understandings about important societal issues.

Theories differ in scope. Some theories focus on the matter just examined such as why an organization behaved the way it did. In these *case-focused theories*, you offer an explanation for what you have learned through the interviews. A study examining why a mayor lost his office might suggest a case-focused theory indicating that the reason she lost political support was because she showed disrespect for citizens. The theory not only speaks to the case in hand, but also suggests broader theoretical concerns by linking the loss of political support to showing disrespect for citizens.

You work toward what is termed *middle-level theory* by asking how far the principles and processes you have discovered in your research might extend. From your study, you might theorize that mayors who act with disrespect toward citizens are likely to lose their jobs, and more broadly, that there is a link between the appearance of political arrogance or public disdain and electoral consequences. To extend your research to a middle-level theory you might briefly examine other similar cases or think about what you have learned in light of other published research on political behavior.

Grand theories are the broadest-scope theories that come about after considerable reflection on the results of a wide array of different studies. Grand theories address a range of issues, with implications extending to many settings, perhaps to many societies, and across time. Because responsive interviewing projects deal mainly with what the researchers have heard directly from their conversational partners, the projects by themselves rarely reach this level of abstraction, but instead provide evidence as others build toward a grand theory.

Most qualitative interviewers work on creating middle-level theory that builds on what was learned from the interviewing and then speaks to issues present in the literature. The entire design of a responsive interview leads step by step toward middle-range theory. You choose only research projects that speak to broader issues and problems. As you prepare questions, you ask yourself why something happened, what concepts are important, and how certain themes might be related—all parts of theory development.

At this stage of analysis you step back a bit and then think how your insights can come together into a coherent theory that explains a broader part of culture or offers an explanation of why things occur the way they do. You build theory by working out which of the themes that you have discovered are related and then systematically create a theory to show how and why they are.

But how do you see which themes fit together? One way is to examine your own questioning patterns, because the questions that emerge during the study reflect your ideas about possible themes. A second approach is to examine your interviews closely to see how your interviewees themselves link together core themes. A third is to think about your own research in light of the published literature, which itself suggests both concepts and linked themes. Finally, you can simply reason out how the concepts and themes might relate to each other. Then with your theory in mind, you go back to your data to see if your reasoning appears to hold.

EXAMINING YOUR OWN QUESTIONING PATTERNS

Throughout a responsive interviewing study, your questions change as you revamp the main questions and work out follow-up queries to explore central issues as they arise. The questions you add reflect your growing understanding of the connections between themes in your data and as such suggest an emerging theory.

In Irene's study of contracting, she wanted to understand the differences local officials saw in contracts for different services. As the project progressed and Irene learned more about what was happening, she asked this question in a variety of ways. She asked how city officials would know if contractors in some service areas were doing what they said they would (concept: *performance measurement and compliance*) and how formal (concept: *formality*) particular contracts were. From what she heard, Irene was able to now say that contracting in some areas, such as water or wastewater, was different from contracting for janitorial services, because clean water was easy to measure, but how clean a building is was much more difficult to measure. Based on further follow-up questions, she concluded that the more difficult outcomes to measure resulted in more formal contract language that specified the number of times *specific* activities were to be performed, such as how often wastebaskets were to be emptied and the number of times the floors were to be mopped. In the questions she asked, she was building toward a theory that brought together ideas on ease of measuring compliance and the degree of formality of contract language.

CONCEPTS OR THEMES DISCUSSED TOGETHER

A second approach to obtain ideas for theory building is simply to look for those places in your transcripts where the coding shows that two or more themes are discussed together. Often these data units will contain stories or extended descriptions of important events in which several core ideas are linked. Once you have seen the connection between these ideas, you then look elsewhere in your transcript where any of the individual themes are mentioned to see if what is said is consistent with your emerging theory about how they relate.

In several of Herb's interviews with community developers, he encountered one story that was repeated about a particular successful community project. Herb examined the story to see how it brought together several themes. The story praised the project and the success of the group that had pulled it off but also mentioned that the community group working on that project was the favorite of the foundations. The story emphasized that community groups do not succeed only on the merits of their ideas but also on the merits of their image with the funders. He then reexamined other places in the interviews in which people talked about success to see whether or not the image with the funders was important, as a step in building a theory of why some organizations succeed.

You have to carefully examine what the interviewees say as you link themes together and pull out broader meanings from their comments. The following story, edited for length, is from an interview conducted as part of Irene's project on municipal contracting. A city official, referred to here as "S," is speaking.

S: In a small community, there is a lot of turnover in the council and on the staff. It is the contractor who stays and trains the new staff. You become dependent on them. They have better relations than you do with the council. They have been taking council members to lunch for five years. You can't let them go. That happens more in the smaller towns that are less professional, but in those communities, just try to remove a long-standing contractor! I have a story on that one.

    When I was the assistant city manager in [city name] . . . Information Technology was contracted out. The contractor had been there for seven years, longer than me or the city manager. The organization was relying on him. He was in lieu of staff; he was a constant, and unofficial staff member. . . . After the first couple of years, he was providing terrible service. He sold us used computers as if they were new. . . . We were going to try to remove him. What he was doing was unlawful. We were just going to claim poor service. . . . The ousted person began calling me and the city manager. We declined to change our minds. He began calling council members and the president of the council. We explained to the council our decision. . . . The council arranged a meeting between me and the ousted contractor and the mayor. We retained our right to dismiss him, but . . .

Irene: The council could still fire you.

S: Yes. The council president wanted to give him six months, to change his act, and for us to develop ways to evaluate his performance. We should have been able to terminate that contract, but we agreed to the six months. We bit our lips. For all the things we wanted to accomplish, it was not worth falling on our swords. I went along with the evaluation period, but I was prepared to quit if forced to keep the contractor after the six-month period.

    . . . The Democrats [on the council] were not close to this computer guy. They said, "No. We want him out." A couple of the Republicans broke rank and agreed with the minority position. They changed their mind, midstream. I called the contractor. He was sarcastic with me. He thought he won. I told him we asked for six months, and they turned us down. He was flabbergasted. So, we got rid of him. . . . But I almost had to quit my job over it.

    Trying to remove a long-term contractor, who is local and politically connected . . . Easiest would have been to accept the

> poor services, and make the best of a bad situation, but you have to do the right thing and let the chips fall where they may.
>
> When it doesn't work out [when you can't remove a contractor for poor performance], it is so disenchanting to be in the public sector. But this time, it worked.

The predominant theme is stated at the end by the interviewee as the moral of the story: "When you cannot remove a contractor for poor performance, it is disenchanting to be in the public sector." But the story contains other thematic material, perhaps the most important of which is that "small cities become dependent on contractors, who act in lieu of city staff, like department heads, which makes it difficult to fire them." Further, two explanations are offered by the interviewee why this happens. The first is that there is high turnover on the council and among the professional staff, so contractors are there longer than anyone who might supervise them and have more historical memory; the second is that contractors wine and dine the council members who then feel obligated to the contractor.

As you build toward a theory, you can see how the themes link up: It is difficult to fire contractors because they act like department heads, which happens because there is high turnover and because the contractors wine and dine the council, with the consequence that when a city official cannot fire a contractor for poor performance, public employees are disenchanted. These linked themes provide a start to a theory, with one main statement, two causes, and one consequence stated. There is also an implied condition, that all this is more likely to happen in small cities, because the small size increases the turnover and hence the dependence on the contractor. Five themes are structurally linked in this one story.

Sometimes secondary themes are not stated in so many words but you note them in the tensions in the stories. For instance, in the contracting story, there is an implicit tension between city employees going along with the poor performance of contractors and not making a fuss (because it is easier and because there are other things they want to accomplish) and not letting contractors get away with subpar performance (because it is wrong and inefficient). A second tension is deeper still between maintaining a faith in the public sector and an erosion of that faith that occurs when the public sector cannot act in an upright and effective manner. Each tension seen by itself is suggestive of a theme. Taken together, the themes suggest a theory concerning problems that public-sector employees face as they try to be good managers and represent the public interest but have to do so in a highly political environment. An analysis of a single passage suggests a middle-level theory relating administration and politics.

You can often find related themes in iconic events or rituals. Sometimes that relationship is one of tension or opposition. For instance, in some weddings, one message (a theme) is that the wife is a form of property: The father of the bride gives the bride away to her future husband, as if she belongs to her father until she is given to her husband to whom she then belongs. The wife is handed to her husband presumably in a pure and virginal state (white dress) so that her child-bearing capacity belongs to her husband. The husband's virginity is not the subject of the ceremony and seems to be irrelevant. Further, the fact that the wedding party is typically paid for by the bride's family thematically suggests that they are paying to have someone take their daughter off their hands. A different part of the ceremony conveys a contrasting message. The future wife is asked, "Do you take this man to be your wedded husband?" and the double-ring ceremony suggests two individuals coming together on equal grounds. In examining descriptions of weddings, we can see tension between the themes of property ownership and of partnership.

BUILDING ON PUBLISHED LITERATURE

In most cases there will be substantial published literature on your research topic. Such literature, especially that appearing in academic publications, describes linked themes that other researchers have found in their data, suggesting to you what might also appear in your own.

The literature on organizational research is rich with suggestions on how organizations perform their tasks and relate to one another and to the environment. Some of this literature talks about how the complexity and changeability of the environment faced by the organization influences the ways in which the organization recruits employees, assigns and supervises work, and rewards good effort. For example, to deal with a complex and changing environment, you need more highly skilled employees who can solve problems, not merely carry out tasks by rote; such individuals are relatively rare, need to be courted (recruited), carefully retained, and recognized and rewarded for creativity. If they are so recognized and rewarded, they are more likely to stay. If you have done a study on organizations and their responses to the environment, you might want to examine the places in your transcripts that you have coded *environmental complexity,* as well as employee recruitment and retention, to see if the themes in the literature appear in your data. Those themes might not be in your data at all. Alternatively, your data might back up what the literature says, or might suggest totally different ways in which environmental complexity affects personnel actions. In any case, you have started toward a theory suggested by the published literature.

Keep in mind with this approach to theory development that you are doing more than simply testing the theories found in the literature. You are also using suggestions in the literature about how particular concepts and themes relate to each other as a starting point to examine your own data. You may find that these concepts and themes relate to each other in a different way than indicated by the literature, or you may find other themes that change the context and interpretation of the results. You are extending ideas and building your own theory using the literature as a jumping-off point. In other words, you are not limiting yourself to testing only those relationships that are already suggested in the literature but instead are building on them to suggest your own theory.

REASONING HOW DIFFERENT THEMES ARE CONNECTED

When you have worked with your data for months or years, you will undoubtedly be familiar with what it says. Based on your feel for the data, you can reason out which themes might be related.

You might begin by examining together concepts and themes that you believe address the same part of your research problem. You then ask yourself a series of questions that help you figure out how the items might be related. Are they *examples* of the same larger process or concept? Are they *opposites* or *in tension?* Does one *cause or influence* one or more of the others? Do several *influence* each other? Are some of them *causes* or *consequences* of some third theme or concept? If the items seem to be linked in any of these ways, you are on your way to developing a theory, though now you have to return to your coded data to provide specific evidence of the relationships.

Herb used this type of reasoning in looking for linked themes in his study of community developers. At one point, he put together various themes that talked about the community organizations' relationship with government. One theme that emerged showed that government regulations for renewal projects delayed the refurbishment of apartments for the poor, whereas another theme was that because of lack of respect for community developers, government is slow in releasing grant money for community work. Together, these two themes formed part of a theory linking non-profit organizations to the public sector: though necessary for development work, government is often an obstacle, not a help.

As part of the same attempt to look at related ideas, Herb also put together from the coded material two seemingly contradictory themes that illustrated how the community groups related to their funders. The first described how community organizations deferred to the whims of their funders and the other indicated that community groups were willing to try to aggressively persuade their funders to support the community groups' ideas. Herb wondered how the community organizations could be aggressive and deferent at the same time. To find an explanation, he returned to his coded conversational units on pressure tactics and this time noticed that many of the pressure tactics were indirect. Rather than the community organizations themselves leading a pressure campaign, they asked supportive funders to talk to other funders on their behalf or they established coalitions whose sole purpose was to take the heat if funders got angry at being pressured. In face-to-face, direct contact, the community groups were deferent; in indirect contacts through a third party, the same groups were more aggressive but less visible. Herb had worked out a mechanism, part of an explanatory theory, through which aggressive and deferent behaviors could be compatible. Herb had started building a middle-range theory of how many marginal community groups survive.

ELEMENTS OF A FULL THEORY

So far, we have talked about building toward a theory, putting together themes that explain your research problem. You might want to stop at this point, or you might want to go on and build a full theory. To do so, you need to have an idea what a full, elaborated theory might look like.

The core of such a theory is a set of main themes. Each of these themes by itself provides an answer to a part of your research problem. At the end, you join these separate themes together as you build toward a theory that explains your overall problem. These main themes form the skeleton of the theory; you can elaborate on these bare bones in several different ways.

If some of your main themes describe what caused an effect, you can ask how this cause brings about that effect, what the steps along the way are. You can also elaborate on your theory by looking for exceptions or countertrends to the themes you have described and explaining what they mean in ways that modify your emerging theory. You can add to your theory by examining each theme and, assuming that the theme is correct, ask yourself what the implications of this theme are likely to be. Finally, you examine your data, perhaps in light of published literature, to determine conditions under which your themes are likely to hold or the situations in which they are not likely to hold. In so doing, you are asking how generalizable your theory might be.

One illustration of how this elaboration process works occurred in Irene's project on federal agencies' responses to budget reductions. Part of that research included agencies whose business was collecting and providing data to other government agencies, businesses, and the public. She concluded from the first stage of her analysis that one of the key resources of such agencies is their reputation for technical expertise and turning out professional products, a reputation that is likely to erode during periods of fiscal stress. She also discovered that government agencies whose budget is threatened were more likely to capitulate to partisan demands, eroding their reputations for neutral competence. Bringing the two themes together, she concluded that fiscal stress erodes the credibility of information agencies. This combined theme provided a start to a theory.

Next, she elaborated the theory by explaining in more detail how the causal relationship worked. She reexamined her data to look for mechanisms to explain the relationship between fiscal stress and reduced quality of their products. She found that the agencies were unable to afford to do studies that would update their database or modernize the measures they reported, could not spend the time or money to check on self-reported data, and were unable to get surveys out and analyzed in a timely fashion. She also found that agencies were more willing to distort or exaggerate the results of some of their studies in accordance with political pressures when their budget and staffing were threatened, because they feared antagonizing potential supporters. These two processes—the inability to provide quality data and the willingness to distort findings—were the mechanisms that reduced the agencies' credibility as neutral providers of information. Combined, these themes suggested an overall theoretical explanation that explained *how* fiscal stress erodes credibility: A poorer product and diminished appearance of professional neutrality together *cause* a reduction in credibility.

Further elaborating on the emerging theory, Irene asked herself what the consequences of reduced credibility were. Again, she returned to her data and noticed that agencies that lost credibility continued to lose political support and did not regain lost funding. This finding suggested the fourth theme, that if information agencies lose credibility by creating a poorer and less professional product, they are destroying the basis for their long-term support and by doing so threatening their own future.

Though Irene's theory was based on a handful of government agencies, she thought that a modified version of it might apply beyond the original research setting: If agencies take the wrong actions in the short term to survive threats from their environment, they can bring about their eventual demise. Based on other agencies in her study, it looked as if this modified theme would apply more generally.

EXTENDING YOUR FINDINGS BEYOND THE RESEARCH SETTING

At the very least, by the end of your study, you should have several summary themes that address your research problem; perhaps you will have a fairly complete midlevel theory that describes your research setting and resolves your research puzzle. At this point, you might want to know if what you have found applies in other situations (see Johnson 1997).

To do so, you can follow three paths. In the first, if you initially hoped that your findings would extend beyond the research setting and so in the original design chose research sites, cases, and interviewees that included sufficient variation to later allow you to extend your results to other settings and situations, you now look over what you have found in these different settings and analyze your data to get an idea of how broadly your theory is likely to apply.

Herb interviewed people in a small number of community development groups compared to the total number that exist, but he intentionally varied the groups he chose to include rural and urban organizations, some in minority communities and others in nonminority communities, and some whose work concentrated more on housing and others more on job creation. Irene selected a range of cases for her study on agencies' responses to budget cuts, including large ones and small ones, information-producing agencies and service-production agencies, agencies that provided services primarily to other governmental agencies and ones that provided services to the public, and agencies that had strong interest-group support and others that had none. Because the design of these studies included a range of cases that covered the differences in organizations that were likely to affect the findings, both Herb and Irene felt comfortable generalizing their findings to similar organizations that they had not studied.

A second approach to extending findings is to look for other cases with similar background conditions to your study. The results from your study might also hold in these similar situations. For instance, in cultural studies, especially when examining ceremonies in which core values are expressed, you can be reasonably sure that the core values found in one setting extend to similar ceremonies carried out by the same cultural group in other settings. In topical studies, you can ask what specific conditions influenced the results you observed in your study and then extend your findings to other situations in which those conditions are present. If you studied a police department to see how it changed after 9/11, the conditions that department confronted were probably widespread, and hence the theoretical findings from your study might apply to the police in many other cities. On the other hand, if you studied Boeing after a major contracting scandal, the particular conditions (of a desperate market situation and military-industry collusion) might be sufficiently rare that your findings would hold in only a few other cases.

The third approach to generalizing your theoretical findings is to examine published literature to see if the theory you have worked out seems to hold in settings and circumstances described by other authors. In his first publications on the community-renewal movement, Herb presented a case-specific theory explaining how the smaller community organizations he studied were able to partially shape the agendas of larger, more powerful groups. Later, Herb came across an ethnographic study by Karen Groenbjerg (1993) that included social-service organizations in which she described at a case-specific level how smaller organizations interacted with their funders in a manner similar to what Herb reported for his community organizations. Because the evidence from her study of social-service providers fit right into the theory Herb had worked out for development organizations, Herb felt comfortable extending his findings beyond his immediate case.

THEORY BUILDING IN THE GROUNDED-THEORY MODEL

Just as grounded theory follows a separate pattern of coding and analysis than responsive interviewing, it also has a different model of theory building. Grounded theorists attempt to build theory solely from the data at hand and in doing so emphasize theory building rather than theory testing (Charmaz 2000, 2001; Strauss and Corbin 1990, p. 57). The core of the grounded theory approach is that theory emerges (in an inductive way) directly from the interview or observational data through a series of steps labeled *analytical induction*. Fielding and Lee (1998, p. 22) summarize the analytic induction process:

Step 1: Identify the phenomenon you want to explain.

Step 2: Formulate a rough definition of that phenomenon.

Step 3: Formulate a working hypothesis to explain the phenomenon.

Step 4: Study one case.

Step 5: Ask "do the facts of this case fit my initial hypothesis?"

Step 6: If the answer is "Yes" go on to study the next case. If the answer is "No" EITHER redefine the phenomenon to exclude the case OR reformulate your working hypothesis.

Step 7: Continue Step 6 until you have a "universal solution," that is, until there is a practical certainty that the emerging theory has accounted for all of the cases which have been considered. However, the occurrence of any negative case must lead to either redefinition or reformulation.

The grounded-theory approach rejects using literature to generate themes, concepts, or relationships between them. Also, because grounded theory is about theory building rather than testing theory, it is less focused on finding the limitations of a study or the extent to which the results can be generalized. All the cases or sites in the study are used to modify the themes and emerging theory, leaving none left over in which the theory can be tested. A grounded-theory study is complete when new cases produce no change in the themes or hypotheses. By contrast, at some point in a responsive interviewing project, researchers are satisfied that they have described the scene or research setting and have an important and useful finding, and then may set out to test the limits of the theory by specifying the conditions under which it is likely to hold.

Computers and Qualitative Data Analysis

Your full interview transcripts and memos should be stored in your computer in ways that allow for near instantaneous retrieval. Beyond storing and retrieving data, how much can computers help in analysis? Qualitative researchers are sharply divided on the answer. Some, such as the Loflands, have moderate expectations:

> A considerable number of software programs for the manipulation and analysis of qualitative data are currently available. . . . We have as yet no solid demonstration of the merits of using these programs for analytical purposes, but there seems little doubt of their value for data storage and retrieval purposes. . . . Transforming data into analysis is a difficult task by itself. Little is to be gained, we think, by compounding the difficulty of the task by adding to it the burden of achieving a high level of computer literacy. (Lofland and Lofland 1995, p. 77)

In contrast, the authors of the numerous computer programs for qualitative analysis—NUDIST, the Ethnograph, CAQDAS, among a dozen or so—clearly disagree. They would argue that learning more elaborate software for coding and analyzing the data pays good dividends by facilitating creative, systematic, and thorough research (Fielding 2001; Fielding and Lee 1998; Fielding and Lee 2002; Gahan and Hannibal 1998; Weitzman 2000; Weitzman and Michael 1995).

Software allows you to quickly regroup interview data, enhancing your ability to link concepts and themes, refine them, and locate evidence. But the software cannot choose for your consideration only those ideas that seem to have high payoff. Left to their own devices, the computer programs may offer a jillion or so possibilities that will overwhelm you. You have to tame this sorcerer's apprentice to make it a useful tool. Ultimately, there is no way to substitute for your own decisions as to what makes sense in your data.

Almost all social, political, and behavioral researchers have been exposed to powerful computer programs, such as SPSS or SAS, that automate statistical analysis. Computer automation has taken the hard work (and some of the need for understanding) out of statistical analysis. Some qualitative analysts may believe that software as easy to use as SPSS or SAS will replace the slow, thoughtful process involved in qualitative analysis. However, as the software expert Eben Weitzman argues, "Software can provide tools to help you analyze qualitative data, but it cannot do the analysis for you, not in the same sense in which a statistical package like SPSS or SAS can do, say multiple regression" (Weitzman 2000, p. 805). Qualitative work emphasizes nuanced, context-dependent analysis that almost by definition precludes a standardized and uniform approach. You cannot give your interviews to a program and have it tell you what your data means. If your expectations are more moderate, however, there are a wide variety of programs that can help in data analysis.

Computer programs differ in how they retrieve data and in what form. (The following discussion loosely follows Weitzman 2000, pp. 805–809.) At one end are text retrievers that search throughout the text for keywords you specify and deliver to you the text associated with those keywords (a paragraph, if you tell the computer to give you the paragraph in which the term appears). Text retrievers can search for terms using Boolean logic, that is, you can request all the passages that contain the terms *money* and *budget* or *money* but not *budget*. You can also ask for all the places where two or more key terms occur near each other. If you ask for the term *minority leader*, the program will not only give you the locations of that term, but also where *minority* and *leader* are separated by a few words. You would get back "leader of the minority party," as well as the more predictable "minority leader."

Some text retrieval programs work without your inserting codes or special markers for the computer to find, treating each word as if it were a key word. The advantage of this approach is its ease; you can search for whatever word occurs to you without coding or recoding the data. The downside is that there may be many passages that refer to the idea of interest but do not use the word you are searching for; the computer has no way of knowing that these other passages also refer to the same idea and cannot return these other passages. To have these data units returned, you have to first put explicit codes in the text.

Another type of qualitative software tries to help you analyze the data through linking concepts and themes. Such software requires you to code the data first, and then the software combines the coded concepts in ways that enable you to pick out those combinations that make sense. These programs have the advantage of thoroughness and highlight possibilities that you otherwise might not come up with but also bring up more choices than you can concentrate on, because the computer cannot limit the options to those that seem most promising. Some programs of this type diagram the relationships between concepts or themes once you have specified the relationships between them.

We refer you to the review article by Weitzman (2000) or the older book by Fielding and Lee (1998) for details on how these programs actually work. Overall, they differ in whether or not you are permanently locked into the initial coding categories or can change them as the analysis continues. Another contrast is in the way the links between the codes are determined, whether imposed by the researcher or based on some measure of association, such as the frequency with which codes appear near one another. A third difference is whether or not the codes are set up to reflect hierarchical relationships—for example, does the program allow you to examine individual references to *cats* and *dogs* while at the same time noting that these animals are grouped together as *pets*?

The most important ways in which the software programs differ is on the assumption of what constitutes meaningful information. Some programs emphasize how many times a concept appears in your text, assuming that what is most common is most important. Other programs emphasize how often particular terms or concepts occur together, implying that what is talked about at the same time is more likely to be related than what is discussed at different times.

Computer programs do help in data analysis, but we remain concerned about what might happen when qualitative data-analysis programs become easier to use. A search for counts and associations among concepts (something that the software facilitates and that takes little experience on the part of the researcher) might gradually replace the thoughtful analysis necessary to qualitative theory building. In the responsive interviewing model, analysis is not about how many times a concept or theme appears, but the strength of the evidence on which those themes and concepts depend and on the importance of the concepts and themes in building a theory. Computer programs are not set up to do these things, and you should not expect them to.

Our personal compromise is to stick with a continually improving code-and-retrieve program called Orbis, which is part of the word-processing package called Nota Bene (and the reason why we adopted Nota Bene initially) and which integrates the search process into the word processor. When you search for a term and find it, you can read it in its interview context and note similar passages on the same topic and then immediately place it into your essay or create a file with all excerpts on the same subject. You designate how much of the text you want returned with each coded item, varying from the line in which it occurred all the way up to the entire interview. Orbis codes on every word as a key searchable term and in addition easily accepts your own coding for each data unit. Because all codes are kept in simple word-processor files, they can be changed through global search commands, which allow you to easily recode, for instance, if you decided to refine the overall code *$badprofessor* to the more specific codes *$badprofessorpersonality* and *$badprofessorlecturer*. As new interviews are completed, you code them and then if they are placed in a specified folder, Orbis automatically adds them to the database.

We use Orbis as an aid to analysis in several ways. To understand the meaning of a concept, we retrieve all passages coded with that concept and then examine them in light of the surrounding discussion. A similar approach is taken to examine themes. To elaborate on the meaning of any concept or any theme, we simply extract a file in which all comments on that theme or concept are placed and then read that file to pull out its meaning. For testing out how concepts and themes are linked, Orbis permits extended and complicated searches (looking for situations that contain both *a* and *b* but not *c*), allowing us to systematically examine situations in which several themes are simultaneously present and to test out a theory, while at the same time allowing us to examine its underlying evidence. Orbis does not automatically produce hierarchical groupings of codes or sophisticated pictures of conceptual networks. For some, that might be a disadvantage, but for us, it is an advantage because it enables us to maintain control as we systematically test out ideas and discover which ones are related.

As a coding and extraction tool, Orbis is easy to use. Its chief advantage to us (and probably its chief disadvantage to those more interested in automating computer analysis of qualitative data) is that we have to think about what themes might be present and which ones to search for rather than let the program make the suggestions. We are comfortable with this division of labor between ourselves and our software. Orbis delivers the advantages of systematic analysis without overwhelming us with options that are unimportant or that are based only on frequencies or associations in the text.

Conclusion: From Analysis to Writing

The goal of analysis is to understand core concepts and to discover themes that describe the world you have examined. Your analysis is done when you can put together a theory that answers your research question and that would be accepted by your interviewees as an accurate depiction of their world and thoughts.

The final stage of the research involves preparing reports that share your findings. In doing the data analysis, you are involved in technical matters, thinking about codes, definitions, theories, and relationships. You may go over the data many times, pick themes, drop them for lack of evidence, modify some, and combine others. You might come up with new themes on a fourth or fifth iteration. In the write-up you cannot just reproduce such an elaborate process; it would be too hard for anyone to follow. Instead, in the write-up you want to present vivid, understandable descriptions while providing convincing evidence for your theoretical conclusions. We describe how to do so in the next chapter.

12

Presenting the Results

By the end of the data analysis, you have worked out the major themes, clarified the concepts, and put together an overarching description of your research findings. The last step in the project is to put this information into a report that is inviting, accurate, thorough, convincing, and rich. When you start to write, you shift your focus from hearing what the interviewees have to say to engaging the interest of your future readers, convincing them to accept your conclusions and possibly to act on them.

You might like to shout your findings from the rooftops but are more likely to adopt the quieter strategy of disseminating your results in writing. You write a report because the problems you have studied are important and you are excited about what you have learned. Writing provides a sense of accomplishment by fulfilling promises you gave to your interviewees to make their problems visible and by influencing an intellectual or policy community, as well as an interested public. The bottom line, though, is that you write because you want to share what you have learned. In a famous musical, *Singing in the Rain*, Gene Kelly, explains why entertainers go through lean times, difficult rejections, and grueling training. His answer? "Gotta dance!" They have no choice: It is who they are, what they have to do. Qualitative researchers "gotta write."

Successful writing requires sustained effort. If you fail to engage the intended audience or your narrative is garbled or the presentation illogical, if there is not enough background provided to make the material understandable or you lack evidence to make the argument convincing, you will be shouting into the wind. No one will hear you, no one will use your work, your insights will be lost, and the voices of the people you represent will remain inaudible.

As you think about your writing, ask yourself four questions. First, *what is the core idea or set of ideas that you want to communicate?*

Are you trying to explain a technical concept, narrate a history of an important political event, share an oral history, work out an academic theory, resolve a policy problem, or something else? Second, *who is the audience you are trying to reach in your writings?* Are you addressing a thesis committee, fellow academics, policy makers, or a broader informed public? Third, *what outlets are available to disseminate your findings?* Will your findings be written up in a policy paper, op-ed piece, internal report, conference paper, journal article, or book? Fourth, *what style and form of writing best communicates the central ideas in outlets that will reach the intended audience?* Should the writing be formal and academic or casual and personal? How much detail can be included? How much of the researcher's or the conversational partner's voice should come through?

In this chapter we try to answer these questions. We focus primarily on writing for formal outlets, including policy reports, dissertations and theses, journal articles and books, and conference papers, though we should note that some qualitative researchers successfully present what they have learned in novels or plays (Ellis and Bochner 1996). We begin by describing a variety of ways findings are disseminated and show how the choice of outlet affects how you present the material. We then examine some writing techniques, particularly focusing on how to express your argument in a logical and coherent way. We suggest ways of evaluating the quality of your writing and then conclude the chapter by explaining the publication process.

Ways in Which Qualitative Reports Are Disseminated

There are many different channels for disseminating your findings, each attracting specific types of readers. You can share your findings through in-house newsletters or publish them in magazines or periodicals aimed at practitioners, in academic journals in your field, in newspapers as freelance articles in the Sunday magazine or as op-ed pieces, or as books, either popular books (called trade books) for a general audience or as monographs for a more specialized academic audience. Both academics and practitioners write papers to present at professional conferences. Increasingly conference papers and in-house reports are posted on the Web. Student research is written up in theses (undergraduate and masters' students) and doctoral dissertations (PhD students). Dissertations and theses are shared on university Web sites, CD-ROMs, or microfilms.

Policy reports help frame issues and provide data to guide decision making. Because policy makers rarely have time for much reading, policy reports are written straight to the point. An in-house study based on exit interviews to recommend changes in personnel policies might be read by only a handful of managers. Other policy reports, often more ethnographic in detail, are intended for a somewhat wider audience. For example, after community activists wondered why many neighborhood organizations in minority communities were being led by nonminority individuals, the think tank Policy Link contracted to conduct a study to answer the question. The resulting pamphlet, *Leadership for Policy Change: Strengthening Communities of Color Through Leadership Development* (Marsh, Daniel, and Putnam 2003), was circulated widely on the Web.

Academic findings are initially shared in conference papers that are presented to groups of specialized scholars. Writings are then circulated more widely in one of hundreds of academic journals that are read by people who are generally informed about the subject matter and are mainly looking for information that speaks to ongoing debates in the discipline. Journal articles can be a bit longer than policy advocacy pieces but are rarely more than 30 typed pages, allowing for the presentation of only a limited number of themes and supporting evidence.

In contrast, academic books allow more space to present a series of related themes or develop a complicated theory, along with supportive descriptive data. For example, Charmaz's *Good Days, Bad Days* (1991) presents a series of linked themes on the problems faced by people with chronic illnesses, working up to a theory on personal coping. In *Renewing Hope Within Neighborhoods of Despair* (H. J. Rubin 2000), Herb presents both descriptions of how community development activists work to renew poor neighborhoods and a theory on why they succeed. In *Balancing the Federal Budget* (I. S. Rubin 2003), Irene explores how the federal government managed for a time to balance its budget and then, based on her descriptions, offers a theory of when and how government learns and how what is learned is stored and recalled. Such academic studies are written for a readership already interested in the specific topics.

Other books based on interview research appeal to a wider audience. Oral histories, usually told almost entirely in the words of the interviewees, transport readers to another time and place. Studs Terkel's oral histories on working and on World War II became best sellers. Mitch Duneier's *Sidewalk* (1999) makes the life of the New York street vendor come alive, and William Wilson's *When Work Disappears* (1996) portrays the dismal employment prospects of inner-city residents showing how poverty breeds despair. In *Troubling the Angels: Women Living with HIV/AIDS* (1997), Lather and Smithies present in (almost) unedited transcripts moving renditions of how women live with this devastating disease. These books are written for a broad public, offer vivid descriptions, and create an empathetic understanding that can lead to changes in social or political policy or help bridge the gap between generations.

Managing Style and Tone

You pick an outlet that is suitable for the kind of report you have done, imagine the readers of that publication, and then write for them. To help you reach those readers and to comply with editors' requirements, you should gear your writing to the *style* and *tone* that generally appear in good examples chosen from that outlet.

Style includes how the writing is physically organized, how headings are used, the way in which notes are handled, page layout—including line spacing, margins, and the presentation of tables, charts, and graphs—and how excerpts from interviews are treated. Style also refers to the length and complexity of sentences and paragraphs and the density of technical information and vocabulary, forcing you to anticipate how the manuscript would sound if you were to read it out loud. Tone communicates how seriously readers should take the findings. Does the writing make the reader laugh or think, rouse anger or conviction, or convey confidence and authority or defensiveness? Is it precise or vague, formal or informal?

STYLE

Stylistic elements differ depending on the outlet, so before writing, look over a series of articles or books in that outlet to see how they appear. Are the writings organized into standard parts, beginning with an introductory section stating the research problem, then a methods section, followed by the presentation of the data and ending with conclusions or recommendations? Is the methodology discussion at the end, in an appendix, or perhaps omitted? Note the length of the paragraphs and the sentences. Though you do not have to match exactly the format of the outlet you pick, doing so may make your manuscript easier for readers to follow.

Another element of style is the extent to which academic trappings—notes, citations, and formal English—are required. Endnotes and footnotes are less central comments that are placed either at the bottom of a page or the end of the text so as not to distract from the flow of the argument. Notes may contain only citations to the literature or they may contain counterpoints, soften conclusions, discuss data sources, or compare the text with other authors' interpretations. Citations are references to the literature referred to or used in the writing. In formal scholarly writing, authors cite every document, article, or book they used, whether the material was directly quoted or only summarized. The goal is to embed the work in the literature while clearly describing what ideas were taken from others.

Scholarly writing builds on formal, written English, not informal, spoken language. Formal English means the writing is strictly grammatical, correctly punctuated, and avoids slang, colloquial expressions, and puns, and emphasizes precision of meaning. In quoting your interviewees, you will use their colloquial expressions and slang because people talk this way, but in the text you must be careful to limit colloquialisms. Formal academic writing avoids slang because it rarely communicates outside the group that created it. Formal English is precise and avoids vague or noncommittal words and phrases, such as *I think*, *it seems*, or *more or less*. Watch out for exaggerations, which may be fine rhetorical flourishes in spoken language but may convey imprecision in written work. If you use a word that has many meanings, define it in the text. Also be wary of language that carries connotations that you do not intend, for instance, labeling someone a *Nazi* when you really mean a *bully*, a *thug*, or a *right-winger*. The word *Nazi* comes with historical and cultural baggage, including supporting the extermination of millions of people in death camps, forced slavery, and biological experiments on unwilling humans. If you do not also mean those things, you should not use the word *Nazi*. More generally, you scrutinize your writing to eliminate inappropriate stereotypes.

It is often difficult to see the colloquial expressions, slang, and stereotypes in your own writing, as they are a taken-for-granted part of your own culture. Stereotypes usually capture a part of what you are trying to describe—some little old ladies have tinted their hair a shade of blue gray, but referring to all older women as blue-haired old ladies is imprecise and may be offensive. Some examples of common colloquialisms, slang expressions, and stereotypes might help you recognize them and learn to avoid them in your formal writing.

Colloquialisms

I knew where she was coming from. (I understood her point of view.)

It was a bad scene. (The situation was awful in some specified way.)

I screwed it up. (I made a mistake with serious consequences.)

She is not all there. (She has emotional problems.)

They bailed out. (They quit or left a difficult situation.)

Slang

Airhead (empty headed, doesn't follow serious news or issues)

Bad (meaning good)

Batman and Robin (inseparable)

In your face (flagrant, obvious)

Stereotypes

Swore like a sailor

Good enough for government work

Butch and femme

Swish

Geek, nerd

Kike-ish

Militant Muslim

Ivory-tower academic

Blue-haired old ladies

Computer jocks

TONE

Style and tone overlap, because the writing style can evoke particular feelings in the reader, but there are additional elements in creating a tone. Two aspects of tone are particularly relevant for writing up qualitative research: one is building in the sense of immediacy, being there, and the other is the feeling of seriousness of the work, which communicates respect for the interviewees and the readers.

Skilled authors can create a mood, make the reader feel he or she is present, watching events unfold or listening to the interviewee answer questions. This feeling of immediacy results from a series of choices of how to present the material, including whether the author uses the first person and the active voice, includes himself or herself in the writing, and uses quotations from the interviewees extensively. Using the first person—*I* chose,

I saw, I decided, and so on—rather than the third person—*the researcher chose, saw,* or *decided,* and so on—gives a more active and immediate tone to the writing. Authors become more visible when they use the active voice although some researchers attempt to make their work sound more neutral, perhaps scientific, by using the passive voice—*it was found* rather than *I found.* Generally, you should follow the style of the publication outlet you want to use, but when you have a choice, use the active voice, as it is more precise, direct, and engaging. To make the author more visible, you include the interviewer's questions along with the interviewees' answers in the quotations you use.

Using extensive quotations from your interviews makes the interviewees real. However, you need to carefully work out how much of the story to tell in the words of your interviewees and how much to summarize in your own words. An essay is likely to be too long if you use just quotations, and as many of the quoted passages need some explanation to be understood, a reader will not be able to follow the argument. You need to balance your explanation and conclusions with the illustrative quotations that make the findings real. Journals differ on their preferences for the length and number of quotations, so pay close attention to the articles you use as your stylistic reference.

You should be careful about which quotations you actually use in your writing. Quotations affect the tone of the writing by both their primary and secondary messages. Primary messages reflect the literal content of what was said, but the word choice, grammar, and hesitations or humor in the quotation may evoke secondary meanings called *subtext.* In one of Herb's essays on community developers, he chose descriptive quotations in which the interviewees described how they obtained funding and overcame a variety of problems in the course of their projects. When he sent this manuscript off to a journal, reviewers told him that the quotes also conveyed a subtext: the dedication and enthusiasm of the activists. In later writings, Herb intentionally chose quotations not only for the overt text (how a building was built) but also for the subtext (the enthusiasm for rebuilding a neighborhood, a sense of possibility) because he wanted the tone of the essay to communicate this mood and message of optimism.

Tone also establishes how seriously the piece is to be taken. You want the writing to communicate that the study is based on solid scholarship, so write in a calm and considered manner—not in an emotional, wry, funny, or mocking manner—to make the reader respond thoughtfully. Scholarly authors make few if any digressions in the text, instead having to march inexorably to the conclusion, each step necessary and in its logical place in the exposition. Scholarly authors try not to tell their readers how to react to a finding, instead providing solid evidence for each key point.

In polemical as opposed to academic writing, the author wants to change an opinion or muster support and may use emotional appeals as substitutes for logic and evidence. If academic writing sounds polemical, the readers may dismiss what is being said. Polemical writing often draws false dichotomies, uses colored words that tell the reader or listener how he or she should feel or leads the reader with a set of inappropriate details. False dichotomies categorize people or answers into two camps in an effort to lead the reader to accept one and reject the other. Being patriotic or being anti-American would be an example of a false dichotomy that forces a reader to accept the label *patriotic*, and all that implies, or wear the label *anti-American*. There is no place for false dichotomies in formal academic writing.

A colored word is a term that evokes emotion, such as loyalty, anger, protectiveness, excitement, or pity, telling the reader how to feel. If you are reporting about a raptor rehabilitation center and describe the birds as noble, *noble* would be a colored word that is intended to evoke support—without the provision of evidence. A polemicist might also pile on unnecessary but loaded details, such as "When I interviewed her, she was wearing a necklace of sculpted silver that must have cost a couple of thousand dollars." This type of description communicates that the interviewee is showing off wealth and makes the reader dislike her, irrespective of what the interviewee actually said. Scholarly writing conveys the story through the evidence, the collected quotations, and the constructed narrative, rather than telling the reader what to feel and how to think.

The overall tone of a written essay should display confidence in what you accomplished. Do not apologize for qualitative methodology by saying, "I used *only* three cases" or "I interviewed *only* 10 people." Instead, you explain why you picked the cases you chose, what they exemplified or what experiences the 10 people you interviewed had that made them important for the study. If you want the reader to take the work seriously, you have to come across as competent and systematic in your methods. A humble, self-mocking, or apologetic tone undermines the competence you want to convey.

Starting to Write

So far, you have an idea of the message you want to communicate, have an audience in mind, and are aware of the style and tone of the outlets for the intended audience. Now you have to start to write. What is important is getting something written and not worrying too much about how it sounds initially, because you will change it a dozen times. We will share our approach to getting started, but if you have another way that works for you, stick with it.[1]

Our writing goes through several stages:

FOCUSED SUMMARY

We begin by thinking about the results we came up with during the analysis phase and ask ourselves what the overall lesson is. The answer becomes a brief summary paragraph that we jot down. If we are still too close to our data, we might end up unsuccessfully trying to summarize everything we learned in one paragraph, a stylistic nightmare, so another approach is required. Sometimes we go back and review the memos we wrote, paying particular attention to the notable quotes that we jotted down when an interviewee said something that summarized a key point in a well-phrased way. We ask ourselves why we felt these quotes were important and then try to write our focused summary to reflect the answer we work out.

Another approach we use is to think about a crucial event or a memorable conversation—how a deal was cut on balancing open space with shopping or how a bureaucratic agency received a larger budget but was then told to prosecute violators less diligently. We ask ourselves why we thought of this incident or conversation; the answer to that question often suggests what to include in the summary paragraph.

An alternative way to come up with the initial succinct summary is to pretend you are answering a question about your research to a specific individual who does not have the patience to listen to a long response. Irene often visualizes speaking to government policy analysts who want to know what her findings mean. Herb has been asked by community developers what he has learned and the brief answers he gives them often suggest the summary paragraph. Academic colleagues are more likely to want to know how your research speaks to broader theory, so your answer to them will focus on the implications for theory.

OUTLINING

Next you organize the material so that the argument moves from idea to idea in a logical way. Outlines provide this organization while helping structure the writing. Though you work out an outline before you write, keep in mind that outlines change as you revise what you want to say.

In an outline you organize the flow of the writing by dividing all the material into different main headings that follow each other logically. An outline visually shows how different themes relate to each other, which ideas come first, which next, and which are main themes and which ones are secondary. The main sections of the outline, which represent the separate core points of your argument, are labeled with roman numerals, the subheadings under each of the main sections use capital letters, and subheadings under those capital letters use arabic numerals. The hierarchical structure makes clear the relationship between specific main points, their refinements, and the evidence supporting them. Gaps in the outline warn you if you are lacking evidence or background for a particular point, are spending too much space on a minor point, or have failed to give ideas of equal import parallel treatment.

We will illustrate using an outline for a typical journal article that contains four main sections:

    I.   Introduction
    II. Methods and Design
    III. Findings
    IV. Conclusions and Implications

In practice, you do *not* work out the details of the outline starting with the introduction. Instead, you outline from the middle concentrating on the sections that provide your findings (in this case, Section III). Under your main heading, you begin to flesh out the details by creating secondary heading (the As, Bs, and Cs) for each of the major themes in your findings, and under each theme, both the evidence as well as the modifications you want to provide (the 1s, 2s, and 3s). Or, you might provide as secondary headings each step of the narrative you are portraying.

If you are working out the findings section of a cultural study, you usually start out with the simplest concepts and themes and then gradually add more complicated ones, and then show the linkages between them. If you are tracing out a narrative of events, the outline headings in the section will be the events that occurred, placed in chronological order. In discussing a complicated social, political, or behavioral problem, each of the subheadings under a main head will describe one part of the overall problem examined, what the problem entailed and what occurred, and then in the last heading a wrap-up that ties the separate parts together.

If you need to make more refinements, you can use small alphabetical letters (a, b, c, etc.) and small roman numerals (i, ii, iii, etc.). As an illustration, we have included below a portion of the outline from the findings section of Irene's project on what contracting entails in local government.

III. Theories, Concepts, and Themes Regarding Contracts
  A. Types of contracts
      1. Professional services (architects, engineers, attorneys, consultants)
      2. Capital projects (design, build, operate contracts; construction)
      3. Service delivery contracts (snow removal, animal control, janitorial)
  B. Experience with contracts over time
      1. Quality tends to deteriorate
          a. Example, wastewater contract—Milwaukee
          b. Example, water contract—Atlanta
      2. Prices go up with change orders
          a. Evidence from capital projects
          b. Intentional deception on initial bid? (Quote from interview)
      3. Contractors may become co-opted, part of the organization
          a. Examples (contract attorneys, water and wastewater management)
          b. Conditions conducive to co-optation
              i. Longer contracts
              ii. Contractor is local
          c. Consequences, blurring of public and private may be result

Section III details the core concepts and themes, starting with illustrations of types of contracts and then describing what happens to the contracts over time. Three themes are as follows: Contract quality deteriorates, prices go up, and some contractors are co-opted by the government agency that hired them—that is, the private companies take on the values of the government agencies.

Irene illustrates each of these themes in a different way. For the theme on the deterioration of quality, she provides detailed examples from two case-study cities. For the price increase theme, she provides evidence from particular projects to demonstrate that the price increases did occur but adds a new point, that these increases might be intentional. For the third theme, she shows that co-optation happens—that is, a contractor may take on a role much like a city employee—and draws out the conditions that facilitate this occurrence, and then describes the consequences of this co-optation. The result here is a kind of minitheory, with a main theme, preconditions necessary for the theme to occur, and consequences of the theme. Some of the examples she uses are just quotes from individual interviews, but others are the result of synthesizing a narrative from multiple sources.

The outline shows much more detail and clarification on co-optation than it does on contract deterioration or price increases. This imbalance suggests that Irene needs to search her interview material more carefully to see if she can make the material in each section of the outline more parallel. Does she know when service quality is likely to deteriorate, or with what consequences? Do her interviewees talk about what causes price increases and change orders or what the consequences are? If not, she might actually want to resume interviewing to track down this additional information. There is nothing wrong with pausing during the writing and returning to the data gathering to obtain the missing pieces.

There is no need for an outline to include each detailed point (as many will emerge only as you write), but you still should avoid creating an outline that is too general, that is, consists of just main headings. Instead, think of what details belong under each category, such as in the following example from the contracting project:

I. Introduction
   A. Statement of the research problem: Government agencies are contracting out more with the private sector; is the public better off as a result? How would we know?
   B. Why the problem is important
      1. Lots of money involved
      2. Threatens jobs of present labor force
      3. Has implications for quality of service delivery, especially for dependent populations
      4. Increases the skills required for managers to supervise contracts properly
   C. History and context
      1. Recent history of increases in contracting out
      2. Recent examples that illustrate impacts on labor
      3. Changes in quality of service delivery over time
      4. Current training for managers with respect to contract supervision
   D. Literature
      1. Polarization of the literature: Some say the public benefits; others say no
      2. Weaknesses in the methodology of prior studies
         a. Don't track actual costs over time
         b. Don't track actual performance over time
         c. Don't track costs of supervision or litigation over time
         d. Don't include comparison groups
      3. Studies limited to garbage pickup—don't address other governmental functions

Note that Irene is providing a lot of detail on the history of contracting because that is the focus of the research, but does not present information on other ways government provides services because that material is irrelevant to her findings. If Irene were later to change the middle portion of the outline, perhaps to include more detail on contract deterioration, she would then increase the material in the introduction to keep the organization of the outline balanced, examining why other literature ignores this problem. When you change one part of an outline, you need to change other parts of the outline to anticipate or reflect the changes elsewhere.

Often, authors wait until they have actually written the findings section before outlining the conclusion. Similarly, the outline for the methods section can be delayed to make sure only needed material is included. In one project, Herb, for example, spent several years interviewing and attending meetings; in a paper based entirely on interviewing, he would not include in the methods section a description of how he went about the observations.

DRAFTING THE MANUSCRIPT

You are now ready to turn the analysis you have completed into a coherent essay. Keep in mind that what you initially write will be changed multiple times. You revise what you have written to improve grammar, flow, and style, but more important, you revise to clarify the ideas, to close the gaps in logic that only become apparent as you examine what you have written, and most important to make sure that what you have written is what you intended to say.

Most academic essays contain four parts: an introduction, a core descriptive/analytical section, a conclusion, and a methodological discussion. In a journal article, the introduction, including literature reviews, runs only a few pages, whereas the body of the manuscript has room for at most a handful of closely related themes. In books, the introduction might spread over two or three chapters in which you describe the overall problem, present background on the topic, as well as a literature review; the conclusions and methodology sections will often run a chapter each, and the descriptive/analytical part will be divided up into a chapter for each theme introduced or each case researched.

Be direct in your writing. Spare the reader the details of how you initially reached your conclusions. Readers want to know what you learned, want convincing, concise evidence for why your findings are interesting and important; they are not interested in the themes you considered and rejected for lack of sufficient evidence. To convince the reader of your case, in each section include an introductory paragraph showing where the argument is going, provide quotations that illustrate or add evidence for your point, and then interpret what was said in light of your own argument.

As you write, repeatedly go down a mental checklist: Does your writing clearly state in words that the reader can follow what each concept or theme means? Are the individual steps in your logic clear? Do the quotations directly and clearly illustrate the point you are making? Do you have sufficient, high-quality evidence for each point? Are you presenting roughly the same length discussion for each major point? If you cannot answer each question affirmatively, you need to make some repairs, choosing clearer quotations, providing better evidence, or cutting some and expanding other parts of the discussion so parallel points are approximately the same length.

When you review the draft of the descriptive/analytical section, make sure you have laid out the transition sentences or paragraphs that relate each individual point to the broader argument. If your argument has several parts that could go in any order, readers can get lost and wonder where you are going unless you remind them now and then. Headings also help in providing organization to your essay, especially if the headings are taken directly from a logical and coherent outline.

Once you have a working draft of the descriptive/analytical section, you can write the conclusion section, in which you briefly repeat the purposes of the research, summarize what you have found, and then describe the implications of your findings for theory or policy action. Your conclusions must emerge from the material reported in your descriptive/analytical section. You can discuss what you have found in light of the literature, modifying, extending, or supporting and confirming what others have written. You can also address the limitations of your study, where the study results might not hold, or what should be investigated in future research.

The content of the concluding section has to match the research problem stated in the opening section, so you write the introduction in ways that anticipate the rest of the essay, which you have already written. In the introduction you describe the research problem, indicate its importance either for policy or theory, present the relevant literature, provide the necessary background for the reader to understand the findings of your study, and anticipate those findings. You show that the research addresses a pressing theoretical or policy problem that has puzzled or eluded other researchers, indicating why your approach should produce new insights or perspectives. Generally, you should not justify the importance of your research on the basis that no one else has studied it, because that often means the problem is not important.

The extent of published writing in almost any area can be immense, so you need to be selective in what literature is referred to in the introduction. Let three principles guide your choice: First, does the book or article provide background necessary for the reader to understand the research question. Second, do these publications summarize the main debates or themes that frame your research. Third, do these writings suggest the weaknesses, omissions, or methodological problems that you intend to fix with your current research?

You can write the methods section almost any time because how you went about the work stays the same irrespective of what conclusions you reached. In articles, the methods section is normally quite brief but still has to include a number of points. You indicate that you gathered data using in-depth qualitative interviews in which you asked open-ended questions that evolved as you learned more about the topic. You describe how you selected interviewees, indicating what different perspectives they represented. If you interviewed at different sites, you describe how those sites differed and why they were chosen. You talk about what role you took, how you negotiated access, and whether you had special relationships with those you studied. You should indicate how many interviews you conducted, how long they lasted, and whether you did follow-up interviews. Also include your approach to coding and analysis and the ways in which you checked your evidence. If your study has the potential of harming your interviewees, describe how you are protecting them. Be brief about how much personal reflection you include, but if you had strong biases or expectations when you began, you may want to mention how they affected the research.

REVAMPING AND REVISING YOUR ESSAY

Good writing comes about only after multiple drafts. Lay the manuscript aside for a few days or weeks, and then pick it up again when you have sufficient distance to be able to see more clearly where your meaning is unclear or your narrative is lacking in logic or evidence.

As you revise, you check to see that the flow of ideas is correct, that you have presented sufficient background so that your readers can make sense of the text, that each argument is convincing, and that the language itself is clear, cogent, and evocative. Work to catch lapses in tone, eliminate as much jargon as you can, and reduce notes to the minimum necessary. Make sure that your spelling is correct and citations are accurate, complete, and in the proper format.

As you rework the essay, pay attention to how you have handled quotations. You cannot just string quotes together; you have to introduce and explain each one. When introducing a quotation, you normally indicate who said it, by name and position, unless you have promised your interviewees confidentiality. In the introduction to the quote, you try to explain briefly why the information should be taken seriously, for instance, by saying, "An official who spent his career in the executive budget office mentioned this about the budget deficit." You can also introduce a quotation by summarizing the theme it illustrates. For example, "A leading community developer funded by the intermediaries still found fault with their policies" would be followed by a quotation from that community developer that was critical of the policies of the intermediary. Alternatively, you may wish to follow a quotation with a sentence or two that links it to the theme you are developing. These introductory and follow-up comments help clarify the meaning of the quotation to the reader.

If you have a short quotation, less than two or three lines, you put quotation marks around it and include it in the text of the paragraph. Longer quotations are set off by indenting them in what publishers call *extracts,* which do not require quotation marks because the indentation tells the reader that the passage is an exact quotation. When you submit your manuscript for publication, the publisher may change the length requirement for extracts to conform to its particular style, but setting quotes of more than seven lines as extracts is a fairly established standard for manuscripts. With indirect quotes, that is, when summarizing in your own words what someone told you, do not use quotation marks.

The quotations are the core evidence that you use, but their meaning might not be all that clear. Most people do not speak grammatically: They interrupt and repeat themselves, leave sentences unfinished, and sometimes use incorrect words or verb tenses. How much freedom do you have to change a quote to make it more understandable? When you put quotations around text, the reader should assume material between the quotation marks is exactly what the interviewee said. If the quotation is hard to understand, look for a substitute example or summarize the point in your own words, without quotation marks. Another way to clarify meanings is to show quotations you are planning to use to those who said them, allowing the interviewees to smooth out what they said. You may lose a little of the flavor of the original, but do not have to worry about changing the intent of the speaker.

Improving the grammar, completing the thought, or eliminating dialect can make the text more readable but might be misleading. Researchers differ in their willingness to modify a quote. The two of us will alter a quote, without explicit permission, but only in limited ways. When we do, we clearly mark the passages so that the reader can tell the changes apart from the original statement. For example, we follow the common practice of editing out repetition and comments that have nothing to do with the topic, putting in elision dots (. . .). As long as the meaning is preserved, the words that are quoted were actually said, and you mark the places where you made omissions, this practice is acceptable. We also insert missing words in brackets that finish up a thought or make it more grammatical, using brackets to show that the original version was more fragmentary. The following excerpt, set as an indented extract, shows how this looks:

> It was a top-down process. [Budget Director] Stockman and OMB determined where [the cuts would be], quickly and, I might say, efficiently. There was not a lot of appeal [from their decision]. Cabinet officers were in sync with the philosophy; it was not a normal policy review. It was almost done by fiat. (I. S. Rubin 1985, p. 81)

Editing the quotations in this manner shows a respect for the interviewee and enhances credibility while making the text easier to understand.

Editing a quotation for style is more dubious. Generally, you want to retain the speech mannerisms of the interviewee. If he or she hesitates a lot, those delays are part of the information being conveyed, as they show how the conversational partner struggled with the question. On the other hand, too many "uhhs . . . ," and "y'knows" are grating and do not add any meaning. You might want to retain just enough of them to suggest the interviewee's speech mannerisms.

JUDGING THE QUALITY OF WRITING

As we make revisions in successive drafts, we ask ourselves whether or not the manuscript has achieved standards of good writing, and if not, try to bring what we have written up to that level. Does the writing engage the reader? Does it communicate the richness and nuance of the world we have studied? Is the argument thorough and credible enough to convince people that what is said is correct? We then seek comments on style and substance from professional colleagues, conversational partners, and peer reviewers, and make revisions based on those comments.

Engaging and Readable

No matter how good your research is, if you cannot lure people into reading the report, it will have no effect. To engage the reader, choose a title that is catchy and that accurately reflects the substance of your report. Authors often use titles with colons in the middle, with the catchy part first and then the explanation, or vice versa. Some examples include *Not Our Kind of Girl: Unraveling the Myths of Black Teenage Motherhood* (Kaplan 1997) and *No Shame in My Game: The Working Poor in the Inner City* (Newman 1999).

Next, make sure you quickly communicate in clear and intriguing terms the subject of the study. For example, "this article examines what happens to people their first few days out of prison." In a book, you have a little more room to grab a reader's interest, perhaps by presenting a brief story that suggests the main themes. Such a story becomes a hook that, like the cane of the barker at the circus, reaches out and brings the audience in by arousing interest.

Hooks have some common characteristics. They are relatively brief, they are interesting and vivid, and they directly suggest the content of the book or article or report. Elaine Bell Kaplan in *Not Our Kind of Girl* (Kaplan 1997) opens with a phone call to a talk show in which the caller blames the social problems of blacks on teen pregnancies. Kaplan contrasts the sentiments in that call with the circumstances and story of a real-life teenage mother. Joseph Shapiro (1993) begins *No Pity,* a book on the political movement of people with disabilities, with quotes from former poster children, contrasting the reality of growing up disabled with the cute and lovable image of the poster child. The hook anticipates the tension that the rest of the book spells out.

To keep the reader interested, you hint at your findings in your introduction, revealing more detailed conclusions one piece at a time. Sometimes you can keep a reader's interest by breaking down the research question into a series of nested puzzles, solving one only to reveal the next.

In the body of the writing you pick examples and quotations that are vivid. The quotations you use should be evocative of the atmosphere and circumstances of the interviewee's world and situation. You might want to use some of the notable quotes you jotted down in your memo file, for instance, the phrase in one of Herb's interviews about "nibbling the hands of funders from time to time" or the quote in one of Irene's interviews about predicting deficits ahead "as far as the eye can see." These phrases evoke a picture; in one case, you can imagine a community organizer chewing on the fingers of a foundation official; in the other, you can visualize a budgeter standing on the edge of a cliff looking out and seeing deficits all the way to the horizon. These images cause the reader to pause a minute and think about what is being said.

Rich and Nuanced Writing

Well-written qualitative reports are nuanced and rich. Nuance means conveying shades of meaning and fine distinctions; richness means the writing includes variations and refinements of the main themes while exploring issues in depth. Richness requires examining a problem in context while dealing with complexity, competing ideas, tensions between values or themes, and mutual causation. Rich reports often contain more than one related story line.

To provide richness and nuance in your writing, you choose quotations that illustrate multiple themes and that perhaps show the tensions between these separate themes. The following passage from an article by Herb illustrates the complexity you can communicate through the use of rich yet readable quotations. An African American interviewee is discussing the relationship of his community development organization to City Hall.

> The other thing that tends to happen . . . is favoritism. You know, if you are in with the bureaucrats on a particular day, then you might fare well. If you are on the outs with them, you don't fare so well. . . . At one time, I had $50,000 in city monies, three or four years ago, to do housing. I used to do a lot of money with the city in terms of community development block grants. But over a period of time the city became increasingly more intrusive [slow and careful choice of words] as a result of that relationship. Meaning that they would demand things of me that had nothing to do with the proficiency of the project. Accounting records.
>
> Or they even went so far as to suggest that I put some Caucasians on my board of directors. So they could say, "You need to expand your board." I said, "What you mean, 'expand your board.'" [They said,] "You know, so you got a more diverse representation on your board." Now I got school teachers. I got business owners. I got directors of alternative education programs. I got an accountant. You know, all of them African-American. But in his eye, he didn't see shit. All he saw was a bunch of black folk down there and you need to expand your board. So I said, "What you mean, expand my board?" [The city official responded,] "Well, you know it is perceived as being a very closed corporation and you know a lot of people won't trust that situation, the way it is, so if you expanded it, you know, a little more expertise, and what not." "So you're talking, put some white people on my board?" "Well that would help, you know, that would help." And, I gave him their $50,000 back. (H. J. Rubin 1993, p. 432)

The richness of the passage is conveyed by the tension between two related themes, first, that the city seemed racist in its dealings with black groups, and second, that the city was concerned with maintaining accounting records. The quotation suggests the unresolved question of to what extent the city's demand for better accounting was racist. Real life is complex, and portraying complexity adds to the richness of the writing.

Thoroughness and Credibility

You revamp your manuscript to make sure that your argument appears thorough and credible. *Thorough* means you followed up different lines of inquiry, paying attention to possible contradictions or unexpected findings, and examined alternative views. *Credible* means that you have presented convincing evidence for each major conclusion. To demonstrate thoroughness, you describe in the methods and design section who you interviewed, what group or faction or perspective or period of time they represent, and how long you spoke to each one, as illustrated in an excerpt from one of Irene's articles:

> Ten people were interviewed for this article on stress between budget staffers and elected officials. They were all senior officials who had spent their lives as budgeters. They represented all the budget agencies at the federal level, including the Congressional budget office in the legislative branch, the Office of Management and Budget in the Executive branch, and the General Accounting Office, which has some responsibilities for monitoring budget and tax processes. Some of the interviewees were retired, others were still active. Three of the interviewees were interviewed more than once, one was interviewed three times. Interviews averaged an hour and a half, with the longest being two and a half hours. (I. S. Rubin 2002)

Thoroughness also means that you followed up on themes and concepts, reinterviewed when necessary, and verified the information you received in your interviews against other interviews, documentary sources, or participant observation. In your methods section, you explicitly describe how you verified information and when you present evidence, especially on controversial subjects, you can show in the introduction to your quotations that you talked to both sides of an ideological divide: "The Democratic leader said . . . whereas the Republican Whip concluded . . ."

When you examine the literature, you show thoroughness by picking the key authors and the relevant publications, covering the relevant time periods and themes, as well as competing schools of thought. Without overwhelming readers with many citations, you need to show that you have mastered the literature and have picked the major trends or themes to sketch the intellectual background of your project.

You make your writing credible by providing solid evidence for each key point in your argument and by describing how carefully you designed—and redesigned—your study. As you reread your drafts, make sure you have backed up each claim and conclusion with the strongest evidence you have. First-hand evidence is stronger than second-hand evidence; pick a quotation from an interviewee who participated in the event you are discussing, who saw the confrontation, and maybe got hit while trying to separate the quarreling parties, rather than someone who read about the brouhaha in the morning paper. You can strengthen the credibility of your report when you quote those conclusions directly from your interviewees with minimal or no insertion of yourself and, hence, minimal possibility of your distorting the results to match some preconceived theory of your own.

To increase credibility, you should describe the experiential base of the interviewees, that is, how they knew what they reported to you. This can be done briefly in the way you introduce a quotation: "As a former budget director for the Department of Housing and Urban Development, Al Kliman argued political appointees sometimes ignore professional staff." In topical studies, naming your interviewees when anonymity has not been promised adds credibility because responsibility for what you say shifts to the interviewee. Readers who are curious can check with your sources to see if they did say what you said they said. It is not usually necessary to name names in cultural interviews, though, because any of a number of people can demonstrate the truth or falsity of your claims.

If you promised an interviewee confidentiality, you cannot identify the individual by name, but you can still demonstrate what kind of experience underlies his or her answers. You can describe your interviewee's background with a lead-in statement: "A longtime observer of the budget process in Washington and former employee of the Congressional Budget Office said . . ." or "A longtime lobbyist on Capitol Hill for social causes told the researcher . . ."

When space permits you can show that you have seen the same pattern in different interviews. Note that the goal here is not to count responses but to make it clear that you have talked to people who hold very different perspectives, who might have seen the same situation from different vantage points, or who come at the subject with different biases but who, despite such differences, all provided compatible and overlapping answers.

If you checked out multiple sources of evidence, include this additional data as support for your conclusions. When you summarize information from an interview—"John told me he was comfortable in public speaking . . ."—you strengthen what you say if you provide an example that shows how you confirmed John's statement: "During the conference plenary session that I observed, John addressed the entire group with poise and humor, pointing out the hypocrisy of the bank regulators. When challenged by a regulator, John responded politely but held his ground."

You can increase credibility by describing in your methods section how you dealt with a variety of obstacles. If readers are concerned that your interviewees gave you distorted or self-serving answers, show how you designed ways of double-checking. Explain how you chose the interviewees and gained access to them and why they were willing to talk openly with you. For example, if you were conducting research in a prison, under whose auspices did you enter the cells and how did you earn enough trust to get reliable and open interviews? How do you know that your interviewees were not lying to you? What steps did you take to verify some of the more outlandish claims? If your design has some shortcomings, explain what impacts they are likely to have on your conclusions and why you were not able to avoid them. For example, if you were not able to gain access to some key figures you hoped to interview, how did that affect what you found? An explicit acknowledgment of what you have and have not accomplished strengthens the credibility of your findings.

Precision in style and tone also helps build credibility. Make sure all of the verifiable details are correct, that you have names spelled correctly, and that dates are accurate. Avoid offering conclusions about details or motivations you could not possibly know. If a mother tells you why her daughter got an abortion, there is no way for you to know that the mother's conclusions about her daughter's feelings are correct. If you have a wrong name of a person or place or an erroneous date, or if you claim to know things you could not possibly know, readers who know about the subject will have a hard time believing the more subtle (and less verifiable) evidence presented.

GETTING FEEDBACK

After you finish with your initial revision of the manuscript, you need to get feedback by seeking comments from professional colleagues, potential readers, and, when possible, from the conversational partners themselves. You will also get reviews from scholars chosen by the publishers to help them evaluate the quality of what you have written. Most of us need someone to read our manuscripts carefully and give us honest reactions to the manuscript, including comments on grammar or citations, suggestions about missing literature, or questions about the credibility of the evidence. When you find people kind enough to read the manuscript for you, you might think about the following questions:

1. Does the writing engage them? Are some passages dull or confusing?

2. Can they describe to you the major themes? When they summarize the major themes, is it what you intended to say?

3. Do they accept the evidence you present and if not, what would make it stronger?

4. Do they follow (and then agree with) the logic of your argument? Is some step missing?

When most people, including us, receive criticisms, their instinct is to try to defend themselves, but in this case, it is better set the defensiveness aside and try to repair the manuscript in accordance with the feedback. Only if the friendly reviewer's comments do not work—maybe they introduce new ambiguity or require data you were unable to collect—should you ignore the criticism and stick to your original approach. The reviewers you choose yourself are not out to tear your manuscript to pieces or prevent its publication; they are trying to help you. When an editor finds a reviewer for your work, as opposed to someone you pick, you might end up with someone who ideologically disagrees with you or has a competing theory, in which case you might get comments you cannot incorporate.

When possible, try to get your conversational partners to review what you have written, asking them to comment on the substance to point out where they think you are correct and where they feel you have gone astray. If your conversational partners tell you that you got something wrong, especially descriptions or the facts of the matter, you probably want to correct what you have written. If they agree with your facts, but disagree with your interpretations, talk with them some more to see if what they say is persuasive. If you still disagree with their interpretation, keep what you wrote; the interpretations are yours, but you might want to add a footnote to indicate that some of your interviewees disagreed.

Most of the time, interviewees will find you have represented their opinions accurately and will recognize their world in the description you created. Every once in a while, though, you might get negative reactions from interviewees. Sometimes these are mild and expected, such as, "Please don't use that quote—I could get in trouble for it" or "Please don't call attention to that set of events, because while it did occur, it wasn't important and it is embarrassing and could cause serious harm." In those cases, you normally accede to the interviewee's request, because doing so will not weaken the argument and will help you avoid harming the interviewees. In a few instances, however, you may get a strongly negative reaction. Then you have to decide what to do.

Example: Dealing With a Negative Response

Irene did encounter one strongly negative response from one of the nine agencies in her recent study on how federal agencies dealt with budget stress. The chapter on that agency went back and forth many times, several officials read and commented on it, and Irene went down the list to see which comments she could accommodate and which ones she could not. Most of them were useful corrections, helpful definitions, and technical changes that she adopted right away, but some were more extensive. One of the agency reviewers suggested a reorganization of the chapter, sorting the information by administrative leaders rather than by theme. That would have made it clearer who in the agency was responsible for what, but it would have made it difficult to follow themes through time.

Their main concern, though, was that Irene suggested that increased efficiency was not enough to make up for budget cuts and that the quality of the agency's work would suffer. Agency reviewers argued that Irene did not have enough evidence to prove that point, so Irene went over her evidence again, carefully examined the interviews for slant, and did indeed find that some of her evidence had come from one interviewee who was biased against the agency. She went through the chapter and pulled out conclusions based on that biased interview. She would not have noticed this bias had the agency officials not charged her with lack of sufficient evidence and pressed her to reexamine the basis for her conclusions.

However, with all the modifications, hedges, and carefully skirted claims, the chapter began to read as if it had been written by lawyers. Irene rewrote the material to correct as many of the faults as she could, but did not eliminate the resulting tone of caution. The chapter still did not satisfy the agency officials, but it was as far as Irene felt she could go and be faithful not only to the interviewees, but also to the audience, who had a right to expect her best judgment of what was going on in the agency.

Getting Published

After revamping the manuscript in response to the comments you solicited, go over it again to make sure that it still has a coherent flow. In-house reports, evaluations, and similar contracted documents will usually be professionally copy edited (to correct grammar, smooth out the writing, and prepare the manuscript for printing), and then printed and circulated. If you are trying to get a short essay published in a newspaper, on the page facing the editorials, you send that manuscript to the newspaper, with a self-addressed, prepaid envelope if you hope to get it back. If you want to publish a popular book, you may need a literary agent, who will shop the manuscript for you to different publishers.

Academic publications follow a different route. For an article, you send your manuscript to only one journal at a time and wait for a response before sending it to anyone else, as submitting a manuscript to only one journal at a time is a strict standard practice; violation of it could result in editors refusing to consider your work. If you receive a rejection from the journal of your choice, you may then submit the manuscript to another journal.

Several considerations influence the choice of journal to which you send your manuscript. Each journal has its own readership, so you pick the journal that reaches the audience you most want to influence. Many academics also consider the prestige of the journal, picking the one that has the highest ranking that they think they might have a chance to get published in. The more prestigious journals typically get more submissions and have a higher rejection rate. The advantages of publishing in a more prestigious journal are that the article is more likely to be noticed and sometimes get more academic credit, and the more prestigious journals often rely on a larger number of reviewers who are specialists in your area. However, acceptance and publication in prestigious journals might entail two or three years of waiting, making your findings obsolete before they appear. You might want to target a specialty journal in your area that has a quicker turnaround time or is read by exactly the experts whom you want reach.

When you submit an article to most academic journals, it does not matter who you are, whether you are famous or unknown, whether you coauthor with a well-known professor, a little-known colleague, or write by yourself, because most journals decide what is published through the use of a blind peer review. Blind peer review means that the journal editor asks peers, experts in your field, to read and comment on the manuscript. Those reviewers do not know whose manuscript they are reading because the author's name is stripped off before the manuscript is sent to them.

The quality and usefulness of the reviews vary widely. At times, reviewers say the manuscript is terrific and recommend that it be published immediately, but more often they will summarize its strengths and weaknesses, comment on the style or tone, clarity of logic, and importance of the contribution, and suggest methodological questions that need to be answered. Better reviewers offer ideas on how to repair the problems they see. Based on these comments, the editor of the journal decides to either reject the manuscript (sometimes suggesting a different journal that might be a better match), accept the manuscript (usually with minor changes required), or offer the possibility of revision and resubmission. The latter response means that if you comply with the critical comments of the reviewers, the editor will look at the manuscript again, and probably, though not necessarily, accept it at that point.

If you receive a *revise and resubmit* from an appropriate journal, it makes sense to revamp the article and resubmit it. You carefully read the comments of the reviewers, paying particular attention to any comments highlighted by the editor. When deciding what to do about each comment, ask yourself if the reviewers understood what you were trying to say, and if not, how you can explain your logic more clearly. You should probably make all recommended stylistic changes, but you can reject some of the substantive ones if you feel they are unjustified. If the reviewers point out that your argument is missing a stage and you have the data for that stage, then include it, but if the reviewers really want a different essay than the one you wrote, you either have to ignore what they said and hope the editor agrees with you or find another journal outlet. At times, an editor chooses a wrong reviewer—perhaps you have ended up with a statistical expert trying to make sense out of your depth interviews—in which case you do not want to try to conform to his or her criticisms. Keep in mind that the final responsibility for the manuscript rests with you, not the editors or the peer reviewers. After you have rewritten the manuscript to comply with whatever criticisms make sense to you, when you resubmit the manuscript, you should probably include a cover letter to the editor explaining which comments you accepted, which ones you rejected, and why.

Be prepared for rejections and do not let them get you down. Most articles go out for review several times before they are finally accepted. If you are patient, persistent, and make the suggested changes, your work should be accepted for publication.

Publishing a book is a little different from publishing an article. When you have a manuscript, you look for companies that have published books on topics similar or related to yours. Some companies are commercial presses that expect bigger sales to wider audiences and may expect repeat sales of books for classroom use. Academic or university presses typically have smaller print runs, sell fewer copies (often to libraries), and can publish excellent books with smaller markets. Academic presses are usually considered more prestigious than commercial presses, but some commercial houses have fine reputations and are better at marketing than academic presses. In addition, the commercial presses tend to respond more quickly and allow you to submit a proposal to different publishing houses at the same time.

Regardless of whether you have chosen a university or commercial press, you prepare a prospectus that describes the content of the book, discusses the importance of the research, summarizes the main themes, calls attention to special features, and compares the book to potential rivals. A prospectus normally talks about the size of the expected market, to whom it would be of interest, what courses might use it, and how many copies similar books have sold. When you send in the prospectus, you can include a chapter of your book and you are expected to attach a chapter-by-chapter outline. Academic presses are more likely to want to see and read the whole book manuscript before they make a decision, but you do not send a manuscript until they ask to see it.

You also need to attach a resumé and include in the prospectus your qualifications to write the book and the level of name recognition that you have achieved. If you are well known in practitioner circles from years of work in agencies similar to those you are studying and the publisher you are aiming for has a way of reaching that market, your project will look more appealing to them. Similarly, if you have published other books that have sold well, your project would be perceived as a lower risk.

You can send a letter of inquiry, describing the book and asking if they would like to see more, or you can send a copy of your prospectus and see what kind of reaction you get. You can send this letter to multiple publishers, but if several academic presses say they might be interested, you then have to figure out which one to send the manuscript to, as you can send a manuscript to only one academic press at a time.

Commercial presses are likely to send your prospectus, including a sample chapter, out for review, especially to professors who might use the book in their courses, because they are interested in the possibility of repeat sales. Academic presses are more likely to send your book manuscript out for review to experts in your field. The kinds of comments you get back might be about ways to improve the organization or readability, citations to the literature that you should have made, and in some cases mistakes found or statements you made without sufficient evidence to be convincing. As with journal articles, you look over these reviews carefully and see what you can change that will improve the manuscript. You can negotiate with the editor, the person hired by the publisher to solicit manuscripts (and often see them through the production stage) about which criticisms are necessary to respond to, which ones are optional, and how many pages you can have to comply with the comments. More pages cost more money in production, so shorter manuscripts may have a better chance of getting published, but in any case, you have to keep your eye on the total number of pages and not let it creep up.

Finally, you get an offer and a contract, some of the terms of which are negotiable, you deliver the manuscript, and it goes into production. In production, books are copyedited by a professional who not only examines the manuscript for any remaining spelling or grammar problems, infelicitous wording, or lapses of tone, but also for accuracy and completeness of citations, and proper format as specified by the publisher. The copy editor simultaneously prepares the manuscript for typesetting, or the electronic equivalent, by marking headings with the proper typeface, marking extracts from your field notes or interviews, and making sure that punctuation and footnotes are visible in the text and are positioned properly on the line. You should get this marked-up copy back to look over and make sure your meaning has not been altered or mistakes made. This is the last time you can make substantive changes without having to pay for them, so you need to take this step seriously and usually do not get much time to do it. You may or may not get galley and/or page proofs to check as the manuscript proceeds through the printing process. Then the book is published.

The publisher normally sends you a few copies of your publication for free, which you may need for your employer and want to give to family and friends, but you might want to get some extra copies to share with your interviewees, especially those kind enough to give you a critical reading and those for whom you promised some public exposure.

With one—or more—publications based on your project, you are finally done with the writing. Now take a deep breath, maybe a vacation, clear your mind, and get ready to begin a new project, perhaps based on the questions that your current research has left unresolved.

Note

1. Ely and her colleagues describe the human dynamics in the writing of qualitative research (Ely et al. 2001).

References

Anderson, E. 1999. *Code of the street: Decency, violence, and the moral life of the inner city.* New York: W. W. Norton.

Anderson, K., and D. C. Jack. 1991. "Learning to listen: Interview techniques and analyses." In *Women's words: The feminist practice of oral history,* Eds. B. Gluck and D. Patai, 11–26. New York: Routledge.

Angrosino, M. V. 1998. *Opportunity house: Ethnographic stories of mental retardation.* Walnut Creek, CA: AltaMira Press.

Aston, J. 2001. "Research as relationship." In *Lives in context: The art of life history research,* Eds., A. L. Cole and J. G. Knowles, 145–151. Walnut Creek, CA: AltaMira Press.

Atkinson, P. 2001. "Ethnography and the representation of reality." In *Contemporary field research, 2nd edition,* Ed., R. M. Emerson, 89–101. Prospect Heights, IL: Waveland Press.

Bart, P. 1987. "Seizing the means of reproduction: An illegal feminist abortion collective—how and why it worked." *Qualitative Sociology,* 10(4): 339–357.

Balshem, M. 1991. "Cancer, control and causality: Talking about cancer in a working class community." *American Ethnologist,* 18(1): 152–172.

Berg, S. 2002. *Local government and municipal citizenship from ancient Greece to modern times: A case study of northern Illinois.* DeKalb: Northern Illinois University.

Berger, P. L., and T. Luckmann. 1967. *The social construction of reality: A treatise in the sociology of knowledge.* Garden City, NY: Doubleday, Anchor.

Boje, D. M. 1991. "The storytelling organization: A study of story performance in an office supply firm." *Administrative Science Quarterly,* 36(1, March): 106–126.

———. 1995. "Stories of the storytelling organization: A postmodern analysis of Disney as 'Tamara-Land.'" *Academy of Management Journal,* 38(4): 997–1035.

Boyatzis, R. E. 1998. *Transforming qualitative information: Thematic analysis and code development.* Thousand Oaks, CA: Sage.

Brajuha, M., and L. Hallowell. 1986. "Legal intrusion and the politics of fieldwork: The impact of the Brajuha Case." *Urban Life,* 14: 454–487.

Cannon, L., E. Higginbotham, and M. Leung. 1988. "Race and class bias in qualitative research on women." *Gender & Society,* 2(4, December): 449–462.

Charmaz, K. 1991. *Good days, bad days: The self in chronic illness and time.* New Brunswick, NJ: Rutgers University Press.

———. 2000. "Grounded theory: objectivist and constructivist methods." In *Handbook of qualitative research, 2nd edition,* Eds., N. K. Denzin and Y. S. Lincoln, 509–536. Thousand Oaks, CA: Sage.

———. 2001. "Grounded theory." In *Contemporary field research: Perspectives and formulations, 2nd edition,* Ed., R. M. Emerson, 335–352. Prospect Heights, IL: Waveland.

Charmaz, K., and R. G. Mitchell. 2001. "Symbolic interactionalism and ethnography." In *Handbook of ethnography,* Eds., P. Atkinson et al., 160–174. Thousand Oaks, CA: Sage.

Chase, S. E. 1995. *Ambiguous empowerment: The work narratives of women school superintendents.* Amherst: University of Massachusetts Press.

Chatterley, C. N., A. J. Rouverol, and S. Cole. 2000. *I was content and not content: The story of Linda Lord and the closing of Penobscot Poultry.* Carbondale: Southern Illinois University Press.

Cole, A. L., and J. G. Knowles, Eds. 2001. *Lives in context: The art of life history research.* Walnut Creek, CA: AltaMira Press.

DeAndrade, L. L. 2000. "Constructing racial and ethnic identity in qualitative research." *Journal of Contemporary Ethnography,* 29(3, June): 268–290.

Denzin, N. 1989. *The research act: A theoretical introduction to sociological methods.* Englewood Cliffs, NJ: Prentice Hall.

———. 1997. *Interpretive ethnography: Ethnographic practices for the 21st century.* Thousand Oaks, CA: Sage.

Devault, M. L. 1990. Talking and listening from women's standpoint: Feminist strategies for interviewing and analysis. *Social Problems,* 37(1, February): 96–116.

Douglas, J. D. 1985. *Creative interviewing.* Beverly Hills, CA: Sage.

Duberman, M., Ed. 1997. *A queer world.* New York: New York University Press.

Duneier, M. 1999. *Sidewalk.* New York: Farrar, Straus, and Giroux.

Edwards, R., and J. Ribbens. 1998. "Living on the edges: Public knowledge, private lives, personal experience." In *Feminist dilemmas in qualitative research: Public knowledge and private lives,* Eds., J. Ribbens and R. Edwards, 1–23. Thousand Oaks, CA: Sage.

Ellis, C., and A. P. Bochner, Eds. 1996. *Composing ethnography: Alternative forms of qualitative writing.* Ethnographic alternatives series. Walnut Creek, CA: AltaMira Press.

Ely, M., et al. 2001. *On writing qualitative research: Living by words.* Philadelphia: Routledge.

Fielding, N. 2001. "Computer applications in qualitative research." In *Handbook of ethnography,* Eds., P. Atkinson et al., 453–467. Thousand Oaks, CA: Sage.

Fielding, N. G., and R. M. Lee. 1998. *Computer analysis and qualitative research.* Thousand Oaks, CA: Sage.

———. 2002. "New patterns in the adoption and use of qualitative software." *Field Methods,* 14(2, May): 197–216.

Fine, M., and L. Weis. 1998. *The unknown city: The lives of poor and working class young adults.* Boston: Beacon Press.

Frisch, M. 1990. *A shared authority: Essays on the craft and meaning of oral and public history*. Albany: State University of New York Press.

Frost, P. J. et al. 1985. *Organizational culture*. Beverly Hills, CA: Sage.

Gahan, C., and M. Hannibal. 1998. *Doing qualitative research using QSR NUDIST*. Thousand Oaks, CA: Sage.

Geertz, C. 1973. "Thick description: Toward an interpretive theory of culture." In *The interpretation of cultures*, Ed., C. Geertz, 3–30. New York: Basic Books.

———. 2001. "Thick description: Toward an interpretive theory of culture." In *Contemporary field research: Perspectives and formulations, 2nd edition*, Ed., R. M. Emerson, 55–75. Prospect Heights, IL: Waveland.

Gergen, K. J. 1999. *An invitation to social construction*. Thousand Oaks, CA: Sage.

Glaser, B., and A. Strauss. 1967. *The discovery of grounded theory*. Chicago: Aldine.

Gluck, S. B., and D. Patai. 1991. *Women's words: The practice of oral history*. London: Routledge.

Goffman, E. 1959. *The presentation of self in everyday life*. New York: Anchor.

Gorden, D. F. 1987. "Getting close by staying distant: Fieldwork with proselytizing groups." *Qualitative Sociology*, 10(3, Fall): 267–287.

Grele, R. J. 1985. *Envelopes of sound: The art of oral history, 2nd edition*. Chicago: Precedent.

Groce, S. B. 1989. "Occupational rhetoric and ideology: A comparison of copy and original music performers." *Qualitative Sociology*, 12(4, Winter): 391–410.

Groenbjerg, K. A. 1993. *Understanding nonprofit funding: Managing revenues in social services and community development organizations*. San Francisco: Jossey-Bass.

Gubrium, J. F., and J. A. Holstein. 1997. *The new language of qualitative research*. New York: Oxford University Press.

Gurney, J. N. 1985. "Not one of the guys: The female researcher in a male-dominated setting." *Qualitative Sociology*, 8(1, Spring): 42–61.

Hammersley, M. 2001. "Ethnography and realism." In *Contemporary field research, 2nd edition*, Ed., R. M. Emerson, 102–111. Prospect Heights, IL: Waveland Press.

Harding, S. 1991. *Whose science? Whose knowledge? Thinking about women's lives*. Ithaca, NY: Cornell University Press.

Harrison, J., L. MacGibbson, and M. Morton. 2001. "Regimes of trustworthiness in qualitative research: The rigors of reciprocity." *Qualitative Inquiry*, 7(3, June): 323–345.

Hollowell, L. 1985. "The outcome of the Brajuha case: Legal implications for sociologists." *Footnotes American Sociological Association*, 13(1): 13.

hooks, b. 1989. *Talking back: Thinking feminist. Thinking black*. Boston: South End Press.

Horowitz, R. 1986. "Remain an outsider: Membership as a threat to research rapport." *Urban Life*, 14(4, January): 409–430.

Hummel, R. P. 1991. "Stories managers tell: Why they are as valid as science." *Public Administration Review*, 51(1, January/February): 31–41.

Hummon, D. 1990. *Commonplaces: Community ideology and identity in America*. Albany, NY: SUNY Press.

Johnson, J. 1997. "Generalizability in qualitative research: Excavating the discourse." In *Completing a qualitative project: Details and dialogue*, Ed., J. M. Morse, 191–208. Thousand Oaks, CA: Sage.

Kaplan, E. B. 1997. *Not our kind of girl: Unraveling the myths of black teenage motherhood*. Berkeley: University of California Press.

Kincheloe, J. L., and P. McLaren. 2000. "Rethinking critical theory and qualitative research." In *Handbook of qualitative research, 2nd edition*, Eds., N. K. Denzin and Y. S. Lincoln, 279–314. Thousand Oaks, CA: Sage.

Lather, P., and C. Smithies. 1997. *Troubling the angels: Women living with HIV/AIDS*. Boulder, CO: Westview Press.

LeCompte, M. D., and J. J. Schensul. 1999. *Designing and conducting ethnographic research*. Ethnographer's toolkit series. Walnut Creek, CA: AltaMira Press.

Levy, J. E. 1975. *César Chávez: Autobiography of La Causa*. New York: W. W. Norton.

Liebow, E. 1967. *Tally's corner: A study of Negro streetcorner men*. Boston: Little, Brown.

Lincoln, Y. S., and E. G. Guba. 1985. *Naturalistic inquiry*. Newbury Park, CA: Sage.

Lofland, J., and L. Lofland. 1995. *Analyzing social setting*. Belmont, CA: Wadsworth.

Lummis. T. 1988. *Listening to history: The authenticity of oral evidence*. Totowa, NJ: Barnes & Noble Books.

Lyman, S., and M. Scott. 1968. "Accounts." *American Journal of Sociology*, 33(1, February): 46–62.

MacLeod, J. 1995 [1987]. *Ain't no makin' it: Aspirations & attainment in a low-income neighborhood*. Denver, CO: Westview Press.

Magolda, P. 2000. "Being at the wrong place, wrong time: Rethinking trust in qualitative inquiry." *Theory into Practice*, 39(3, Summer): 138–146.

Marsh, D. S., M. H. Daniel, and K. Putnam. 2003. *Leadership for policy change: Strengthening communities of color through leadership development*. Oakland, CA: Policy Link.

McCall, M. M. 1990. "The significance of story telling." In *Studies in symbolic interaction, volume 11*, Ed., N. Denzin. 145–161. Greenwich, CT: JAI Press.

McCormack, C. 2000a. "From interview transcript to interpretive story: Part 1—Viewing the transcript through multiple lenses." *Field Methods*, 12(4, November): 282–297.

———. 2000b. "From interview transcript to interpretive story: Part 2—Developing an interpretive story." *Field Methods*, 12(4, November): 298–315.

McMahan, E. M. 1989. *Elite oral history discourse: A study of cooperation and coherence*. Tuscaloosa: The University of Alabama Press.

Merritt, M. D. 1998. *A case study of rulemaking for DoD procurement policy: Effects of policy changes for mergers and downsizing of defense contractors considering congressional oversight and executive branch administrative responsibility and industry roles*. DeKalb: Northern Illinois University.

Merton, R., M. Fiske, and P. L. Kendall. 1990 [1956]. *The focused interviews: A manual of problems and procedures*, 2nd edition. New York: Free Press.

Moerman, M. 1988. *Talking culture: Ethnography and conversation analysis.* Philadelphia: University of Pennsylvania Press.

Miles, M. B., and A. M. Huberman. 1994. *Qualitative data analysis: An expanded sourcebook.* Thousand Oaks, CA: Sage.

Moody, M., and M. Musheno. 1997. *Justice in the delivery of government services: Decision norms of street bureaucrats.* Data archive. NSF Grant #sbr951169.

Naples, N. 1997. "A feminist revisiting of the insider/outsider debate: The 'outsider phenomenon' in rural Iowa." In *Reflexivity and voice*, Ed., R. Hertz, 70–94. Thousand Oaks, CA: Sage.

Newman, K. 1999. *No shame in my game: The working poor in the inner city.* New York: Alfred Knopf.

Oakley, A. 1981. "Interviewing women: A contradiction in terms." In *Doing feminist research*, Ed., H. Roberts, 30–61. London: Routledge.

Padilla, F. 1992. *The gang as an American enterprise.* New Brunswick, NJ: Rutgers University Press.

Paredes, A. 1977. "On ethnographic work among minority groups: A folklorist's perspective." *New Scholar*, 6(1): 1–53.

Poland, B. D. 2002. "Transcription quality." In *Handbook of interview research*, Eds., J. F. Gubrium and J. A. Holstein, 629–650. Thousand Oaks, CA: Sage.

Prasad, P. 1991. "Organization building in a Yale union." *Journal of Applied Behavior Science*, 27(3, September): 337–355.

Psathas, G. 1995. *Conversation analysis: The study of talk-in-interaction.* Thousand Oaks, CA: Sage.

Reinharz, S. 1992. *Feminist methods in social research.* New York: Oxford University Press.

———. 1997. "Who am I? The need for a variety of selves in the field." In *Reflexivity and voice*, Ed., R. Hertz, 3–20. Thousand Oaks, CA: Sage.

Reissman, C. K. 1987. "When gender is not enough: Women interviewing women." *Gender & Society*, 1(2, June): 172–207.

Rogers, M. B. 1990. *Cold anger: A story of faith and power politics.* Denton: University of North Texas Press.

Rubin, H. J. 1973. "Will and awe: Illustrations of Thai villager dependency upon officials." *Journal of Asian Studies*, xxxii(3, May): 425–444.

———. 1984. "The meshing organization as a catalyst for municipal coordination." *Administration and Society*, 16(2): 215–238.

———. 1988a. "The Danada farm: Land acquisition, planning and politics in suburbia." *Journal of the American Planning Association*, 54(Winter): 79–90.

———. 1988b. "Shoot anything that flies, claim anything that falls: Conversations with economic development practitioners." *Economic Development Quarterly*, 2(3, August): 236–251.

———. 1993. "Understanding the ethos of community-based development: Ethnographic description for public administration." *Public Administration Review*, 53(5, September/October): 428–437.

———. 1994. "There aren't going to be any bakeries here if there is no money to afford jellyrolls: The organic theory of community based development." *Social Problems,* 41(4, August): 401–424.

———. 1995. "Renewing hope in the inner city: Conversations with community-based development practitioners." *Administration and Society,* 27(1, May): 127–160.

———. 1997. "Being a conscience and a carpenter: Interpretations of the community based development model." *Journal of Community Practice,* 4(1): 57–90.

———. 2000. *Renewing hope within neighborhoods of despair: The community-based development model.* Albany, NY: SUNY Press.

Rubin, I. S. 1977. "Universities in stress: Decision making under conditions of reduced resources." *Social Science Quarterly,* 58, 242–254.

———. 1982. *Running in the red.* Albany, NY: SUNY Press.

———. 1985. *Shrinking the federal government.* New York: Longman.

———. 1992. "Budget reform and political reform: Conclusions from six cities." *Public Administration Review,* 52, 454–466.

———. 2002. "Perennial budget reform proposals: Budget staff versus elected officials." *Public Budgeting and Finance,* 22(4, Winter): 1–16.

———. 2003. *Balancing the federal budget: Trimming the herds or eating the seed corn?* New York: Chatham House.

Schegloff, E. A. 1992. "Repair after next turn; the last structurally provided defense of intersubjectivity in conversation." *American Journal of Sociology,* 97(5): 1295–1345.

Schein, E. H. 1985. *Organizational culture and leadership.* San Francisco: Jossey-Bass.

Schutz, A. 1967. *The phenomenology of the social world.* Evanston, IL: Northwestern University Press.

Schwandt, T. A. 1999. "On understanding understanding." *Qualitative Inquiry,* 5(4, December): 451–464.

———. 2000. "Three epistemological stances for qualitative inquiry: Interpretivism, hermeneutics, and social constructionism." In *Handbook of qualitative research, 2nd edition,* Eds., N. K. Denzin and Y. S. Lincoln, 189–214. Thousand Oaks, CA: Sage.

Shapiro, J. P. 1993. *No pity.* New York: Times Books.

Snow, D., R. D. Benford, and L. Anderson. 1986. "Fieldwork roles and informational yield: A comparison of alternative settings and roles." *Urban Life,* 14(4): 377–408.

Spradley, J. P. 1979. *The ethnographic interview.* New York: Holt, Rhinehart, and Winston.

Strauss, A., and J. Corbin. 1990. *Basics of qualitative research.* Newbury Park, CA: Sage.

Tannen, D. 1990. *You just don't understand: Women and men in conversation.* New York: Ballentine.

Terkel, S. 1974. *Working: People talk about what they do all day and how they feel about what they do.* New York: Pantheon.

———. 1984. *"The good war": An oral history of World War II.* New York: Pantheon.

Thomas, J., and J. Marquart. 1988. "Dirty information and clean conscience: Communication problems in studying 'bad guys.'" In *Communications and social structure*, Eds., D. R. Maines and C. J. Couch, 81–96. Springfield, IL: Charles C Thomas.

Thomas, M. D., J. Blacksmith, and J. Reno. 2000. Utilizing insider-outsider research teams in qualitative research. *Qualitative Health Research*, 10(6, November): 519–528.

Tierney, W. G., Ed. 1999. "Writing life's history." *Qualitative Inquiry* 5(3, September): 307–312 Special Issue.

Tixier y Vigil, Y., and N. Elasser. 1978. "The effects of ethnicity of the interviewer on conversation: A study of Chicana women." *International Journal of the Sociology of Language*, 17, 91–102.

Turner, D. D. 1997. "Reconstructing the history of musicians' protective union local 274 through oral narrative method." In *Oral narrative research with black women*, Ed., K. M. Vaz, 177–196. Thousand Oaks, CA: Sage.

Van Maanen, J. 1978. "The asshole." In *Policing*, Eds., P. K. Manning and J. V. Maanen. New York: Random House.

Warren, M. R. 2001. *Dry bones rattling: Community building to revitalize American democracy*. Princeton, NJ: Princeton University Press.

Weitz, R. 1987. "The interview as legacy: A social scientist confronts AIDS." *Hastings Center Report*, 17(3): 21–23.

Weitzman, E. A. 2000. "Software and qualitative research." In *Handbook of qualitative research, 2nd edition*, Eds., N. K. Denzin and Y. S. Lincoln, 803–820. Thousand Oaks, CA: Sage.

Weitzman, E. A., and M. A. Michael. 1995. *Computer programs for qualitative data analysis: A software sourcebook*. Thousand Oaks, CA: Sage.

Werner, O. 1998. When recording is impossible. *Field Methods*, 11(1, August): 71–76.

Whyte, W. F. 1955. *Street corner society: The social construction of an Italian slum*. Chicago: University of Chicago Press.

Wilson, W. J. 1996. *When work disappears: The world of the new urban poor*. New York: Alfred A. Knopf.

Yarwood, D. 2003. "Humorous stories and the identification of social norms: The senate club." *Administration & Society*, 35(1, March): 9–28.

Zinn, B. M. 2001. "Insider field research in minority communities." In *Contemporary field research, 2nd edition*, Ed., R. M. Emerson, 159–166. Prospect Heights, IL: Waveland Press.

Index

About the Authors

Herbert J. Rubin is Professor Emeritus of Sociology at Northern Illinois University. He is the author of *Applied Social Research* and (with Irene Rubin) three editions of *Community Organizing and Development*. He has written articles based on in-depth interviewing that explore rural development in Thailand, suburban land-use fights, cooperative housing, and economic and community development. Both his monograph on Thailand, *The Dynamics of Development in Rural Development,* and his book on community renewal in the United States, *Renewing Hope within Neighborhoods of Despair: The Community-Based Development Model,* are based on participant observation and hundreds of in-depth interviews. He is currently using open-ended in-depth interviews to study organizations that advocate for the poor.

Irene S. Rubin is Professor Emeritus of Public Administration at Northern Illinois University. She is the author of *Running in the Red: The Political Dynamics of Urban Fiscal Stress, Shrinking the Federal Government, Class Tax and Power: Municipal Budgeting in the United States,* and *Balancing the Federal Budget: Eating the Seed Corn or Trimming the Herds,* all four of which rely extensively on qualitative interviews. She has written journal articles about citizen participation in local-level government in Thailand, how universities adapt when their budgets are cut, and fights between legislative staffers and elected and appointed officials about unworkable policy proposals, all based on qualitative interviews. She is in the middle of an interviewing project about how local officials view and use contracts with the private sector and with other governmental units to provide public services.

Herb and Irene have both taught qualitative research at Northern Illinois University, with an emphasis on in-depth interviewing. Their students have helped them improve this edition by pointing out what sections of the first edition were not sufficiently clear and the authors thank them. Also, the authors thank their students for providing them with examples of their experiences in conducting in-depth interviewing, some of which have been included in the this edition.

About the Authors

Herbert J. Rubin is Professor Emeritus of Sociology at Northern Illinois University. He is the author of *Applied Social Research* and (with Irene Rubin) three editions of *Community Organizing and Development*. He has written articles based on in-depth interviewing that explore rural development in Thailand, suburban land-use fights, cooperative housing, and economic and community development. Both his monograph on Thailand, *The Dynamics of Development in Rural Development,* and his book on community renewal in the United States, *Renewing Hope within Neighborhoods of Despair: The Community-Based Development Model,* are based on participant observation and hundreds of in-depth interviews. He is currently using open-ended in-depth interviews to study organizations that advocate for the poor.

Irene S. Rubin is Professor Emeritus of Public Administration at Northern Illinois University. She is the author of *Running in the Red: The Political Dynamics of Urban Fiscal Stress, Shrinking the Federal Government, Class Tax and Power: Municipal Budgeting in the United States,* and *Balancing the Federal Budget: Eating the Seed Corn or Trimming the Herds,* all four of which rely extensively on qualitative interviews. She has written journal articles about citizen participation in local-level government in Thailand, how universities adapt when their budgets are cut, and fights between legislative staffers and elected and appointed officials about unworkable policy proposals, all based on qualitative interviews. She is in the middle of an interviewing project about how local officials view and use contracts with the private sector and with other governmental units to provide public services.

Herb and Irene have both taught qualitative research at Northern Illinois University, with an emphasis on in-depth interviewing. Their students have helped them improve this edition by pointing out what sections of the first edition were not sufficiently clear and the authors thank them. Also, the authors thank their students for providing them with examples of their experiences in conducting in-depth interviewing, some of which have been included in the this edition.